SCIENCE AND CULTURE SERIES
JOSEPH HUSSLEIN, S.J., Ph.D., GENERAL EDITOR

TOTAL EMPIRE

OTHER BOOKS BY THE SAME AUTHOR:

1. *The Fall of the Russian Empire*, 1927, Little, Brown Co., Boston

2. *The Last Stand — An Interpretation of the Soviet Five Year Plan*, 1933, The Atlantic Monthly Press, Boston

3. *Ships and National Safety*, 1933, Georgetown University

4. *The Woodcarver of Tyrol*, 1935, Harper Brothers, New York

5. *Les Principes Fondamentaux de la Vie Internationale*, 1936, Recueil Sirey, Paris

6. *L'Évolution de la Diplomatie Aux États-Unis*, 1939, Recueil Sirey, Paris

7. *Total Power — A Footnote to History*, 1948, Doubleday and Co., Inc., New York

Total Empire

The Roots and Progress of World Communism

BY

EDMUND A. WALSH, S.J.

Vice-President, GEORGETOWN UNIVERSITY
Regent, SCHOOL OF FOREIGN SERVICE

THE BRUCE PUBLISHING COMPANY
MILWAUKEE

Acknowledgment is gratefully made to the publishers for permission to cite certain passages from:

The Fall of the Russian Empire, by Edmund A. Walsh (Boston: Little, Brown and Company, 1928).

The Last Stand, by Edmund A. Walsh (Boston: The Atlantic Monthly Press, 1931).

Total Power, by Edmund A. Walsh (New York: Doubleday and Company, Inc., 1948).

The Bolshevik Persecution of Christianity, by Captain Francis McCullagh (London: John Murray, 1924).

Marxism — An Autopsy, by Henry Bamford Parkes (Boston: Houghton, Mifflin, and Company, 1939).

Karl Marx, by Otto Rühle, translated by Eden Cedar Paul (New York: Viking Press, 1929).

The Coming Defeat of Communism, by James Burnham (New York: The John Day Company, 1949).

Winged Power, by Arnold and Eaker (New York: Harper Brothers, 1941).

Preface by the General Editor

FOR many years the author of this book has been a close observer of the Soviet regime and Communist tactics. Having resided in Communist-dominated countries, he became familiar with their ways and doctrine, not by hearsay, but by direct observation.

Two years of penetrating study in this most acute of all present-day problems were spent by him in Russia itself. This initial experience was followed by twenty-five years of research, by much delving into Communist thought at the roots, and by prolonged travel in many foreign lands. In particular, Germany and Japan were further scenes of his untiring activity in securing the fullest possible information on this most threatening evil, whose promoters at the present hour dominate actually a third of the population of the entire civilized world. Ruthlessly, Communist Russia is determined to bring under its single despotic power the remaining two thirds as well.

There, then, is the danger threatening us, which never can be taken too seriously. It must be met with all the resources at our command. And the first requirement is clearness of understanding. What the conquest of the world by Communism would actually mean the author makes fully clear in the pages of this book.

Eighteen years ago, before the international situation had assumed its present seriousness, two conferences on this vital subject were held by the author himself with the then President Roosevelt. The circumstances and significance of those conversations are discussed in the present volume.

May this book, then, make clear that no inhibition exists on the part of our Communist foe as to the use of even the most deadly weapons that science can invent for the destruction of human freedom. Such means are even now, the author shows, in the hands of an enemy without conscience, without belief in God, and hence without any regard for humanity itself except as it can be used to bolster up the Communist cause. For what, in their theory, are mortal men but an evolution at the best from insensate plant or animal life to the human stage? The conclusion from this creed is coldly and relentlessly applied in its ultimate disregard for the dignity of human life and personality.

It is with strict facts only and not with mere imaginings that the author is concerned, and with the clear exposition of the ultimate determination of Communism, if not now prevented, to extend its rule over all the civilized earth. These are the facts that must be made known for the safety of society, for the welfare of our country, and for the preservation of the spiritual basis of Western civilization.

Partly biographical, the text embodies pages of the author's own Russian diary never yet presented to the public. A further attempt is made to lay bare the very roots of the Russian Revolution itself in order to demonstrate the historical continuity and basic consistency of the Soviet policy. And all this is done in a manner readily intelligible to everyone.

Fortunately, too, the author has chosen the present most opportune moment to make public his research of a quarter of a century in a book, no less interesting than important. May it reach out far and wide as its subject matter deserves. High time, indeed, that the world should learn to know the truth, only the truth, and the full truth concerning this most vital and important subject of our day that even now has begun to impinge directly and most closely on our lives.

JOSEPH HUSSLEIN, S.J., PH.D.

General Editor, Science and Culture Series

Contents

APPENDICES

BOOK I

The Seeds of Contradiction

CHAPTER I

Leaves From a Russian Diary

THE present writer was an eyewitness of the Russian Revolution during its adolescent years and has been a constant observer of its progeny, World Communism, for upward of a quarter of a century in many regions of the earth. Some twenty-eight years of such observation, interspersed with frequent debates, both public and private, with advocates of the Marxist system, gave rise to certain basic convictions and guiding principles. There is something fundamental, though elusive, about the Soviet mind which our people have not yet fully comprehended, though they are much more conscious of the realities today than ever before. Korea was the latest revelation. And the President's proclamation of a national emergency on December 16, 1950, was an official if late recognition of a public record. The Revolution never relaxes though it has sometimes stumbled. It changes tactics and personnel but never renounces its program of planned chaos. It shifts gears and reduces speed but never loses direction or sight of its objectives. It gains or loses momentum but never changes its inner nature or renounces responsibility to itself. It substitutes new forms and places of attack but never relents in its conspiracy for world domination. It swaps the blockade of Berlin for most of China. It concedes you a dime but pockets a dollar. It pretends to love peace and justice but sponsors an aggressive war in Korea. It damns and vilifies the American government from the rostrum of the United Nations but wines and dines with American delegates outside office hours.

It is sometimes possible, in retrospect, to put one's finger on a point in time, on a date, or a set of circumstances which can be recognized as having exercised a measurable influence on one's intellectual growth. Ruskin tells us of such a determinant in his progress toward appreciation of natural beauty and art forms. In his tender years he had been taken to an enchanting spot called Friar's Crag, overlooking Lake Derwentwater in the Midlands of England. It is a tranquil promontory looking down on the oval lake which is set in an amphitheater of encircling mountains, one range overlooked by others of greater height. The panorama, he records, impressed itself indelibly on his young and susceptible mind, a mind that was later to give us *Stones of Venice* and *The Seven Lamps of Architecture*. Derwentwater was Ruskin's first introduction to natural beauty, and he never forgot the moment. Similarly, though under wholly different circumstances, a sequence of specific happenings left their traces on my own education to an understanding of the inner nature and outward characteristics of the Russian Revolution.

They began during the period when the government of the United States had refused to enter into diplomatic relations with the Communist regime and had maintained that position since 1917 through a succession of Republican and Democratic administrations. The policy had been originally established by the Democrats under Woodrow Wilson. But, in common with most Americans, I had accepted that aspect of the matter as a political decision, without having direct personal experience of the full weight of the reasons behind the fact. It is, consequently, an accurate statement to say that I first entered Soviet Russia in February, 1922, with a wholly open mind and in a spirit of friendliness toward its people. It required nearly two years of residence in Soviet territory to recognize the deep gulf which separated the Christianity of the West from the new religion of denial enthroned in the Kremlin. What actually stood revealed was a cult of national and international violence, which included a program of organized assault on the freedoms of democracy as well as on revealed religion.

Face to face with the realities as they developed day by day in those formative years of the Revolution, one could not deny the testimony of his senses. Some 200 of us, members of the American Relief Administration, were laboring wholeheartedly and with singleness of purpose, in 1921–1923, to break the backbone of the most devastating famine in the long and turbulent history of the Russian State. With neither political nor social prejudice beclouding our vision or impairing our efficiency, but with sincere good will toward a very lovable people whose qualities are admirable in many respects, we, as a band of American relief workers, under the direction of Colonel William N. Haskell, were performing a task of Hercules. Stretched in a thin line from the Gulf of Finland to the Caucasus Mountains and stationed at remote posts ranging from the Polish frontier to the Urals, as dispensers of international good will we were conducting in snow and ice the most extended feeding operation of the period following World War I. We had to wage daily battle with the elemental forces of a rigorous climate, epidemic disease, a wrecked economy, a crippled transportation system, and the general disorganization of normal life resulting from a world war that had been followed by social upheavals complicated by bloody internal conflict between white and red armies. Approximately 70 million dollars worth of free food, medicines, and clothing from America was eventually distributed. Although this sum is not too impressive in comparison with the astronomical figures of public finance in 1951, it represented in 1922 and 1923 the princely generosity and the spontaneity characteristic of American charity.

At the peak of the operation we were feeding eleven million needy Russians every day, the quota under my direct responsibility being 156,000 mouths to feed every twenty-four hours. The flow of contributions and supplies continued for two years, until the Soviet Government declared, in the summer of 1923, that famine conditions were no longer existent and that Soviet agencies would be able thereafter to meet the remaining needs without assistance of the American organization.

*   *   *   *

The first key to understanding the Soviet concept of permanent revolution was vouchsafed in the form of two incidents arising from the organization of relief headquarters for the Crimea in the city of Eupatoria, on the shores of the Black Sea. It was late in the summer of 1922. At the outset, an attitude of cordiality and co-operation was manifested by the local commissars toward the foreigners bringing gifts and food. Comrade Bulle, the liaison officer from Moscow, endeavored, as far as we could judge, to create an atmosphere of civilized reciprocity. Thus, he invited me one evening to a sort of caucus of the Communist Party, a preliminary convention where delegates were to be chosen for the forthcoming All-Union Congress in Moscow. Composed of peasants and workers, the assembly faced a platform on which were gathered the Communist authorities of the town and the Party candidates. Around the sides of the hall and across the back was arranged a cordon of Bolshevik soldiers, armed as always.

As the only guest, I was seated on the stage where courtesy imposed a certain protocol. I applauded at what seemed the proper moment and rose at the end for the singing of what turned out to be the *Internationale*. The voting was particularly revealing. A spellbinder delivered an impassioned address which rose to a climax. Pointing to the elite seated on the platform he eulogized them as the cream of the Crimea. Then he put the question: "All who are opposed to the Party candidates will signify by raising the right hand." At this the Red guards made noises with their boots and with their rifle butts. Obviously nobody stirred or raised a finger. "Now," continued the orator, "all in favor of the Party candidates will signify their vote." The air was straightway filled with waving hands and fluttering digits. The Red guards relaxed and the Secret Service men sauntered approvingly along the aisles. But that was not all. An exact count was made and the unanimous election was recorded for transmission to Moscow and the news services.

At the conclusion of the ceremonies, toward midnight, I retired with my chaperon to the house where I was quartered. It was a fairly substantial building, though in general disrepair after the years of revolution and civil war. Eupatoria, once a picturesque, but in 1922 a wasted, half-ruined city, had been one of the most frequented watering places of the old regime. Not far from where we sat — the spot could be reached in an hour — the allied British and French forces landed in September, 1854, during the Crimean War. Once a favorite resort for Russians seeking relief from the summer heat of Petrograd and Moscow, it still showed evidence of something more than vanished gentility in the palatial whitestone villas that dotted its water front. But these remnants of a fallen empire were mostly ruins now, plundered for loot or despoiled in search of wood for fuel; their roofless walls stood stark and bare with the empty window spaces silhouetted against the sky like the eyeless sockets of a human skull that had passed through fire. The city had been cruelly devastated by the successive waves of invasion that had passed over it — first the Germans, then the retreating armies of Denikin, then the triumphant Bolsheviks again. With the waters of the Black Sea rippling up to the beach outside, and by the light of a candle stuck in the neck of a bottle, I discussed the Russian Revolution with my friendly Commissar.

We sat the whole night out and burned many a candle to the stub. He was filled with zeal and enthusiasm, I with curiosity and a sense of special opportunity. It was agreed that each could be perfectly frank, asking and replying as he deemed proper, no offense intended. He was a seasoned Marxist, I an unconvinced bourgeois.

"What you saw and heard tonight," he said, "is going on at this time throughout the entire Union of Workers and Peasants. Nothing can stop the dictatorship of the proletariat."

"The world revolution that Mr. Saïd Galaiev spoke about," I asked, "will it also come in my country, the United States of America? . . . I live far away."

"Eventually, yes. But not for a long time. It will come late, probably last, to the United States."

"Why this — pardon the expression — privileged exemption for so long a time?"

"The revolutionary leaders who drafted your Constitution were wiser than European rulers. They included in your organic law shrewd provisions which anticipated the future awakening of the masses. They made your Constitution flexible and elastic, capable of being modified to keep pace with popular demand and social developments. When exploitation of the workers threatens your bourgeois state, you Americans add an amendment in response to the pressure from below."

"I do not believe they all came precisely in that way; ten were added immediately from above — but let that pass."

"Our Russian state was like cast iron. A rigid system cannot bend, so we broke it."

Comrade Bulle had obviously retained no little of his indoctrination in the social history of the United States. But he had missed the informing spirit of the American Constitution as well as the genesis and historical background of the Bill of Rights. He knew nothing of the three principles of balance required by James Madison for the organic law he did so much to draft:

1. Separation of powers, including checks and balances;
2. The natural limits to the power of numerical majorities in republics operating over a large area;
3. Federalism, reserving a portion of governmental authority to the states.

What my Commissar held as incontrovertible was the firm conviction that all non-Communist States must eventually succumb to the new order established by Russian Communism. It was my first personal and authentic contact with the Party Line in the flesh.

But these cordial relations were soon to be rudely interrupted. Whether new tactics had been ordered from Moscow or instinctively adopted by the local commissars at a prearranged moment I could not ascertain. What became extremely important was the purpose underlying the typical maneuver which now transpired. After considerable difficulty and overcoming of unnecessary obstacles, our kitchens and feeding facilities were finally ready for operation. Exercising the freedom of choice guaranteed in the Relief Agreement signed by the highest Soviet authorities, I had recruited a staff of secretaries, interpreters, bookkeepers, and miscellaneous assistants. Knowledge of foreign languages was of prime importance; hence the office personnel were chosen from the native population on grounds of competency irrespective of politics, religion, or social status. People were starving to death in the streets of Russia and no time was to be lost. Quick, efficient distribution of the food from America was our sole objective. But the secret police, then known as the Cheka, had other ideas: to plant their secret agents in foreign relief missions for espionage purposes was classic procedure. Hence, the chief of the political bureau of the town, the Ispolkom, demanded of me that I discharge the staff recently chosen and accept the nominees of the local Communist Party.

A delegation descended on me in force, coming, like Nicodemus, by night. It was a weird consultation in an improvised office. As electricity was not available we conferred by the flickering light of two candles stuck in the necks of empty beer bottles. The visitors gravely announced that the persons already chosen were "criminals" and, as such, "ineligible for positions of trust." On inquiry as to the nature of their criminality, I was informed: "This one previously owned a house in this city; hence, he is a bourgeois exploiter of the proletariat. The other, over there, was the wife of an officer who fought as a White Russian during the civil war," and so forth, and so forth, down the approved list of ideological crimes during the Revolution. Unable to agree that a mission of mercy to the hungry, the sick, and the dying should be turned into an instrument of party politics or transformed into a weapon of revolutionary vengeance, I declined their proposals. A deadlock ensued. The kitchens were not opened; affixing seals on all supplies, I left the Crimea for Moscow to lay the case before the highest Soviet authorities. The old familiar pattern was there resurrected: "Oh, yes, that was some local subordinate official; he could not have known of the agreement. He will be removed. But, now, you send a telegram, opening the kitchens, and we will then send an order canceling the interference." Eventually the feeding stations were opened, and 40,000 people of the Crimea were saved from starvation — but not in the sequence required by Moscow. The order canceling the violation of the agreement was first dispatched and the kitchens were promptly opened *after* its arrival. We were all learning very rapidly.

These relatively unimportant and far-off incidents would seem trivial in 1951 if they did not reveal something that is neither trivial nor incidental: the permanent psychology and unchanged inner workings of the Soviet mind, which transcend time and place and reveal themselves with continuity and uniformity in issues great and small.

This form of harassment by unilateral assumptions, by constant pressure and attempts at browbeating, reached its climax at a higher level on October 1, 1922. By that time the American organization was approaching peak development in its battle against famine and disease, with huge quantities of food and medical supplies concentrated at strategic points, particularly in the valley of the Volga. This service to the Russian people was not without physical danger. I shall not easily forget those Russian winters nor the hours I spent in Moscow at the bedside of American relief workers as they gasped for life under attacks of pneumonia and typhus. Two others, in more distant stations, could not be saved and they died at their posts, one probably a victim of murder. Another had to be escorted with care and charity back to a sanitarium in the United States, his mind shattered by what he saw and experienced in the famine area. Suddenly, on the date indicated, the director of the American Relief Administration in Moscow was presented with a document from the Kremlin which turned out to be a virtual ultimatum requiring him to turn over the administration of the relief supplies to the Soviet government, which would dispense them thereafter without American supervision. Summoned to headquarters from the billet called the Brown House on that evening in October, I was delegated by Colonel Haskell to condense the long, involved document to cable length for transmission to Washington. "You are a schoolteacher," he observed, "so you make the précis."

The tone and wording of the text clearly meant complete repudiation of the agreement signed by Litvinov at Riga before the feeding operation began. The terms and conditions under which American assistance was to be administered had there been spelled out with great accuracy and much detail. Now that huge quantities of American supplies were safely concentrated in Russia, the treaty was suddenly denounced and surrender of supplies and of the guarantees of autonomy was demanded. Fortunately, the director of the A.R.A. was a leader of men, with the foresight of a statesman as well as the courage of a soldier. Surrender on that vital point, he knew, meant total and continued surrender. He held his ground. Orders were prepared for all units to prepare to move out of Russia, taking supplies and equipment with them, although Colonel Haskell was doubtless well aware, in his heart of hearts, that the 200 men under his command could not have moved a pound of food, supplies, or medical equipment — if, indeed, they could have extricated themselves from the widely scattered areas where they were stationed, should Soviet forces oppose them.

Excitement and suspense mounted in Moscow and in the districts as this conflict of wills progressed. Colonel Haskell refused resolutely to be seduced into the interminable negotiations by which Soviet dialecticians always hope to smother the facts, confuse the issue, and exhaust their opponents. The Soviet ultimatum, he replied, was clear, and the document spoke for itself. The Communist government was given a deadline, set at some forty-eight hours later, for an answer without equivocation.

To its great credit, Washington backed up its representative in the field. The Kremlin retreated many hours before the deadline, replying in the form of an "explanation." "It was all a mistake. . . . The offending document had been sent by error to the great American Relief Administration, whereas," it was soothingly explained, "the text was really intended for certain minor relief agencies, whose assistance was negligible. . . . The clerk who had made the error would be punished," and so forth, and so forth. Obviously, it was a face saver, and a crude one. Every line of the document, the specific references and the description of the colossal feeding operation could apply only to the American Relief Administration. Had appeasement been the fashion at that period instead of honest, firm, and patient maintenance of the equities, that great operation would have passed into history as a huge failure. We all breathed a sigh of relief, returned to our posts — and waited for the next crisis.

It was not long in coming. Attacking from another angle, the Soviets, who, by agreement, were committed to assume some of the administrative expenses, called for an "important conference" in January, 1923. With much display of statistical wizardry, the

Marxian accountants produced a set of figures showing that the American overhead was running to something like 30 per cent of the total value of the relief supplies. Such an unreasonable expense, it was argued, indicated inefficiency and raised serious doubts of the practicality of the entire relief operation as conducted by Americans. The American accountants promptly produced their bourgeois records, from which it was shown that distribution costs had been kept down to 3 per cent, one tenth of the alleged expense. Were the Marxist acrobats embarrassed? Far from it. "Oh, yes," they replied, "a decimal point has slipped."

        ❊   ❊   ❊   ❊

The second stage in penetrating to the depths of the antagonism between the Soviet State and the Christianity of the West was reached during the closing days of a famous trial in Moscow, in March, 1923. Violent religious persecution was then the order of the day; fourteen Catholic ecclesiastics were on trial before the Revolutionary Tribunal, including the only remaining representative of the Catholic hierarchy, Monseigneur Jan Cieplak, Archbishop of Mogilev. At that stage in the evolution of Soviet policy, the procedure was much more direct, less subtle, far more reckless than at present, and wholly uninhibited. Thus, in my own hearing — I was present in the courtroom as Vatican observer — the Soviet Public Prosecutor, Krylenko, addressed to the Archbishop and to all prisoners in the dock a clean-cut ultimatum:

"Will you stop teaching the Christian religion?"

"We cannot," came the uniform answer. "It is the law of God."

"That law does not exist on Soviet territory," replied Krylenko. "You must choose. . . . As for your religion, I spit on it, as I spit on all religions."

Here was and is the authentic mind and voice of Marxian Communism. Although Krylenko was soon to be eliminated from public life and pass into the waiting shadows, the accuracy of his interpretation remains. Basic principles can never be compromised; in a clash to the finish between fundamental opposites, one or the other must prevail. The weakling who attempts to reconcile the root differences between Marxian Communism and

Christianity is engaged in biting on granite. He can only end in breaking his teeth and degrading his intellect. The Soviet Union is the first sovereign State, to my knowledge, which has elevated the negation of God to the status of a principle of political philosophy.

The direct challenge was met by the victims of 1923 with unequivocal refusal to surrender; the anticipated penalties were then swiftly imposed: death, exile to labor camps, various terms of imprisonment, ranging from two to ten years. The formal condemnation was pronounced at midnight on Palm Sunday, 1923. Monsignor Budkiewicz, vicar of St. Catherine's in Petrograd, had his brains blown out in a dungeon of the Lubyanka on the following Good Friday. The others disappeared behind the Iron Curtain of Soviet prison life.

It was shortly after the close of the trial that an incident occurred which revealed a measure of sadism the more repulsive because it was anonymous. Charged by the reigning Pontiff, Pius XI, with the duty of negotiating a peaceful solution of the *impasse* between the Soviet government and the Petrograd clergy, I held myself in readiness for any possibility. When it became evident that certain of the accused would be executed — though eventually we managed to save the life of Archbishop Cieplak — a request was addressed to the Soviet Department of Justice that I be allowed to assist the condemned at the end, as a priest in attendance. The text of my letter made reference to the fact that spiritual ministration to persons condemned to death was a courtesy which civilized nations commonly granted. No answer was vouchsafed. An appeal for commutation of sentence was rejected and experienced newspaper correspondents assured me that Monsignor Constantine Budkiewicz was certainly doomed.

Resolved to go to the prison, if permitted, I sat waiting on the night of March 30 in the dwelling assigned to the Papal Relief Mission on Spiridonovka — waiting alone, since all our Russian employees had been released from their duties in view of the danger of arrest always present for Russian nationals employed by a foreigner. Even my very faithful personal interpreter, Walter Kurrol, had been dismissed for that night, a circumstance I shall never cease to regret, as my knowledge of Russian was too limited to conduct a conversation in the vernacular, should the necessity arise. How it did arise and what transpired I leave to an English writer, Francis McCullagh, an experienced journalist then working in Moscow. He knew the ways of the Bolsheviks and was an adept in ferreting out news. He has the following passages in his *The Bolshevik Persecution of Christianity*.[1]

At twenty minutes past one on the night of Good Friday, March 30, the telephone bell in Dr. Walsh's office suddenly rang. We hated to go into that room because it was a front room and was, when the electric light was turned on, commanded by the silent and inscrutable eyes on the other side of the street; it seemed, consequently, to be permeated, especially at night, by some influence, occult and intensely malignant. The doctor answered the telephone, but was greeted only by a roar of savage laughter, by ribald singing, and by remarks which he could not understand, and which seemed to come from a room full of people. The same mysterious performance was repeated four times that night and no explanation of it was afterwards forthcoming; but from that moment the Papal delegate gave up hope as completely as if he had seen Mgr. Budkiewicz shot. That telephone call came, he surmised, from No. 11, Bolshoi Lubyanka, in the cellar of which the unfortunate priest was murdered; and it probably came from the murderers.

McCullagh's allusion to the silent eyes on the opposite side of the street refers to the constant espionage directed against all foreign missions. Controlling all houses and lodgings, it was an easy task for the secret police to install its agents directly opposite any selected dwelling and maintain constant surveillance. The account continues:

The Papal Mission had been allowed to send packets of food to each of the prisoners. Next day the chocolate addressed to Mgr. Budkiewicz was returned, broken as if by a hammer, and by another route came to a Russian friend a scribbled message: "Budkiewicz has been taken away from us." On April 3 the *Pravda* published the following curt announcement: "On March 31 the death sentence was carried out on Mgr. Budkiewicz, who was sentenced in connection with the trial of the Catholic counter-revolutionaries."

No details of the martyr's last moments have so far been published. The Reds still refuse to give the hour and the place of the murder, or to say where the corpse has been buried. From a good source, however, I have obtained the following information: Mgr. Budkiewicz was conveyed to No. 11, Bolshoi Lubyanka, on the night of Good Friday, and was immediately made to descend into one of the cellars. The method by which the murder was

---

[1] London: John Murray, 1924.

carried out was deliberately arranged with the object of making the martyr die in as undignified a manner as possible. He was stripped naked and made to traverse a dark corridor leading to another cellar, where an experienced executioner was awaiting him. On reaching the end of this corridor, Mgr. Budkiewicz found himself in a room lit up by a powerful electric light that made the unfortunate priest blink and stagger back awkwardly. Before he had recovered himself, the executioner had shot him through the back of the head; and the bullet, coming out through the center of the face, had rendered it unrecognizable.

Having satisfied themselves that their victim was dead, the Bolsheviks wrapped the body in a cloth and carried it into a motor-lorry which was waiting. This motor-lorry brought it to Sokolniki, a summer resort near Moscow, where it was buried with the bodies of nine bandits which had been awaiting interment.

McCullagh's account is substantially correct. Three times that strident telephone rang, at various intervals, and three times I asked the unknown voice to speak English or German or French. But the only reply from the unidentified was a torrent of Russian in a tone unmistakably hostile and vituperative. I shall never know what he was saying or what the background of confused noises might signify; it sounded as if several persons were gathered at the other end of the line. When the telephone rang the fourth time, toward 4 a.m., I let it ring unanswered. One thing, however, we were able to establish: Msgr. Budkiewicz had been executed sometime between midnight and dawn. It was a ghoulish practice, I was told, for the executioners of the G.P.U. to taunt the family or relatives or acquaintances of their victims by anonymous telephone calls. Captain McCullagh's reference to the smashed chocolate bars is wholly accurate; I found them on my doorstep the following morning, left there by I know not whom.

Among the condemned ecclesiastics was one commanding figure whose defense, when he spoke his last word, went to the very roots of an insoluble issue. Meeting this man for the first time in Moscow during the dark days of 1923, I instinctively knew that I was in the presence of an Athanasius. Appointed by Benedict XV, in 1921, as Exarch for Catholics of the Slavonic rite in Russia, Leonidas Feoderov was indefatigable in defending the claims of conscience and the right of Union with the Apostolic See. Clad always in the long, sweeping purple of his office, with flowing hair black as a raven's wing and with a noble beard in the Byzantine tradition, his handsome figure arrested attention in any gathering. But it was the nobility and asceticism of his countenance, the piercing tranquillity of his deep-set eyes, and the sharp contour of his aquiline nose that made his profile such a striking symbol of otherworldliness that he might have served as an artist's model for Christ in the streets of Moscow. Often, during the Terror, when the relentless net of the G.P.U. was tightening around its predestined victims, I was enabled to supply food and to be of service to this intrepid shepherd of a tiny flock that was still unafraid, though marked for certain extermination. His vision of the Calvary that lay before the Church in Soviet Russia was singularly accurate and his counsel for the future was marked by an intuition of the future role of World Communism that has proved prophetic and circumstantial. Among my most treasured possessions are his letters, veritable pastorals filled with encouragement and breathing the calm confidence of one who views all earthly phenomena in the light of eternity. Some of them were composed even in the prison of Sokolniki and smuggled out. One of them requested me to permit no steps to be taken for his exchange or ransom, as prisoners so released by the Bolsheviks were sure to be exiled. His life, he argued, his intellect, and his entire earthly allegiance belonged to his native land whose return to the ancient faith was the consuming flame that illuminated the little study where we first conversed and sustained him throughout the twelve subsequent years of Soviet brutality.

Lost among the eager spectators who attended that trial and saw him arraigned to make a Soviet holiday, I shall not soon forget the final scene. After four days of public and bitter denunciation thinly veiled under a pretext of legal procedure, each accused was permitted to make a final statement before the preordained sentence was imposed. If the Soviet tribunal hoped that mental anxiety and physical fatigue would weaken Leonidas Feoderov, they were roundly deceived. He arose with alacrity and for upward of an hour faced his prosecutors with a courage and nobility of bearing that left them wavering between indignation and respect. Russian of the Russians as he was, born in St.

Petersburg and speaking the language of Pushkin, Dostoevski, and Turgenev much more correctly than his judges, he waved aside the mendacious charge of conspiring with Polish counter-revolutionaries. Of humble origin — his father was a baker — he refuted the conventional charge of reactionary sympathy with the Tzarist regime under which, in point of fact, his faith had been bitterly persecuted and his oriental rite particularly penalized. He himself had suffered imprisonment for several years under the Tzars, as Archbishop Beran of Prague had suffered in Dachau at the hands of the Nazis.

On one point only was he adamant and uncompromising: "If the Soviet government orders me to act against my conscience, I will not obey. As for teaching religion, the Catholic church lays it down that its children will be taught their religion, no matter what the law says. That obligation is above even Soviet law. No law which is against that right can bind." Unable to find other grounds beyond his loyalty to the Catholic religion, the Public Prosecutor, Krylenko, revealed the very essence of Communist jurisprudence when he replied: "We condemn you not only for what you have done, but for what you are capable of doing."

If the Communists hated Cieplak and Budkiewicz, they feared Leonidas Feoderov. So, instead of murdering him outright, they decided to crush his great heart and silence his fearless tongue by degrees. To destroy his spirit, they transferred him from prison to prison, subjecting him to the Soviet process of slow disintegration in the prison camps on Solovetsky Island and elsewhere. But they never broke his spirit. They accomplished their inexorable death sentence in exactly twelve years, at Viatka. On March 7, 1935, the Angel of the Judgment summoned the unconquered soul of Leonidas Feoderov to a higher tribunal. A painting of that heroic figure hangs opposite me at this moment and the remembered eyes gaze tranquilly at me as I pen these lines.

There was a sequel to the tragic events of that Good Friday of 1923; it came in a form that tranquilized one's nerves and set things in a calmer perspective. On Easter Day, while Moscow was still vibrating with the events of the previous week, I motored alone to a hill outside the city to seek a more composed atmosphere for meditating on a crucial problem. The spot is called *Vorobevye Gory*, Sparrow Hills; it was there that Napoleon stood in 1812 and gazed in bewildered anger down on the evacuated stronghold of the Tzars which was eventually to conquer even his Grand Army and shatter his dream of universal empire. From that eminence one commands a sweeping panorama of the plain and the valley of the Moskva River. Below, in the center of converging routes and railroads, sprawled the many-towered capital of the Soviets, a huge, colorful mosaic of tiled roofs in many a hue, slender spires, glittering domes, and graceful minarets. By the riverside, dominating that scene of oriental splendor, rose the historic Kremlin, a red flag floating over the dome of its central building.

The problem was urgent. What was to be done? What answer should the director of the Papal Mission return to the numerous proposals and indignant protests that had reached his desk during the troubled fortnight that had just ended in blood and wholesale condemnation? Funds for famine relief had been generously contributed from the Catholic world and many a telegram had arrived from donors in Europe and America demanding immediate cessation of our activities in the face of such violent persecution. Representations in various languages had been communicated to the Soviet Government from many chanceries in Europe. Secretary of State Charles Evans Hughes had sent a vigorous note on behalf of the Government of the United States. . . . And what were they thinking on another hill overlooking the Tiber?

Unable to resolve my doubts and reach a firm decision, I returned to my headquarters at 32 Spiridonovskaia Ulitza and there reread a recent batch of mail from the Vatican. One paragraph in a letter from the Cardinal Secretary of State held my attention: "I think it opportune that you should not speak of eventual suspension of the aid in case of persecution. The supplies are sent through a spontaneous spirit of charity to the suffering people of Russia without distinction of politics or religion; while requests made to the Government in favor of Catholics are proposed on grounds of justice and equity." The decision was made. The

Papal Relief Mission continued its feeding of the poor and caring for the sick for another year and six months.

❊   ❊   ❊   ❊

The next formative circumstances in my education occurred during two conferences with President Franklin D. Roosevelt in October, 1933. The President had done me the courtesy of inviting me to the White House on the very day when he announced to an astonished press that he had just dispatched an invitation to the Soviet Government to send a representative to Washington for the purpose of negotiating an agreement involving diplomatic recognition of the Soviet Union. It was shortly after four o'clock. The President had ascended from the executive offices to the Oval Room on the second floor of the White House. He was in an exhilarated mood and reflected in his outer bearing the thrill he always experienced in letting fall some new bombshell. After some few preliminaries of courtesy and protocol, we discussed with complete frankness the nature of the announcement which, at that moment, was circling the world on the wires of the newspaper agencies. I shall not here recount the complete substance of that extraordinary interview. One phrase, however, was particularly revealing. In reply to certain observations I had made respecting the difficulty of negotiating with the Soviets, he answered with that disarming assurance so characteristic of his technique in dealing with visitors: "Leave it to me, Father; I am a good horse trader."

This first interview terminated with his request that I prepare two reports for him, one dealing with my personal recommendations respecting religious liberty in Russia, the second with the personality and background of Maksim Litvinov, the Soviet negotiator then preparing to leave Moscow for Washington. The latter request was occasioned by my look of amazement when the President remarked:

"Did you have any dealings with Litvinov? I understand he is a renegade Catholic."

My reply was to the effect that somebody must have been pulling the Presidential leg, as Maksim Litvinov was well known to be a Jew who had passed under several aliases, his family name being Finkelstein. Mr. Roosevelt tossed his head back, moving it from side to side in one of his characteristic gestures. Then, with a laugh, he fished into his pocket, and extricated a crumpled package: "Have a cigarette, Father?"

The two documents were duly prepared and ready for delivery before Litvinov could reach Washington. The first memorandum, in accordance with the President's request, dealt with the Soviet attitude on religion and the provisions of current legislation in that field. It covered nine typewritten pages, legal size, followed by an Appendix of fifty-eight printed pages containing the supporting evidence derived from Soviet sources. Convinced that Mr. Roosevelt had made up his mind to exercise his constitutional prerogative and re-establish diplomatic relations with the Kremlin, I presented no argument against recognition. The sixteen-year-old debate on that subject was now at an end. But in the course of the written statement certain facts were brought to the President's attention. Governments which had already recognized the Soviet Union and exchanged ambassadors had frequently regretted that they had not first required concrete evidence of good faith instead of relying on vague and slippery promises. Hence the memorandum stated:

"Should the same ineffective course be again adopted, the last chance will be lost for a distinguished service to humanity. The United States is the last government in a position to effectively implement such guarantees. This can be done by requiring appropriate and explicit clauses to be inserted in any proposed agreement — and published *before recognition or at least simultaneously*. The unusual circumstances and the extraordinary importance of the issue justify unusual and extraordinary measures. While it is true that recognition without the conditions I have outlined could not, in justice, be interpreted as condoning the notorious political and religious tyranny within Russia, it is equally true that recognition without them would have the practical effect of helping to perpetuate conditions that are matter of public record. Such assistance, though indirect and involuntary, would be wholly alien to American ideals and abhorrent to Christian instincts. There is precedent, too, in

American diplomatic history for the procedure I have here outlined."

Urging the President to profit by the example of governments which had failed to obtain specific and unequivocal performance, the memorandum continues:

"Unless concrete results are achieved before recognition it is the mature judgment of the undersigned, based on long experience with Bolshevik negotiators, that the liberties now being assailed in Russia will never be restored. Soviet negotiators hitherto have beguiled foreign governments into postponing proof of good faith until *after recognition*. That rose once plucked, they have invariably continued their previous offensive policy and referred the inevitable complaints to mixed commissions and other tedious forms of procrastination, or else replied with flat denials of fact and acrimonious counter-charges in unrelated fields. They are masters in all forms of evasion, concealment and in diverting attention away from damaging facts.

"Where diplomatic relations have been established with no tangible accomplishment of fact but only of vague promise, Soviet treatment of diplomatic representatives has been cavalier and often impertinent. Witness the recent treatment of the British Ambassador, Sir Esmond Ovey. Similar rebuffs have greeted similar representations made after recognition by other foreign diplomats. The only time, consequently, when American proposals will have weighty effect is prior to and as a condition of recognition. They have always expressed admiration for Americans and the American way. The undersigned invited the Soviet Government in 1923 to arrange their church problem as we have done it in the United States, where for one hundred and fifty years, there has been complete and harmonious co-operation between Church and State, with no accusation from the government that the population is priest-ridden, ignorant or plunged in superstition. That invitation still stands. They may now be prepared to do something concrete in amelioration of religious persecution in order to secure what they most need from the United States; the public record supports my contention that they would do little should recognition be safely obtained without concrete concessions. And they would doubtless enter it as another victory over the 'bourgeois' world. Mr. Litvinov has already given some inkling of his mind in his Berlin statement that the forthcoming negotiations, as far as he is concerned, need not take more than half an hour."

The second document is entitled *Aide Memoire on Maxim Litvinov* and covers five typewritten sheets, legal size. After a short biographical sketch the text makes the following comments on Litvinov:

"He is persistent, obstinate, incapable of rebuff in the accepted sense, knows exactly what he is after, an excellent intriguer, and capable of gross impudence when he feels he is in a strong position. Knowing the national politics and policies of the various European powers, he skillfully plays one off against the others and in consequence has scored signal successes in the diplomatic field. This was greatly facilitated by the mutual jealousies, conflicting interests, contiguous borders and mutual suspicion which are characteristic of the European powers. In the case of the United States, however, situated far from the European concert and furnished by nature with independence of outlook and judgment, Litvinov should encounter a new set of conditions. His case may now be judged on its intrinsic merits and with a detachment that would be impossible in the traditional nervous atmosphere of European conferences. . . .

"His tactics will probably be to admit nothing and claim much. The Third International he will dismiss as a private organization and he may make reference to Tammany by way of an analogy. When the obvious differences are pointed out he will shift to some other defense. If the President is unable to accept the stereotyped claim of irresponsibility on the part of the Soviet Government Mr. Litvinov may then declare that the world revolutionary programme and influence of the Comintern has been so modified of recent years that it no longer presents a serious obstacle. He will not want to hear that as late as January 22, 1933, the Communist International issued instructions to all Communist groups throughout the world to renew activities and to reverse the policy of quiescence which has been alleged in certain quarters. This reversal of front was published in the form of a manifesto signed by the Executive Committee of the Third International under date of January 22, 1933, but not published until March 6, 1933, in *Pravda*. It was directed particularly against Germany, which is convincing proof of Moscow's policy to shift allegiance when deemed opportune. Germany, Soviet Russia's first ally, was once Moscow's main hope and was considered the second possible link in the chain of world revolution — until the recent measures of Hitler against Communists alienated Moscow. So, she revived the Third International on January 22, this year. This must cause both disappointment and chagrin to those who have honestly argued that the hope of World Revolution having faded, the Third International had been quietly shelved these latter years. It is impossible to reconcile that contention with the facts mentioned above, or with the instructions printed in *Pravda* October 11, 1932, addressed to American members of the Communist Party. In precise and circumstantial language the American Comrades are instructed how to turn minor local disturbances in the United States into major revolutionary outbreaks against constituted American authorities.

"As set forth in the accompanying Memorandum on Religion, definite, frank action, not promises, is the only proof of good faith left to Mr. Litvinov. The acid test of Moscow's sincerity will come when she demolishes and abolishes the Third International with the same finality with which she founded it in 1919. So long as she keeps that instrumentality shielded, fostered and protected in her capital as a weapon of social offense to be unsheathed when opportunity offers, her claims to be considered a friendly government are insincere and unconvincing.

"The comparative inactivity of the Third International in recent years is part of the zigzag method of approaching a permanent objective. The deviations to right and left leave the ultimate goal unchanged. So in his retreat from integral Communism during the NEP, Lenin encouraged private trading and certain forms of Capitalism. But the crisis over, the Party struck the bourgeois again and launched a violent new offensive. The same tactics are followed in international relations.

"The unchanging nature of the Soviet objective is clearly set forth in the Constitution of 1923, preamble, closing sentence: . . . 'a decisive step towards the union of the toilers of all countries into a World Soviet Socialist Republic.' The same Constitution of

1923 maintains that the structure of the Soviet power is *'international in its class character.'*

"This is a matter for serious reflection, as these claims to a universal jurisdiction are not the irresponsible rhetoric of a soap-box orator, but the organic law of the land, embodied in the Constitution.

"Confronted with this objection, the Soviet Party has frequently replied that these passages of the Constitution must not be taken too seriously as they are intended largely for domestic consumption. On the other hand, when complaints and protests have been lodged with respect to persecutions and other excesses, the answer had always been: 'We are only applying the laws of the land as any government must do.' They cannot have it both ways."

The two documents were delivered by me personally on October 31, 1933, at twelve o'clock noon, President Roosevelt receiving me this time in the executive office in the west wing of the White House. On entering the room, I perceived that we were not to be alone. At my left, toward the North wall, a man was apparently working on a clay model of the President's head. It was Mr. Jo Davidson, a well-known sculptor, born in Russia, who at that time and for many years thereafter was an enthusiastic advocate of causes considerably left of center. I understand that Mr. Davidson's affection for Moscow has cooled considerably in recent years. But on the date here under discussion, and because of the circumstances of my visit, I found his presence within easy hearing distance of whatever I might say so curious a coincidence that I chose an attitude of extreme reticence. This conference was short, due to the reservations suddenly imposed on me by the eavesdropper at my elbow. I have reason to know, however, that the President did give a measure of consideration to my documents; they were later transmitted to the State Department with certain notations by his own hand in the margin.

It was President Roosevelt's confident assertion that he would be able to cope with the situation which deepened my foreboding for the future. His attitude gave rise even then to many questions: Does he realize that he will not be dealing with a horse trader from Arkansas but with an experienced conspirator, born Joseph Vissarionavich Dzhugashvili, now known as Joseph Stalin? Is he

familiar with the odds against him? At the Moscow end of Mr.
Litvinov's cables would be sitting an icy-cold revolutionist who
had been bred to ruthlessness and deceit, skilled in double talk
from long encounter with Tzarist police, accustomed to trading
in kingdoms, thrones, and dynasties, and who had beaten the
brilliant Trotsky at his own game, pursued that Machiavelli over
two continents, finally cornered him in Mexico, and hounded him
to death even in a closely guarded retreat.

It took less than two years to reveal how cavalierly Moscow
was to regard the solemn guarantees made in the first Soviet-
American agreement of 1933, particularly in respect to non-
interference in the internal affairs of the United States. Mr.
Cordell Hull in his *Memoirs* describes the stages of disillusionment,
beginning, as they did, with the usual friction and arbitrary
demands from the Kremlin. Although he had sincerely welcomed
the resumption of diplomatic relations with Russia, the Secretary
of State was soon to see his hopes go the downward way of so
many previous precedents and subsequent false starts. The initial
occasion, as customary, was a unilateral demand made within
four months by the Kremlin for something never promised but
which Soviet authorities maintained was what they had really
meant, irrespective of what the American negotiators understood
them to mean at the time of the agreement.

Mr. Hull replied with directness to Ambassador Troyanovsky:
"I must be entirely frank with you. The President, Mr. Bullitt,
Assistant Secretary Moore, and others who took part in the
Russian debt conversations with you, or with Mr. Litvinov, were
greatly disappointed to learn that Mr. Litvinov had offered a
contention and version of the debt understanding entirely different from anything they were thinking about. The misunderstanding is so wide that perhaps it would be best to bring all
commercial and financial relations to a standstill until it can be
clarified."

A few lines further on in the chapter devoted to these incidents,
Mr. Hull described the situation prevailing in 1934, in language
which was prophetic of 1948, 1949, 1950: "An unbreakable
deadlock ensued, despite months of negotiation."

The leopard has not changed his spots.

Then came the ultimate affront to good faith. At the Seventh World Congress of the Communist International held in Moscow in the summer of 1935, Mr. Stalin openly welcomed a delegation of American Communists, among them Mr. Browder and Mr. Foster; he encouraged them in the usual way to renewed activity in their conspiracy for overthrowing the government of the United States, all in patent violation of the Roosevelt-Litvinov agreement. On full and accurate documentation from the American Ambassador in Moscow, Mr. Hull dispatched a vigorous protest against the violation of the plighted word. Not only was the American note repudiated but it was declared unacceptable in a form and in language which demonstrated that the honeymoon was over. The reply was not even signed by Litvinov, then Commissar of Foreign Affairs, but by one of his subordinates. Mr. Hull described the Soviet argument as "an astonishing assertion." Recounting the incident in his *Memoirs,* the former Secretary of State concluded: "We were now back almost to where we had started . . . no bedrock of friendship and co-operation." He finishes his account of the lost horizons of 1935 with the old, familiar, but always late discovery: "Negotiating with Russia was not like negotiating with other powers. In every approach to Moscow I had to bear these things in mind."

In a résumé of similar violations of agreements, of obstruction and sabotage of peace by Soviet Russia, the State Department, on May 18, 1948, published a list of 26 clear instances. Again, on May 23, 1950, the governments of Great Britain, France, and the United States transmitted official notes to the Kremlin accusing the Soviet government of having violated its postwar agreements by establishing in Germany a so-called police force of 50,000 men which was in reality a completely organized military contingent equipped with machine guns, howitzers, antiaircraft cannon, mortars, and tanks. The American note declared that such an organization was not a police force but a German army in direct violation of Soviet pledges given in the Crimea Conference of February 11, 1945, repeated at Potsdam on August 2, 1945, confirmed on September 10, 1945, and embodied, with Soviet agreement, in Control Council Law No. 34, dated August 20, 1946.

* * * *

What has been called the cold war has its roots deep in Soviet psychology: possibly they lie so deep as to remain beyond the sight of the common man. But why the core of the conflict should have so long been missed by responsible statesmen and makers of public policy has not yet been satisfactorily explained. The genius of America produced brilliant technicians and alert experts whose technology and electronic inventions could detect hidden land mines, locate submarines lurking in the depths, and pinpoint hostile aircraft at great distances. Each new military challenge was countered by a new defense, new ingenuity, and by superior weapons such as radar, the Norden bombsight, the proximity fuse, the bazooka, and the Garand rifle. Research and achievement in the physical sciences left little undone. The harnessing of atomic energy to assault and defense marked the logical response from the laboratories. In step with the tempo of the times, jet-propelled aircraft, guided missiles, and torpedoes that seek their own target are now rushing to their appointed places in the mobilization of matter for national defense. It is too facile a solution to hint that a similar responsiveness of mind in the conduct of international relations and diplomacy was deliberately balked by treason in high places, or caused by misplaced confidence or by unwarranted appeasement of Moscow. Some or all of these human forces may indeed have been at work in recent years, as we shall see in a later chapter. But, in all conscience, the ax must be laid closer to the roots of a disturbing paradox in our national character: genius for the practical and concrete phenomena of life, coupled with a kind of tone deafness toward the role of the abstract and metaphysical in the unfolding of world history.

CHAPTER II

To See Life Steadily and See It Whole

IN A previous volume, *The Fall of the Russian Empire* (1927), I expressed the conviction that the Russian Revolution of 1917 was the most significant single political event in the history of Western civilization since the decline and disappearance of the Roman Empire. The years that elapsed since that first publication saw the rise, the full zenith, and the total defeat of the attempted Nazi revolution which temporarily challenged both Western Europe and the Communist World Revolution. Circumstances permitted me to observe both these historic events at firsthand — the Nazi gamble for total power in Germany, and the course of events in Soviet Russia itself during the early years of the Bolshevik regime. A later, though shorter, residence in Japan and examination there of the documentary evidence produced in connection with the trial of Tojo in 1948 furnished additional material for comparison of these three attempts to establish by force cognate forms of empire in three widely separated regions of the earth.

Two of the gigantic conspiracies were defeated at a cost in human lives and material resources which is still felt in the shattered economy of the entire world. The third revolution not only survived but today stands dominant over 800,000,000 people, with its dynamism undiminished in Korea, its enhanced power threatening Western Europe, its subversive activities affecting the internal economy as well as the security of the United States, and its agents infiltrating into the still unconquered states of Asia. The sources of this vitality and the causes of its continuity must be examined if we are to understand why American soldiers had to die in Korea and why this country was again faced, in December, 1950, with the dread necessity of mobilizing for national defense.

Intellectual honesty will not permit us to limit the diagnosis to the narrow orbit of political and economic issues. The roots of the tragedy strike deeper into the soil of history and human motivation. One must mount, as it were, an eminence of the mind, a watch-tower above the sound and fury of the contemporary scene, and contemplate the stream of human experience, cutting its way like a majestic river through the landscape of single events. From such a detached position one will observe that the flow, the vicissitudes and variations in the panorama are marked by recurrent character-istics as the constants in human nature assert themselves. The move-ment of men and nations as their interests clash, the rise and progress of civilizations, the growth of cultures, states, governments, and social institutions do not follow a rectilinear channel, though the general direction of the current may be uniform. History rarely unfolds in sudden leaps but by transitions. There are roots of causality discernible in every past chapter, palpable consequences in every present, and probable dangers in every future. The observer will recognize many a period when progress was tranquil, fairly constant and forward; but, at other times, the waters are troubled and surge violently to right or to left as events multiply and produce crises which result in transitions to other forms of social control, some of which prove better, some worse, perhaps, than those of preceding generations.

These are the moments of choice and high decision in the evolu-tion of the race, which are recognizable by historians and sociolo-gists as veritable crossroads of history. The conscious will of man, exercising freedom of choice in one situation or submitting to forces beyond his present powers in another, changes his way of life for good or evil and thus sets in motion new ferments which serve as prelude to further progress — or result in degeneration as the sequel may reveal. But through this moving tide of change, which to some appears to be mere motion without design, plunges the greatness and the littleness of man obedient to a final cause that holds him like a magnet to his essential course. He wavers, weakens, and is sometimes submerged, only to rise to the surface again and press forward in his ceaseless, unsatisfied urge to bridge the gulf between the finite and the infinite.

Each age, each epoch, may be said to have its own identity. Each has significance and place in the continuity of history; even the evils of them have value, though negative, perhaps, and admonitory in the retrospect of philosophic history and certainly in their relation to man's progress toward eternity. This consciousness of causality in great events — or in small affairs, too — is one of the elements distinguishing a civilized mind from the barbarian who sees no farther than Nietzsche's gross egotism: *"Satan prince of this world — then, be Satanic."*

* * * *

Assuredly the birth of Christ marked such a crossroads of history, introducing, as it did, a profound spiritual and cultural transformation in the ancient world of paganism. His appearance divided even the calendar into two recognizable epochs of time. Man emerged from the mass of indistinguishable humanity as a personality endowed with an individual dignity unknown to the pagan privileged castes of pre-Christian civilizations, though Plato and Aristotle had touched the hem of the revelation. It was the turning point in the spiritual history of the race, the fusion of the complete with the incomplete, which reconciled the freedom of man with the sovereignty of the Omnipotent. The Fall of the Roman Empire introduced ages of political fragmentation in Europe, as the unifying control of Roman law and consular administration gave way to the anarchic localism and feudal psychology of the next thousand years. The discovery of America opened up new vistas for exploration, exploitation, and colonization by the great maritime powers — Spain, Portugal, France, England, and Holland. Their rivalries ushered in a period of conflict for control of the overseas riches which directly affected both the old and the new world for the next three centuries. . . . The Fall of Constantinople in 1453 channeled to Italy and other centers of southern Europe that migration of oriental scholars, precious manuscripts, and classical traditions which gave form and substance to the Renaissance. The revival assuredly constituted a transitional stage in Western culture by exalting unduly the cult of an earthly humanism and laying the foundations of capitalism. The consequences are still with us.

The Italian Renaissance left an indelible imprint on the soul of Europe. It gave to scholarship the Vatican library and an accumulation of beauty in art forms that made the Italian peninsula the richest museum of the age. But it gave us Machiavelli as well, and the riotous venality of Renaissance *condottieri*. Its prodigious intellectual energy and worship of form, line, and color created the golden age of painting, architecture, sculpture, letters, damascened silks, and colorful pageants; but it also condoned a succession of unspiritual pontiffs and publicly dissolute cardinals whose example bred a cancerous heritage of scandal and undisciplined morals that paved the way for the religious revolt of Germany and the northern nations in the sixteenth century. The Eternal City lost much of the pristine quality once attaching to the central shrine of Christianity as its ruling minds became fascinated with the artistry and aesthetic niceties of an exhumed pagan naturalism. The subsequent revolution in faith, dogma, and religious loyalties split the once Catholic Europe into two hostile camps. Under the leadership of Martin Luther and by stimulation of secular princes serving their own interests, the seamless robe of Christ was rent in twain. Christendom divided itself into Catholic and Protestant states which rapidly transformed their theological differences into permanent political animosities. Thirty years of savage, fratricidal war was the evil fruit of reckless seeding. When the great cleansing came in the Tridentine period and in the succeeding General Council it came as a Counter-Reformation in time to prevent complete disintegration of the ancient faith but too late to preserve the unity of Christendom.

The Peace of Westphalia in 1648 consecrated and perpetuated the Balkanization of the Christian Commonwealth by validating the concept of separate sovereignties and legalizing the principle of self-centered and jealous nationalism. The modern State system, as contrasted to a universal Christendom, became the political counterpart of the new theological doctrine setting up individual and private interpretation of the Scriptures as the sole norm of religious belief and moral conduct. The social and political consequences were implicit in the theological premises of the successful religious revolt. If each individual man was to become the private interpreter of the rules for obtaining eternal salvation — no Supreme Court acknowledged — it was starkly logical for kings, princely rulers, and national States to demand the same untrammeled sovereignty, i.e., freedom from external control, in the conduct of international relations.

The American Revolution of 1776 marked another transition to new channels of thought. The successful challenging of the hitherto dominant principle of monarchy by thirteen English colonies strung along the Atlantic seaboard had immediate effects not only throughout the Western Hemisphere but in Europe as well. The idea set fires that were reflected in the flames of the French Revolution consuming the residue of Feudalism, and in the series of revolts which ended the last vestige of monarchy in Latin America.

The Industrial Revolution of the late eighteenth century, originating in England with the harnessing of steam power to machinery, enlarged the factory system, multiplied productivity, transformed economic processes, and accelerated the rise of Finance Capitalism. But, despite its acknowledged contributions to the conveniences of life and its miracles of increased productivity, the fascination of material achievement created false values, gave undue license to a *laisser-faire* economy, embittered relationships between capital and labor, and furnished the Marxist agitator with some of his most telling accusations of exploitation and enslavement of the masses.

We come finally to the greatest of all crossroads in modern history, the successful seizure of power by Communism in Russia on November 7, 1917. One epoch ended and an age of special conflict began. It is with that far-reaching social upheaval and its consequences that the following pages are concerned. An attempt will be made to probe to the core of the reasons why the Russian Revolution alone has survived and prospered in contrast with the two similar attempts that proved abortive within recent memory.

✿   ✿   ✿   ✿

The changed circumstances and the new conditions created for the United States by events in Korea, though far from canceling out optimism or weakening our determination to achieve eventual victory, make it imperative for us to consider soberly and realistically the odds against us. We must cease imagining that victory in every war, great or small, is a national inheritance. The bare fact that we were victorious in every previous armed conflict is a historical truth which, like the Scriptures, can be twisted into error and self-destruction. The humility of understanding and the understanding of humility must underlie our thought processes and discipline our mental attitudes. General James Wolfe, in an order to his troops before Quebec in 1759, wrote: "Next to valor, the best qualities in a military man are vigilance and caution." The warning applies to those charged with safeguarding the political, economic, and social existence of a State as well as to military leadership.

The long history of the republic as a form of government in ancient Rome, if re-examined, will suggest many a fruitful meditation for those who are impressed with the duration of Democracy in the United States. There were over 400 years of popular rule in Rome, treated by historians as the Early, Middle, and Late Republic. Then followed the oligarchy and finally the Empire of Augustus in 27 B.C. The final disappearance of the greatest political organization of antiquity, in the fifth century A.D., was not due to external assaults alone but to the slow and corroding disintegration of the physical and moral foundations of Rome's ability to meet her far-flung obligations and preserve the *Pax Romana*.[1] The powerful framework of Roman rule — the greatest thus far known — collapsed from inner rot complicated by the assault of younger, undisciplined civilizations, leaving the mistress of the world to become, in Byron's haunting phrase, "the lone mother of dead Empires."

---

[1] Toward the end of the Republic, in Cicero's days, the approaching storm was often lamented by the great orator. Thus, in his celebrated oration *Pro Lege Manilia* he says: "It is difficult, fellow citizens, to describe in words how hated we are by the nations abroad because of the abuses and the greed of the men we have sent with plenary power to rule them during these past years." The following paragraphs deal with the type of official sent to the provinces to represent the occupying power.

That historic event, as we have noted, profoundly influenced the subsequent history of Europe. It was not a single, colossal crash, as if some mighty edifice suddenly collapsed at a given moment with a deafening roar heard round the world. The phrase is a descriptive expression, not a definite date that can be precisely determined and recorded on the calendar. The collapse was a long process which entered on its final stage after the line of so-called Antonine Emperors — let us say sometime around the beginning of the third century A.D. It was preceded by 200 years of Roman supremacy in stability of government, in policing of large areas of Europe, Asia, and Africa, in road making, law enforcement, art, literature, and in general excellence of the material and outward aspects of civilization. But after the Antonine Emperors a distinct downward grade is observable as the Empire fell into the hands of upstart soldier-emperors; it was often put on the auction block by the Pretorian Guard and knocked down to the highest bidder. Economic crises recurred, progressively deeper, and at shorter intervals. The currency was debased; art and literature palpably degenerated, descending from Golden Age to Silver Age to the brass of mercurial scribblers and lascivious potboilers. Even architecture showed a coarsening of the virility and purity of the Greco-Roman arch, pillar, and architrave.

Simultaneously, morals, both public and private, sank into the cesspool of iniquity which Juvenal lampooned so vigorously in his satires, particularly the prevalence of divorce and the easy exchange of wives. Small wonder, then, that the barbaric tribes from the North and pirates in the Mediterranean gradually infiltrated to the very heart of the Empire and destroyed its prestige and culture. They found an ennervated and effeminate civilization, ripe for the ruthless invasions of Huns, Goths, and miscellaneous plunderers of Germanic and Oriental origin. As one analyst writes: "In part, at least, the economic crisis was due to the heavy burdens of government and defence, and to the oppressive and erratic system of taxation; in part, perhaps, to a fatigue of spirit. . . . Each Emperor chose his own successor. . . . The military power absorbed all the functions of government. . . . Besides the separate and elaborate administration for each territorial unit, the emperors had an extensive central bureaucracy — e.g., the *magister officiorum* — the personnel manager, who was very powerful because he had a finger in every department. . . . "[2]

By A.D. 308 this enormous machine, corroded by corruption, was clanking to disaster. Emperors found themselves at war with their generals; generals proclaimed themselves emperor at the drop of a hat. A new capital arose in 330 at Constantinople and the Empire was divided; domestic rivalries increased, as the external menace grew stronger and more insolent. Britain was evacuated of Roman troops in 407; Alaric sacked Rome in 410; Attila invaded Italy in 452. Murder became a fine art obligatory on every aspirant to the royal purple, until in 476 the last Emperor of the West was deposed by Odoacer, a barbarian commander, at Ravenna — the circumstance which traditionally marks the end of the Roman Empire, after a decline of some 276 years. Like all previous and later civilizations which met disaster, it was not murdered; it committed slow suicide. During the process, it followed an observed degenerative pattern: monarchies and oligarchies decline from the head downward, democracies decay from the roots upward.

❋   ❋   ❋   ❋

If examined chapter by chapter, the course of the Russian Revolution demonstrates the presence of competent and continuous staff planning. Although at times during the thirty-four years of its span the tactics may have seemed unrealistic and erroneous, yet as end result, the Revolution outdistanced and outmaneuvered its more orthodox and cautious opponents. The cumulative effects stamp it as the revolution of revolutions in respect to both the quality and quantity of change it has introduced in such large and important areas of international life. Whether these transformations of values in the Nietzschean sense will endure as permanent political and amoral standards, only time can tell. What may with propriety be attempted is to relate the Revolution to its historical antecedents and seek to discern its probable future.

Among the more striking social achievements may be recognized a concrete realization of Vilfredo Pareto's celebrated theory on the

---

[2] *Encyclopedia of World History,* Compiled and Edited by Prof. Langer of Harvard University, 1940, pp. 117–122.

circulation of the elite. The Italian sociologist, combing through the wealth of data he culled from the history of revolutions, concluded that they all reveal certain constant characteristics affecting social classes.[3] Though overmuch fascinated by a kind of mathematical sociology, he correctly emphasizes one constant phenomenon. Power passes upward, i.e., from stocks once considered inferior by the ruling classes but who eventually displace the privileged groups of the old regime. The transfer is not a mass transfer but is accomplished by the elite, by the more capable leaders among the previously submerged groups — men who correspond at their social level to the same smaller elite which controlled power for and in the name of the privileged upper strata. In both classes there is found a governing elite and a nongoverning elite.

In normal times, rise to political power by individuals from the humbler level is possible and frequent, as happened in the case of Abraham Lincoln in this country and Count Witte under the Tzars in Imperial Russia. What revolution accomplishes is to speed up the process and increase the velocity of class circulation, the *circulation des élites* as the French put it. One group is pushing its way up the stairs to political power while another is descending to the exit. History, Pareto concludes, is a graveyard of aristocracies which have lost their vigor, squandered the residue of values inherited from more robust ancestors, and entered on the inevitable process of physical decadence and intellectual decay. Superior intellects accumulate in the lower strata and, conversely, inferior minds become more numerous in the upper class. And the rising consciousness of the hitherto submerged group is not adverse to using force at a given moment, whereas the upper class, through the fatal inertia of wealth, becomes more disposed to buy off its adversaries by bargains and concessions — until it is too late and the first leg is over the wall.

To be sure, there was no earth-shaking social discovery in Pareto's leisurely and rich documentation of this lesson of history. It is cited here for the purpose of noting the new element of international challenge introduced by the Communist revolution of November 7, 1917. The circulation of the elite, in the Soviet

[3] *Trattato di Sociologia Generale*, published in English as *The Mind and Society*, 4 volumes (New York: Harcourt, Brace, 1935).

logistics, is not to be limited to citizens of any one country ripe for revolution: it is to become a world-wide transformation in which the units involved are no longer individuals or groups of citizens in a given State but governments, nations, and continents. The verses of the *Internationale* which visualized the entire human race were neither rhetoric nor metaphor. That is the aspect which, by a sort of reverse English on the ball, makes the rise of the Communist State comparable to the influence of the fall of the Roman Empire on the history of Europe and on the cultures which derive from it.

What of the American Revolution in this day and generation? The form of government which it created has survived substantially unaltered under one continuing Constitution for a hundred and sixty-two years. It has witnessed the progressive elimination of monarchies in Europe and Asia since 1789 until kingship is now limited to a handful of countries in the entire world. But dictatorships are on the increase, and the American Democracy finds itself at war with one of them in Korea at this moment. Are we witnessing the extension of the Monroe Doctrine to meet the challenge of Soviet doctrine in Europe and Asia?

The suddenness and surprise of the invasion of South Korea by a Communist satellite army reveal the emerging pattern and main logistics of the Russian Revolution in its current phase. Direct conflict with America is definitely assumed and included in the Soviet program, as will appear in the chapters of this study dealing with Lenin and Stalin. The manner and timing of that eventual clash probably constitute the main preoccupation of the technicians charged with scheduling the progressive stages of world revolution. The decision to move into South Korea in June, 1950, was, in all probability, not taken with intent to precipitate a general war at that time but as a localized operation of a limited, raiding character. The withdrawal of American troops in 1949 and the inviting opportunity thereby created, apparently, was deemed sufficient argument for a calculated risk involving no commitment of Soviet troops. This abstention from a full-dress military invasion, but rather reliance on the Trojan Horse technique, has characterized Soviet tactics since 1945; the record of success in other satellite lands gave every hope for a similar "liberation" of South Korea.

When all the evidence is in and reliable information becomes available, one need not be surprised to find that the North Koreans were used as expendable pawns in a game of chess — in which Russians have long excelled. Neither king nor queen was in danger, and the game itself was at its early stage. The unexpected firmness of the United States, and the unforeseen support of 52 out of the 59 members of the United Nations in a unified resistance, obviously checked the cautious gamblers in the Kremlin, without however forcing them into a position of complete checkmate in their favorite game.

A more disastrous alternative, however, is wholly possible and cannot be ignored. The Korean adventure resulted in disruption of Soviet Russia's immediate program and endangered her grip on satellite lands by reason of the demonstrated resolve of the United States to face the Revolution with finality and challenge its advance. Desperation or anger, or both, then forced the Kremlin to reverse its tactics. It decided to deploy its controlled mercenaries in Manchuria and China in order to drive United Nations' forces out of Korea. That accomplished, the Revolution could equally well transfer the pressure elsewhere and siphon off American power to other threatened sectors, including Berlin, and thus prolong the present tension for an unpredictable number of years. Europe was once plagued with a Hundred Years' War between France and England, lasting from 1338 to 1453, characterized by sustained campaigns, fragile truces, victories, defeats, the ravages of the Black Death, peasant revolts, foreign alliances, stretches of dreary peace, English monarchs proclaimed kings of France, Paris occupied, and Joan of Arc burned at the stake. The smell of warfare was in the nostrils of three generations.

So now, as an alternative to the pattern of local wars and constant attrition, the Russian Revolution may judge that the hour has struck to cast the "ifs" and "buts" into its favorite "dustbin of history" and abruptly pour its millions of reserved troops into several Armageddons of its own choice for the final, direct encounter with the entire non-Communist world. Such a momentous decision may indeed not be imminent; but who shall say what is proximate, ultimate, or penultimate in the Soviet strategy? In August, 1950, Mr. Winston Churchill declared that the West had not more than two years of breathing space to prepare and by preparing possibly head off World War III.

Whatever hypothesis becomes reality, whatever alternative the Politburo may choose, several grim eventualities remain crystal clear. The government of the United States, committed to a road from which there is no turning back, faces the gravest crisis of responsibility in the history of its international relations. The viewpoint developed by our only living ex-President, Mr. Herbert Hoover, in his broadcast of December, 1950, represented the attitude of many Americans. We would best serve our cause, this school maintains, by recognizing our limitations and retiring from defense of continental Europe and Asia. We should limit our commitments to a cordon of oceanic bases, including Japan, Formosa, and the Philippines in the Pacific and Britain — if she so desires — in the Atlantic. With our available air and sea power focused on these attainable objectives, adequate protection would thus be available to make the Western Hemisphere a "Gibraltar of civilization." The opposition, in dissenting from Mr. Hoover's analysis, maintained that such a policy would be cowardly abandonment of friendly peoples to whom we have already pledged military assistance in case of Communist attack. Former Secretary of War, Robert P. Patterson, called Mr. Hoover's proposal a "counsel of discouragement, despair, and defeat."

On one point, however, the debaters could not help being in agreement. Western Civilization, as a whole, confronts the most formidable challenge since the barbarian hordes from the North overran the capital of embattled Rome during the twilight of the Empire. The scepter of the Caesars passed to Byzantium and from thence to Moscow where Ivan III assumed the heritage, after the fall of Constantinople in 1453. It was then that the escutcheon of Muscovy for the first time included a double-headed eagle facing east and west; a new title, *samoderzhets,* autocrat, was likewise appropriated by Ivan. His Marxist successors in the Kremlin feel the same stirrings of the messianic spirit which impelled the Princes of Moscow to declare that the first Rome had fallen, that the second succumbed to the Moslems, and that now: "The third Rome, Moscow, stands, and a fourth there will not be."

*   *   *   *

The present managers of the Russian Revolution have not relied on power alone to achieve their ambitious program. They added psychological warfare to their arsenal of weapons and have developed that technique as vigorously as military modes of assault. They rode the wave of history with intelligent understanding of the phenomenon which Professor Quincy Wright analyzes in his monumental *Study of War*[4] published after sixteen years of preparation and research. In the course of a summation dealing with wars in modern times, this laborious delver into the sociological aspects of armed conflict notes an important change in the causes of such clashes between governments. Wars occurring in the early stages of civilization, he finds, were usually fought over political and economic issues, with territorial expansion or integration of an existing civilization as the specific objective. But with growth in the size of political units and because of the increasing interdependence of states . . . "political and economic ends became less tangible and cultural patterns and ideal objectives assumed greater importance."

Pitirim Sorokin in his four-volume work, *Social and Cultural Dynamics,* likewise provides a wealth of information and historical data covering twenty-five centuries of recorded wars and revolutions. He concludes that the twentieth century of the Christian Era will undoubtedly "prove to be the bloodiest and most belligerent of all the twenty-five centuries under consideration." The upswing of the war indicator, he concludes, is due to the nature and causes of modern belligerency, i.e., to social and cultural crises leading to a climax of catastrophe.[5]

G. K. Chesterton, in *A Short History of England,* when dealing with the racial fatalism that first came to Elizabethan England in the war with Spain, has an arresting passage on . . . "the idea of *natural* wars, not arising from a special quarrel but from the nature of the nations quarrelling."

Such a climax of conflicting ideas and ideals, in its full intensity, may or may not, as yet, be actually upon us. But that we are caught in its movement and sweeping toward the consummation can hardly be denied. The direction imparted to the tide by the

---

[4] Pages 1288–1290.
[5] *Dynamics,* Vol. III, Chaps. 9, 10, 11.

calculating policy of the Politburo sitting in the Kremlin, with an outpost in the United Nations, is as clearly recognizable as are the volume and content of the upheaval. The fact that it is the weight and the might of Russia which lend stimulus and give character to the present international turmoil derives from three qualities of the Russian temperament.

Historically, no nation has a longer background of revolutionary preparation, revolutionary leadership, and revolutionary technique; as a result, the literature and theory of revolution in modern times bear the hallmark of their Russian origin. Although the ideologues of the French Revolution contributed something in their time to the stock of ideas and methods, and although Sorel and Proudhon wrote in French and Marx, Kautsky, and Engels in German, the leading exponents of the art were Herzen, Bakunin, Leo Deutsch, Stepniak, Pisarev, Prince Kropotkin, Plekhanov, Nechaiev, Gorki, Radek, Trotsky, Bukharin, Preobrazhensky, Lenin, and Stalin. Their combined output of revolutionary writings and organized agitation in the concrete gives them a unique pre-eminence in what came to be recognized as a special profession (see Appendix III).

Spiritually, the Russian people were alienated from Western Europe at their very infancy as a nation. The predominant religion of the land inherited its special character and organizational structure from Byzantium in A.D. 988. Unlike the Western Slavs who had experienced the influence of the Roman Empire and continued much of the Latin tradition even after the disappearance of Roman consuls and administrators, the Eastern Slavs received their first official introduction to Christianity from sources in spiritual rebellion against the West. The Russian Church, moreover, by origin and later by compulsion, became allied with Caesarism. Under the growing power of the Grand Duchy of Moscow, as it developed across the centuries into the autocracy of the Tzars, the Orthodox Church, though cutting loose from Constantinople in 1589, lost its independence and the ability to develop effective spiritual or social leadership. Ivan IV, called The Terrible, simply had his strangler murder the metropolitan of Moscow, Archbishop Philip, when that saintly churchman remonstrated against the Tzar's brutalities. The ultimate subjection came in the reign of Peter the Great who abolished the Patriarchate in 1700 and humiliated the Church to the status of an inferior agency, subservient to the imperial will. This subordination of the spiritual to the secular had profound consequences on the subsequent history of the Russian State. Lenin regarded Peter as the first Bolshevik and declared that he was his political ancestor.

The finer minds of the Orthodox Church — and there have been many among clergy and laity alike — often longed for the opportunity to exercise the leadership so often manifested by the Western Church in its frequent conflicts with ambitious kings, arrogant emperors, robber-barons, and miscellaneous oppressors of the common folk. But the Crown, working through the Holy Synod, had a genius for transferring to Siberia any priest or bishop suspected of inclination, or even capacity, to assume the role of an Ambrose of Milan before a Theodosius, the royal murderer of Thessalonica. It was as if a Cabinet officer of an American administration had the power to transfer Cardinal Spellman from New York to Anchorage in Alaska, or order Bishop Dun to quit the Protestant Episcopal Cathedral in Washington for a parish in Guam. There has been no Canossa in Russian history.

Together with this outward Erastianism in State-Church relationships went the long-standing inner animosity of mind toward Latin Christianity in the West. The great ecclesiastical schism inaugurated at Constantinople by the usurping Patriarch Photius, in A.D. 857, was consummated by his successor, Michael Caerularius, in 1054. This period of turbulent conflicts over dogma, doctrine, and jurisdiction coincided with the period of the conversion of the Eastern Slavs from paganism to Christianity. The Eastern schism was in the making and headed for the unhappy climax of 1054. It was not Rome, then, but rebellious Constantinople that predisposed the Russian soul to contradiction and signed the baptismal certificate. The contemporary polemics in the United Nations reveal something of the historical origins of the vituperation hurled at the Western Allies by Gromyko, Molotov, Malik, and Vyshinski. Thus, Nicetus Pectoratus, a monk favoring the schism of Caerularius called his Western opponents "dogs, bad workmen . . . hypocrites, and liars." The archschismatic himself, Caerularius, anticipating Lenin, described his Western adversaries as "insolent, boastful, rash, arrogant, and stupid."

By the beginning of the twelfth century, Russia was lost to anything resembling unity of religious doctrine with Western Christendom and was well on her way to the political and cultural separation which characterizes her national attitude at the present time. The brief truce and short union effected at the Council of Florence in 1439 ended in failure and a gradual renewal of the ancient animosities. Even that short-lived union, like the previous attempt at Lyons was not a basic meeting of minds; it was largely an act of prudence on the part of the Byzantine Emperor, John Paleologus, faced as he was by the threatened assault on Constantinople by the Turks. There were many sincere advocates of peace in the Eastern camp, such as the learned Bessarion, Archbishop of Nicea, and the energetic Isadore of Kiev. But the full record suggests that the maneuver, from the political point of view of lay Byzantium, was not unlike the temporary alliance made by Stalin with the Western powers after Hitler had invaded Soviet Russia in 1941. It would be difficult for an impartial historian to affirm the sincerity of the Byzantine emperors for religious reunion.[6]

Russian canonical writings, from the Metropolitan Leontius (1004), George (1072), Ivan II (1089), and Nicephoras I (1121) down to the lay writings of Khomiakov and the present Soviet-sponsored Patriarch, are implacably hostile to the Roman. Their position was historically determined, whether the term Roman be used to connote the predominantly Latin origins of Western civilization or to denote specifically the religious organization centered on the Papacy — which is considered the true schismatic. Rudyard Kipling, though more concerned with secular appearances than with theology, touched on the core of the problem. Russia, he wrote, must be considered not as the most Eastern nation of the West, but the most Westerly nation of the East. The new Tzars have continued the Romanov system by utilizing selected leaders of Orthodoxy as endorsers and props of the Soviet Empire.

This is not to insinuate that the Church in Russia did not have its martyrs and confessors during the Revolution. On the contrary, there was a long succession of courageous Orthodox bishops, priests, and laymen who held their Christianity above Marxism and

---

[6] *Catholic Encyclopedia*, Vol. VI, p. 765.

suffered death, exile, or degradation for their constancy. The present writer paid willing and unequivocal tribute to their memory in a previous work.[7] So too, Orthodoxy in the United States has registered its protest against the subjection of the mother Church in Russia to the purposes of world Communism. In a national *Sobor* (Council) convoked on December 5, 1950, at New York, the Russian congregations repudiated the jurisdiction of the present Soviet-controlled Patriarchate and erected themselves into an autonomous body, the North American Orthodox Church. By an open ballot of 231 to 7, the Council voted against retaining in the liturgy the commemoration for Alexsey, the Patriarch of Moscow, who had warmly praised Stalin and condemned the United States as an aggressor.

Psychologically, the Russian people — upon whom the Revolution is based and without whose acquiescence it could not have been launched or so long sustained — have always revealed qualities of frustrated mysticism which inclines them to constant acceptance of contradictions and paradoxes. The nonlogical, if appealing, can produce moods and exaltations in their souls wholly at variance with their better selves. Those who have had frequent contact with representative Russian intellectuals, particularly with those of Slavic temperament, often marvel at the versatility with which in one conversation they range the whole gamut of inquiry from metaphysics to nymphomania with an alert, restless curiosity that betokens something more than mere emotional frivolity. In their years of suffering, when I first knew them in Russia during the early years of the Revolution, the more thoughtful among them seemed forever drifting rudderless in an immense sea of speculation but grasping always at the infinite, searching everywhere for God. That is why their favorite mood was melancholy tempered by resignation. *Bogoiskateli*, seekers after God, is a term that occurs often in their literature to describe themselves.

It was the genius of one of their greatest word artists, Anton Chekhov, to weave the national temperament into his plays, novels, and short stories with a haunting and intimate simplicity that is

---

[7] *The Last Stand — An Interpretation of the Soviet Five Year Plan* (Boston: Atlantic Monthly Press, 1931), pp. 169–219.

often more revealing than the harrowing and soul-searchings of Dostoevski and Tolstoi. In the second act of *The Three Sisters,* Chekhov makes Colonel Vershinin say: "Well, if we can't have any tea, let's philosophize, at any rate. . . . Let us meditate . . . about life as it will be after our time." Despite the perpetual frustration of their little hopes, the three sisters, marooned in a dull provincial town, never quite abandon their fading dream of getting back to Moscow. One by one their friends depart, the last symbol of desolation being a group of artillery officers making their farewells to the music of the regimental band:

Màsha. Oh, how the music plays! They are leaving us, one has quite left us, quite and for ever. We remain alone, to begin our life over again. We must live . . . we must live. . . .

Irina (*puts her head on Olga's bosom*). A time will come when every one will know what all this is about, what all this suffering is for, there will be no more mysteries, but meanwhile we must live . . . work, only work! To-morrow I will go away alone, I shall teach at the school and give my whole life to those who may want it. Now it's autumn, it will soon be winter, the snow will cover everything, and I shall be working, I shall be working. . . .

Symbolical of passive fatalism is their brother, Andrei, who had gradually degenerated from an ambitious aspirant to a professorship in Moscow down to the slackness of a bored bureaucrat of the municipality to whom an aged and deaf messenger is constantly bringing documents to be signed. Falling into melancholy, the brother soliloquizes on his past also, on his lost opportunities and his unfulfilled destiny. The particular lot of each character is identified with the universal. . . . The curtain falls on more documents still unsigned.

In another of Chekhov's classics, *Uncle Vanya,* the motif of felicity far off but still to be achieved is expressed by Sonya at the conclusion of the play:

. . . and there, beyond the grave, we shall say that we had suffered, that we had cried, that our lot had been bitter, and God will take pity on us, and both of us, uncle, dear uncle, shall see a life lofty and tender and beautiful, we shall know gladness and look on our present predicaments with affection, a smile — and we shall rest.

We shall rest! We shall hear angels, we shall see heaven all diamonds, we shall see how all evil drowns in the mercy that shall engulf the whole world, and our life will be peaceful and tender and sweet, like a caress. . . .

In Pushkin's poem-novel, *Eugene Onegin,* we find the classic type of "the eternal wanderer" whose proud rebelliousness is forever seeking a better world in Russian terms, but wasting his genius without making it fruitful for mankind.

It is in the works of Dostoevski, however, that one can best recognize that reconciliation of good and evil which is so easy of achievement by Russian intellectuals. In him the religion of suffering found its most characteristic Russian expression. He himself, in his work *Humbled and Outraged,* described it as "mystic fright." The paradox reaches its climax in *Crime and Punishment.* Raskolnikoff, a murderer, accepts the necessity of expiation and throws himself at the feet of Sonya, the prostitute who supported her parents in the only way open to her: "It is not before thee I kneel — I prostrate myself before the suffering of all humanity." Raskolnikoff, conquered by remorse, confesses his crime and is condemned; Dostoevski makes Sonya teach him how to pray and has them both go tranquilly to Siberia, the house of the dead, in expiation of their sins. For Dostoevski, Russia — and in sum all humanity — is a penitent forever seeking salvation, wandering in uncertainty, and suffering in the darkness of welcomed agony.

Tolstoi continued the tradition of the Russian intellectual forever seeking a true course — and ending in Nihilism. Among the gallery of individual portraits that adorn the pages of *War and Peace,* and reflect the contradiction that obsessed other Russian thinkers as well as his own soul, Tolstoi paints a full-length specimen in Prince Andrew Volkonsky, the proud, cold, refined skeptic. Lying wounded on the field of Austerlitz, he stares at the sky and meditates: "That distant sky, high up there, eternal. . . . If I could only say 'Lord, have mercy on me.' . . . But to whom shall I say it? Either to an Indefinite Power who is inaccessible, whom I cannot even define in words; the Great All or the Great Nothing — or is it the God which is contained in this charm given me by Mary? . . . Nothing, nothing is certain, except the Nothingness of everything I can conceive and the majesty of something I cannot understand."

It would be an error to imagine that this mournful mysticism was confined to the intelligentsia. If anything, it was deeper and more elemental among the "black people" of the soil. The Russian muzhik when steeped in vodka reveals a sordid grossness and a slumbering animality limited only by physical capacity. But, the orgy over, he will weep with you in brotherly understanding, condone thieves (was there not a good thief on the right hand of the dying Saviour?), shield murderers with compassion, and manifest instantaneous sympathy with all suffering fellow pilgrims in this vale of tears. He pities himself and you, and murmurs to the stubborn earth, as he plows and hoes it in his unending task of wringing a bare subsistence from the soil, "*Gospodi pomilui! . . . Gospodi pomilui!* — Lord, be merciful!"

Despite this fundamental anchoring of life in religion — noted, as it has been, by every discriminating traveler in Russia — the historical fact remains that its people for over 32 years have been forced to tolerate an anti-God government and supply the man power necessary for the expanding Soviet domination of Europe and Asia. The apparent transformation of the traditional compassion characteristic of the Russian soul into the nihilism, the gross inhumanity and exploitation practiced by Russian armies in occupied Europe would seem to be flat negation of the quality of pity so prevalent in Russian literature. One asks himself if the former reputation was a sham? Or have the wells of motivation been poisoned by some evil influence that worked corruption of heart and mind throughout an entire nation?

The paradox becomes intelligible if we consider two elements in the complex Russian, one psychological and permanent, the other material and contemporary. Grossness and brutality, crime, punishment, war, peace, sheer sensuality, and spiritual sensitivity dwell side by side in one breast without the slightest inconvenience. The juxtaposition fills the pages of representative Russian writers, notably those already cited — Chekhov, Tolstoi, and Dostoevski. Stephen Graham, though an Englishman, caught the mood when he contends that Russians are always spiritually *en route* to some place . . . and however mean, ugly, and strange an individual Russian's life may seem, it is, nevertheless, a part of his great pilgrimage. The theme runs unceasingly through peasant thought and was found in Dostoevski's personal joy that he had suffered a term of penal exile in Siberia.

Whether the mysticism be authentic or a myth, the next fact

is equally clear. The Politburo has capitalized on it with great shrewdness and political profit. The men in the Kremlin have now had an entire generation at their mercy and fashioned it to at least passive conformity with the Marxian vision of paradise through economics. They created an earthy counterpoint as response to the dominant note of Slavic psychology. They made flesh and matter the Logos that came to dwell as god among men. They thus substituted a new divinity to fill the nostalgia in Russia's soul and set up a new Jerusalem for Ivan Ivanovich's unending pilgrimage. Whether or not he accepts the new theology in his heart of hearts we have no sure way of knowing, as he dwells behind an iron curtain or disappears by millions into concentration camps; his voice, as a people, is as mute as was the tongue of his patron saint, Seraphim of Sarof, who spoke not a word in his hermitage for 35 years even while Napoleon was invading Holy Russia. There is no record of the first word he spoke when he broke his silence.

We have no indication as yet of the day and the manner of Russia's liberation from its latest form of despotism nor of the activities of any organized domestic underground comparable to the French and Polish resistance in World War II. Its people are a long-suffering race accustomed to the yoke fashioned by successive rulers who ranged in technique from the Tatar conquerors to Ivan the Terrible and the present Politburo.[8] Throughout her long and tumultuous history Russia has rarely been governed by the masses or by the proletariat, nor has her destiny depended on informed acceptance of the true issues involved in a given instance. At this point one may question that word "rarely" and ask — "Was she ever governed by the people in contradistinction to an autocracy?"

The answer must be that she once was so governed. There existed a vigorous and independent democratic tradition in the Slavic civilization of former centuries. Autonomous republics such as Pskov and Novgorod were city-states as jealous and assertive of their freedom as was ever Ghent, Venice, or Florence. The

---

[8] This is not to suggest that underground resistance is impractical in the satellite countries, nor to seem unaware of claims in some quarters that a substantial resistance is developing inside Russia.

Court of Yaroslav at Novgorod saw true popular assemblies of free men, the *Vecha*, determining the character of their political institutions six hundred years before the Mayflower reached Plymouth; its Declaration of Independence was drawn up seven centuries before the Philadelphia masterpiece of Thomas Jefferson and was much shorter, too: "If the Prince is bad, into the mud with him." But the growing power and appetite of the near-by principality of Moscow gradually snuffed out liberty in those primitive and boisterous democracies of the steppes, until by 1570, Moscow became what it still is, the despotic center and sole mouthpiece of old, free Russia. From the days of Ivan the Terrible, down to the present apotheosis of Joseph Stalin, Russia has obeyed the autocrat or dictator in command, whether authority took the form of a hereditary dynasty or a self-appointed Politburo. The ruling power always relied on that intangible but gripping love for Mother Russia which historically bound her people to their land, even when the bond was a fetter and the burden heavy.

This folk trait runs through Russian psychology in a manner quite different from the stereotyped blood-race-soil argument of Hitler and his doctrinaire propagandists. The Nazi Chauvinism was of the head — arrogant, domineering, and argumentative. The Russian love of native land comes from the heart — tender, understanding, and forgiving. It is not a reasoned habit of mind nor a consciousness of civic duty. It does not aspire to be called an ideology. It does not argue; it feels, and leaves syllogisms to Poles and Latins. It permeates Russian legends, poetry, and sagas, from the *bylini* to the latest Soviet panegyrics; it tolerated an Ivan the Terrible in spite of his murderous record and his thousands of slaughtered victims — because his savagery was clothed in mystical service to Russia; it burned Moscow, beloved Moscow, to the ground in 1812 rather than see it profaned and occupied by Napoleon's Grand Army; it sustained peasant Russia through the long and oppressive centuries of serfdom and expressed itself stubbornly in the celebrated peasant rejoinder to landowners: "We are yours but the land is ours." Its roots grow from what Upsensky, one of the most talented portrayers of Russian peasantry, had in mind when he wrote:

It is the same soil which you bring home on your rubbers in the form of mud, it is the earth you see in your flower pots, black, wet earth; it is, in a word, the most ordinary, natural earth.

That sentiment prevailed notably in 1914, on the outbreak of World War I. During the months preceding the crisis, there had been open rebellion in the streets of St. Petersburg; on May 1 a huge strike was in progress in that city, with 130,000 workmen clamoring for reforms, while Cossacks were charging barricaded strikers, leaving dead and wounded strewn on the pavement exactly as they had done on Bloody Sunday, 1905. But Russian psychology is gloriously independent of political realities when Holy Russia is menaced. Political differences and revolutionary slogans were buried under outbursts of passionate patriotism and fierce Slavic fealty to the land and homes threatened by Teutons. The declaration of war acted as a hot iron fusing all classes and parties into a common purpose. Milling crowds ranged themselves before the winter palace and knelt at the appearance of the Tzar. The revolutionary slogans were transformed into a chanting of the imperial hymn and the clamors for redress of grievances became vows of allegiance to the throne. . . . The same common front would probably again greet any foreign attempt at invading Russia, at any time, no matter what the form or quality of the domestic government might be.

What counts for the world, then, is the political psychology and the declared objectives of Russia's small governing class at any given period, not the mute and captive aspirations of her 200,000,000 inhabitants. They are not the real enemy.

In the meantime, the only public voice we hear speaks the flagrant falsehoods and distortions of reality dictated to Communist spokesmen by the Kremlin and repeated by Mr. Malik in the name of his government from the unique vantage point provided by his presidency in August, 1950, over the Security Council of the United Nations. The same pattern revealed itself in the ominous diatribes of the Chinese revolutionist, General Wu, during his appearance before the United Nations in December. To interpret the contemporaneous phase of the Russian odyssey and make concrete the Politburo's adaptation of a people's antecedents to new international ends requires much analysis of the record and citation of chapter and verse. The author is aware that such an account must, at some stages, run heavily to Communist dialectics and probing of Soviet apologetics. The process is often tedious and boresome, because of the repetitions, involved structure, and profusion of invective in the Marxian language. But that hazard is inseparable from any attempt to lay bare the working of the Marxist mind behind the Russian power. To ignore or omit that aspect of the deepening tragedy would be a staging of *Hamlet* without the Prince of Denmark. Without patient assembling of the antecedents in the case and steadfast continuity of understanding, Soviet policy would indeed be an enigma, a puzzle, and a mystery — which it is not.

CHAPTER III

The Lengthened Shadow of Three Men

MARX — ENGELS — LENIN

THE term "cold war" applied to events between 1945 and 1950 caught the popular imagination in a manner which illustrates how easy it is to oversimplify and condense a great historical process into a single phrase. Soviet Russia, in point of time, had by 1950 been conducting a cold war against the United States for over thirty years. The interval 1941–1945 was a period of truce, an interruption made advisable because of the Nazi invasion of Soviet territory. The underlying and permanent belligerency began on the day when Lenin engineered his coup d'état, seized the government of Russia, founded the Soviet State, and declared a state of siege against the whole non-Communist world. A generation of Americans was born and came to maturity since that epochal event; but it is doubtful if they or their elders have as yet fully grasped the fundamental challenge and social implications of the Third Russian Revolution.

Flexibility of tactics, combined with oneness of purpose, is a constant theme in Lenin's writings. Since his words and every scrap of paper bearing his handwriting are preserved in the Lenin Institute at Moscow as a sort of sacred scripture for his followers, it becomes extremely important to know what the master revolutionist taught, and how he acted under given circumstances.[1]

---

[1] His collected works (*Sobranie Sochineniy*) run through some 30 volumes; in addition, his miscellaneous writings comprise 30 supplementary volumes (*Leninskie Sborniki*).

His letters from Switzerland, where he was living as a political exile at the moment of the abdication of Nicholas II, furnish a revealing documentation and starting point for understanding the subsequent course of Soviet foreign policy. The monarchy was falling and the line of Romanov Tzars reaching back three hundred and four years was at an end. That chapter was finished and a blank page was spread before the several contestants for imperial power. The future lay in the grasp of the first resolute will and the hand quick enough to write the command in terms agreeable to the released hopes and aspirations of the Russian people.

The news of events from Petrograd threw Lenin into a fever of expectation. This is not to suggest that Lenin's influence on history began in 1917 nor that his writings on the art of revolution are directed exclusively or even mainly to the Russian case. That would be to ignore the voluminous treatises, analyses of social organization, controversy, polemics, and concrete agitation that poured from his pen over some thirty years. He ruled the Soviet State less than seven years; he had been advocating an international revolution and preparing for it for a quarter of a century. What is meant is that all his planning and theories now came alive, focused at white heat on the lucky chance awaiting exploitation in his native land. Had revolution come first in another country he would have welcomed it with impartiality. That it had first come to his own land was a windfall twice welcome, since no obstacles would now intervene on the side of language, psychology of the masses, knowledge of traditions, or acquaintance with geography and the social landscape. Now was the appointed hour, and his instructions to fellow conspirators on the spot in the demoralized capital on the Neva reveal the pattern and shape of things to come.

He is impatient to take command of the Revolution but until he can arrive on the battlefield he must content himself with stopgap communiqués to his staff officers. Thus, his letter of March 16, 1917, warns his agents that the "first stage of the first revolution bred by the war will be neither final nor confined to Russia . . . by all means a combination of legal and illegal means . . . agitation and struggle for an international proletarian revolution."

On the following day he speeds new instructions to Madame Kollontai: ". . . . refuse all confidence and support to the new government . . . keep armed watchfulness; armed preparation of a broader base for a higher stage." In the original text of this letter the word "higher" is italicized. On March 30 his instructions to J. S. Hanecki rise to impassioned heights: ". . . the workers should be told the truth. They should be told that . . . only then will they have the right to demand the overthrow of all kings and of all bourgeois governments. For God's sake try to get all this into Petrograd and into the *Pravda*. . . . Implacable propaganda of internationalism. . . . Kamenev must realize that on his shoulders rests a responsibility of historical and universal import."

These two ideas — the universal scope of the Revolution, and Russia's function as the brains and dynamo of a gigantic upheaval — remained the hard core of Lenin's revolutionary leadership; he always sang the same tune although with minor variations and in different keys. The vision of a world aflame with social revolution became for him and for his apostles "the idea of ideas, about which the splinters of all other thought revolve like the planets around the sun." His successors down to the present day have added only detail and body to the blueprint blocked out by the master architect.

It would be an error to imply that Lenin lacked the ability to draw up specifications. On the contrary, his genius visualized manner, methods, and tactical maneuvers to an extent that placed him in the forefront of revolutionary practitioners. Even during the critical years following the seizure of power when the crushing burden of providing administrative agencies for a sprawling empire suddenly bereft of disciplined officials might well have engaged the undivided energy of any man, he did not relax in production of theoretical treatises and handbooks of revolutionary procedure for the conquest of power on an international scale. Time and space permit but bare mention of selected specimens. As early as April 20, 1917, four days after his triumphant arrival in Russia, he published a popular treatise on *Problems in Tactics*. At the end of April came *Class Character of the Revolution*, followed in rapid sequence by *Dual Authority*, *After the Uprising*

(July); *Constitutional Illusions; Lessons of the Revolution and International Tactics.* Then in November came the final crisis, and it was resolved as much by the pen of Lenin as by the sword of Trotsky, although considerable blood was shed in the final phase.

The unflagging ideology of Lenin then plunged into analysis of remaining problems and his facile pen turned out treatise upon treatise, tract after tract, such as *The Constituent Assembly; Peace and Our Task; The Problem of Organization; Management and Production; Democracy and Proletarian Dictatorship; The Old Order and the New; The International Revolution;* etc., etc.

Running through the collected works of this founding father we find one consistent warning, repeated dozens of times in one form or another: "Without a revolutionary theory there can be no revolutionary movement . . . only a party guided by an advanced theory can act as vanguard in the fight." On another basic dogma he is particularly frank and vocal. In an address delivered at the Third All-Russian Congress of the Russian Young Communist League, October 20, 1920, he declared unequivocally that the Soviet concept of morality is independent of all other norms and derives exclusively from the class character of the Revolution. " . . . In what sense do we repudiate ethics and morality? In the sense according to which they were preached by the bourgeoisie, who declared that ethics were God's commandments. We, of course, say that we do not believe in God. . . . we repudiate all morality that is taken outside human, class concepts. . . . We say that our morality is entirely subordinated to the interests of the class struggle of the proletariat. . . . What is this class struggle? It is overthrowing the Tzar, overthrowing the capitalist, abolishing the capitalist class."

It was upon this welcomed precedent that Nazi jurisprudence was established and formulated in its day and generation. Thus Frank, Hitler's Minister of Justice, defined right and wrong for Nazi jurists at Leipzig in a conference held there October 2–5, 1935: "Justice means whatever is useful to the German people and injustice whatever harms them." Both doctrines led logically and ruthlessly to class consciousness, class hatred, class warfare, class justification of barbarism such as the wanton murder of captured American soldiers in Korea and the atrocious tyranny of class legislation in the satellite lands.

There was a significant difference, however, in the manner of applying the measuring rod of good and evil. Hitler's division of humanity was by a vertical line which ran through all classes of men; those who were Nordics and Aryans were acceptable as first-class citizens in his projected empire, whether classified individually as royalty, aristocracy, bourgeois, or proletarian. The test was racism, Germanic blood and non-Jewish origin. Those falling on the other side of the line were either tolerated aliens or pariahs marked for destruction. The Lenin-Stalin criterion runs horizontally through the mass of humanity on a basis of social and economic status; men are either proletarian or bourgeois and that ends the testing, no question raised of blood, race, color, or nationality. Neither the Nazi nor the Communist revolution accepted man as man, but submitted men to certain prescribed tests determined in one instance by the Politburo, in the other by the Führer's sovereign decree. Both agreed on the manner of dealing with recalcitrants. Life was to be fitted schematically to the pattern ordained by the ruling camarilla; if life refused to be so regimented, death or imprisonment or exile became the logical alternative.

As a craftsman of revolution Lenin was immeasurably superior to Hitler and his cabal. In nothing is this more apparent than in his practice of the twin virtues of flexibility and adaptability to circumstances. Hitler was rigid, unyielding, and possessed of the arrogance common to an amateur suddenly elevated to a position of supreme command. He was emotional, sometimes hysterical, and always opinionated.

Lenin knew when to strike, but he had an equal instinct for retreat when compromise was needed. His program, published to the Russian people during the duel with Kerenski from April to November, 1917, spelled out all the promises and blandishments characteristic of a skilled politician. The document is preserved in Lenin's collected works and is reproduced in Volume I, pages 332–343 (English edition). What was promised to the Russian people would do credit to Thomas Jefferson and the framers of

Magna Charta: freedom of religion and of the press; immunity in their homes; inviolability of person and possessions; universal suffrage; equal, direct, and secret ballot; freedom of labor and occupation; local self-government; freedom to strike; and the right of any distinctively national State to secede from the Union. His fighting slogans were especially attractive to a people long thirsting for just such gifts: peace, land, bread, the factories and manors to the workers and peasants, all power to the Soviets. "They are rightfully yours. . . . Take them — take them now. You have nothing to lose but your chains." But once in the saddle and supported by an organized minority, his cool repudiation of every guarantee appalled the tricked and unorganized majority. Those who murmured or protested were arrested as "counterrevolutionaries." Their opposition was described as "a unanimous chorus of wolves, jackals, and mad dogs." Obviously, freedom of the press was the first thing to go. State control of all printed words is a prime condition, as every tyro knows, for the erection of a dictatorship. The Social Democrats protested: "Our newspapers are shut down." The reply was immediate. "Naturally," Lenin retorted, "but unfortunately not yet all. Soon they will be shut down entirely. The dictatorship of the proletariat will put a complete end to this disgraceful sale of bourgeois opium."

This quick transition to a bolder psychology and a more ruthless handling of the opposition marks a definite moment in the chronology of events. The nascent years of the Russian Revolution were marked by that combination of legal and illegal measures which historians discover in every violent transfer of supreme power in a state undergoing social transformation. Revolution, by its definition is, strictly speaking, illegal; it is a direct challenge to existing law and prevailing custom. Hence, the skilled revolutionist, knowing that he and his party always constitute, at first, a small minority of the total population, must justify his claims in terms acceptable to the level of intelligence, the traditions and psychology of the broad masses. Revolt must bear the outward appearance of reform and must use that door. Lacking the authority and legitimacy enjoyed, at least outwardly, by the old regime, he must not overplay his hand so long as the forces of revolt are without sufficient power to impose their program on a hesitant people. The transition from tactical to open illegality and to complete rupture with the past must be wisely calculated and it is his sense of timing which reveals the quality of a revolutionist's mind.

Power safely in hand, he then proceeds to the next daring objective: the creation of revolutionary legality expressed in sweeping changes promulgated in the name of the people but preserving for a time the vocabulary and outward forms of conventional law-making. If the changes are, at bottom, designed to create a new civilization and a new culture, legal terminology will then press forward toward that ultimate goal, discarding on the way its previous appeal to revolutionary necessity. That baggage is no longer needed. The Russian Revolution after several internal modifications reached that degree of mastery under the Constitution and New National Policy of 1936. Soviet judges now consciously render decisions in terms of Socialist legality. The word "revolution" had progressively dropped out of court proceedings and an impression of stabilized normalcy was cultivated as a substitute for legitimacy. That is why late-comers to the study of Soviet jurisprudence, arriving from the outside, are frequently trapped into false conclusions by the mechanics of the machinery at work in the evolution of Soviet justice. Paralleling the public Soviet courts, non-judicial and secret Communist tribunals continue to impose heavy penalties, including death or imprisonment in concentration camps. To instill fear of the government still remains the device by which a usurper government covers up its own fear of the people.

Confronted with power in the concrete, Lenin, however, was quick to recognize and respect the argument. The German armies had crossed the Dvina in February, 1918, and were on the march toward the inner citadels of Bolshevism. Consecrated above all else to World Revolution, he recognized the danger and staked his all to save Moscow and Petrograd. It was not patriotism or love of Slavonic culture that moved his soul: it was the Revolution that counted. The hotheads of the Party were all for continued resistance. With his back to the wall, Lenin argued for surrender and for breathing space even against the advice of his most respected counselors of the Central Executive Committee. He won by sheer force of his dominating personality — and saved the Revolution. The vote was 126 to 85 and the Treaty of

Brest Litovsk, though sacrificing much in territorial values, averted an imminent danger. "Their knees are upon our chest," Lenin protested to his committee, "and our position is hopeless. This peace must be accepted as a respite. . . . The proletariat of the whole world will come to our aid. Then we will renew the fight." He called it a Tilsit peace and explained the reference: "When Napoleon I forced Prussia in 1807 to accept the Tilsit peace, the conqueror had defeated all the German armies, occupied the capital and all the large cities, established his police, compelled the conquered to give him auxiliary corps in order to wage new wars of plunder by the conquerors, and he dismembered Germany, forming an alliance with some German states against other German states. And, nevertheless, even after such a peace, the German people were not subdued. They managed to recover, to rise, and to win the right to freedom and independence."

Such realism and sense of timing for the Revolution was apparently native to Lenin's character. As a boy of 17 in Simbirsk he received, with a certain hardening of resolve, the news that his brother Alexander had been hanged at St. Petersburg for complicity in a plot to assassinate the Emperor Alexander III. It is said that his comment was: "We shall never get there by that road."

When no power was available to an opponent, Lenin struck with directness, speed, and ruthlessness. A Constituent Assembly elected under democratic pledges convened in Petrograd in January, 1918, with a popular mandate to determine the permanent form of the Russian State. But a count showed that Lenin's party was outnumbered by delegates committed to a democracy in fact. A crucial resolution introduced by the Soviet minority in order to secure immediate priority for their measures was voted down by an overwhelming majority; consequently, Lenin dispersed the members by a summary decree on January 19. This turning point in the history of the Russian Revolution was accomplished physically by a single sailor, his rifle slung over his shoulder. Approaching the speaker's rostrum he whispered into the ear of the presiding officer, Victor Chernov, that it was time to end the proceedings and go home. As machine guns had already been set up near by, the delegates had but small choice.

Russia was again dragooned into obedience as it had been coerced by organized autocracy for over three centuries.

The Tauride Palace, where the Constituent Assembly met, was encircled by Lenin's Red guards; armed to the teeth, they thronged the corridors also and packed the galleries, booing, hooting, and jeering at the delegates. One of the supporters of this last brief attempt at representative government commented: "On our side were legality, great ideals, and faith in the triumph of democracy. On their side were activity, machine guns, weapons." Lenin's decree dissolving the Constituent Assembly set the form and style for similar writs in many languages: the Assembly, he declared, was "serving only as a cover for the struggle of bourgeois counter-revolution for the overthrow of the power of the Soviets."

In order to lend point to their contempt for those who had listened to the siren promises of the previous June, the Soviet authorities decided on a little object lesson. It might have been awkward to turn machine guns on the whole assembly and butcher them *en masse*. But somebody remembered that one of the most prominent intellectuals of his day, an elected member of the assembly, Andrew Shingarev, was lying ill at the near-by Mary Hospital. During the night, as the sailors and Red guards were waiting to murder the most freely elected assembly Russia had ever known, a group of official assassins entered the sick chamber and approaching the bed bayoneted to death Shingarev and Kokoshkin, his friend.

The dissolution of the Constituent Assembly by armed troops thus early in the history of the Soviet State marked the end of the Russian Revolution properly so called and ushered in the counterrevolution. It halted the orderly processes toward a constitutional government which had been the goal of every liberal in the long struggle against the totalitarianism of the previous three centuries. It checked the growth of a viable democracy and set back the clock of civil and religious liberty far beyond the point reached by Alexander II, emancipator of the serfs, in 1861. Lenin's comment on the event is worth recalling: "Naturally it was a great risk on our part that we did not postpone the convention — very, very unwise. But in the end it is best that it happened so. The breaking up of the Constituent Assembly by

the Soviet power is the complete and public liquidation of formal
democracy in the name of the revolutionary dictatorship. It will
be a good lesson." Trotsky describes the dissolution of the
assembly as a "tragicomic episode" and takes a contemptuous
fling at the "rear guard of democracy" departing from the scene
armed with candles and sandwiches.

With the Soviet power now in control of a huge laboratory
of social experimentation it might have been supposed that
domestic reconstruction along Marxist lines would be a task
sufficiently absorbing to engage the full capacity of Lenin's
available energy and material resources for a long period of time.
Such was not the case. Convinced that integral Communism in
Russia was unattainable and the Russian Revolution never secure
so long as the new State remained an island of collectivism
surrounded by a sea of capitalism and free enterprise, he straightway began to prepare his campaign of international social
revolution and launched it in February, 1919. To imagine that
Communist Russia could exist alone and unsupported was, in
his judgment, an infantile delusion.

As early as April 20, 1917, which means four days after his
arrival in Russia, he had published in *Pravda* his theses respecting
the tactics essential to achievement of a World Revolution. These
propositions formed the backbone of a policy which, though
elastic in timing and application, was never repudiated or modified in essentials during his lifetime, nor abandoned by his
successors. He pours his usual scorn on the "hypothetical Marxists,"
on the "milk and water Louis Blanc," on "the sugary Kautskian,"
and on all temporizers who recoil at the immediate seizure of
power. Hence the ninth thesis calls, domestically, for a "government Commune," a reference to the Paris Commune of 1871
which Lenin always considered the prototype of his projected
Revolution, though with certain correction of errors in the
technique of the Communards of 1871. In addition, he proposes
that the name of the Party be changed. Instead of Social Democrats he required that his party thereafter be known as the
Communist Party, since, he explains, the official leaders of Social
Democracy throughout the world had betrayed Socialism in 1914
by going over to the bourgeoisie and supporting the war effort

of their respective governments. The tenth thesis called for the revival of the International, a revolutionary International, against "the social patriots and the center." He defines "center" as "those elements, v.g., Kautsky and Co. in Germany, Lonquet and Co. in France, Cheidse and Co. in Russia, Turati and Co. in Italy, MacDonald and Co. in England."

The eight months of conflict with the Provisional Government and the breathing space required for consolidation of the triumph of November 7 delayed the convocation of the proposed Third International, but only until February, 1919. Pending the organization of specific agencies of revolt throughout the world, the task of preparing revolutionary upheavals outside Russia was committed to Soviet diplomatic representatives in virtue of a decree issued in No. 31 of the official governmental *Gazette*, December 13, 1917:

> *An Ordinance Assigning Two Million Rubles for the*
> *Needs of the Revolutionary Internationalist Movement.*
>
> Taking into consideration that Soviet authority is grounded on the basis of the principles of international solidarity of the proletariat and the brotherhood of the toilers of all countries, that only on an international scale can the struggle against war and imperialism lead to complete victory, the Soviet of People's Commissaries considers it necessary to come forth with all aid, including financial aid, to the assistance of the left internationalist wing of the workers' movement of all countries, entirely regardless of whether these countries are at war with Russia, or in alliance, or whether they retain their neutrality.
>
> With these aims the Soviet of People's Commissaries ordains: the assigning of two million rubles for the needs of the revolutionary internationalist movement, at the disposition of the foreign representatives of the Commissariat For Foreign Affairs.
>
> > [*Signed*]
> > President of the Soviet of People's Com-
> > missaries, Ulianoff (Lenin)
> > People's Commissary for Foreign Affairs,
> > L. Trotsky
> > Manager of Affairs of the Soviet of
> > People's Commissaries, Bonch-Bruevich
> > Secretary of the Soviet, N. Gorbounov

Published by the Soviet government less than five weeks after its assumption of power, this decree served as a temporary measure for sustaining a permanent objective. Finally, in response to a summons sent out over government wires to selected revolutionaries in foreign countries and signed by Lenin as Premier and his Secretary of War, Leon Trotsky, the first Congress of the new Communist International convened in Moscow, in March, 1919. The initial group numbered 52 delegates, largely Russians, with a minority group of representatives from near-by countries. In the second meeting of 1920 we find 218 delegates, among them several Americans. By 1928 the roll call of professional revolutionaries who assembled for the sixth Congress shows 532 delegates, each a picked man and a schooled agitator. It marked the apogee of the Comintern, revealing the world-wide ramification thus far achieved and the complete co-ordination of all revolutionary elements under a unified command.

The official stenographic report of that Congress lies before me as I write — 1766 printed pages, quarto size, in double columns. It recounts activities that range from Buenos Aires to Tokyo, from Java, South Africa, and Afghanistan to New York, Chicago, and Detroit. But all were directed, sponsored, and controlled from the city of Moscow by a Central Executive Committee of which Mr. Joseph Stalin was an important member. It is interesting to note that the American section was headed by a Japanese, Katayama.[2] In 1929, ten years after its foundation, the Comintern numbered 43 sections in as many lands; 20 of them were illegal. The total number of members registered in the legal sections was, as of that date, 394,000, without counting the Communist Party in Russia, which was then given as 1,605,000. If we add the 2,400,000 members of the Communist Youth, there resulted an army of approximately 5,000,000 men — the international shock troops of World Revolution; but these were only the leaders, as affiliated organizations throughout the world must be added to ascertain the total strength of Marxism. In Germany alone Party members numbered nearly 6,000,000 by 1933.[3]

---

[2] Later replaced by a certain Weinstein.

[3] In 1950, the world membership of the Party was declared by Moscow to be 25,000,000. The Russian Communist Party is the largest with 7,000,000 members; the Chinese Party came second with 4,000,000 members; the Italian Party claimed 2,532,000 adherents; Czechoslovakia listed 2,300,000; Poland, 1,360,000. In France only 800,000 were listed, as against 1,300,000 in 1947. By 1951 membership had substantially declined throughout all western Europe.

With the organization and functioning of the Third International a new and important agency of World Revolution appears in the history of international relations. There had been Socialists and Socialist parties before, secret societies during the French Revolution, Syndicalists of the Sorel School, Anarchists led by Bakunin and Kropotkin, Illuminati and Babeufs, Proudhonists and every variety of miscellaneous rebel against government since the world began. There was an active First International from 1864 to the Hague Conference in 1872, after which it expired peacefully in New York, whither Karl Marx had transferred it for decent interment. There was a Second International, organized in 1899, which disbanded itself automatically in 1914 at the outbreak of World War I. But revolutionary organizations hitherto had been debating societies, with no sanction or effective weapons beyond propaganda, platonic alliances, cryptic confederacies, and occasional assassination. With November 7, 1917, however, the Communist leaders found themselves for the first time in physical possession of one of the major governments of Europe, whose entire apparatus, foreign and domestic, became the instrument for the execution of Marxian Communism and supplied the formidable elements of practicality, authority, unity of program, and world-wide ramification so conspicuously absent from prewar internationalism.

* * * *

Underlying the popular and easily understood slogans which had triumphed on November 7, 1917 — peace, bread, land, factories, all power to the Soviets of workmen, peasants, and soldiers' deputies — reposed an integrated philosophy of social transformation. Without a theory of revolution, Lenin perpetually insisted, there can be no successful achieving of revolution. With triphammer frequency he repeats and reiterates this basic premise. Primitive and electrifying slogans, amplified and popularized in everyday language, would suffice for arousing the masses in the streets, in factories, and on the land. But for the directors and managers of the revolution an organized and comprehensive theoretical framework, an ideology of revolt, a body of dogmas, and a system of strategical metaphysics was imperative.

The ABC of Communism by Bukharin and Preobrazhensky laid the foundations and developed the grammar school concepts. Translated widely and made adaptable to local conditions in all countries, this basic and official text reduced Marxian economic and social doctrines to practical political conclusions. The English version, rendered by Eden and Cedar Paul, in 1922, was described by the publishers as being "a book for all — easy to read; impossible to misinterpret — the very essence of Communist theory — a world classic." Using terms of modern applicability, it developed the Marxian conception of production and distribution, the theory of social labor as the determinant of value, the necessity of planned economy under public control, the materialistic interpretation of history, the gradual withering away of the State and the substitution of statistical bureaus which would determine the needs of each citizen and the distribution of labor hours. "Within a few decades," the textbook promised, "there will be an entirely new world with new people and new customs." Class consciousness, class distinctions, class warfare, the dictatorship of the proletariat through a Communist World Revolution are elaborated logically though less offensively in the *ABC* than in many other equally authoritative expositions of the Communist programme. It avoids the "blood-soaked reality," the "conquest of power on a world-wide scale," and "the deadly challenge to the bourgeois world" published in *Pravda* on September 9, 1928. But in the field of religion the attitude of Marx, Lenin, and Engels is followed without deviation. Chapter XI deals with the necessity of extirpating all forms of religion, as they are all "opium for the people." No Communist can be a believer in any religious creed and no religious believer can be a Communist.

The authors of the *ABC*, however, make a highly significant observation at one point. Advocating direct and State-directed assault on the supernatural and on any expression of humanism which recognizes the divine in man, these two leading spokesmen of the Party warn Communists that the suppression of religion must be conducted in a cautious way among the ranks of workmen. Great patience and prudence will be required there, as well as energy and perseverance. "The credulous crowd is extremely sensitive to anything which hurts its feelings. To thrust atheism upon the masses . . . would not assist but would hinder the campaign against religion."

Friedrich Engels also composed an ABC of Communism in his time, which, though reducing the essentials of Marxism to brief formulae, entered more subtly into the field of history and sociological economics. Written in 1847, it took the form of question and answer — *Grundsätze des Communismus* — and may be found in the German collection, *Marx-Engels Gesamtausgabe,* Berlin, 1932. A few specimens will illustrate the mordant style of the man who rescued Marx from complete unintelligibility by editing his voluminous manuscripts, disorderly notes, and disparate memoranda and arranging them systematically into the volumes now known as *Das Kapital.*

1. *Question:* What is Communism?
Answer: Communism is the science dealing with the conditions for the emancipation of the proletariat.

2. *Question:* What is the proletariat?
Answer: The proletariat is that class of society which draws its livelihood exclusively from the sale of its labor and in no way from the profit of capital investment; people whose happiness and distress, whose life and death, whose whole existence depends on their search for employment, and depends also on good and bad times, as well as on the fluctuations of a system of unrestricted competition. The proletariat or the proletarian class, in one word, is the working class of the nineteenth century.

3. *Question:* Were there not always proletarians?
Answer: No. There were always poor people and a working class, and the working class were generally poor. But such poor, such workers as lived in the given circumstances, i.e., proletarians, did not always exist no matter how free and unrestricted was the competition.

4. *Question:* How did the proletariat come into existence?
Answer: (A long description of the Industrial Revolution.)

5. *Question:* Under what conditions does this sale of a proletarian's work to the bourgeoisie take place?
Answer: (A technical exposition of the viewpoint that labor was a commodity whose price was considered as one of the costs of production.)

6. *Question:* What kind of working classes existed before the Industrial Revolution?
Answer: (A catalogue of workers in different stages of antiquity and medieval times.)

7. *Question:* How does a proletarian worker differ from slaves?

Answer: A slave is sold once and for all; a proletarian must sell himself daily, and hourly. The individual slave, private property of a master, led a secured existence, though it might have been miserable, because that was for the interest of his master; the individual proletarian has no assured existence, as he is, so to speak, the property of the whole bourgeois class, and his labor will only then be bought when someone of them needs it. This is the only existence assured to the proletarian class. The slave lives outside the realm of business competition, but the proletarian lives inside it and experiences all its fluctuations. The slave is valued as a thing, but the proletarian is acknowledged to be a member of bourgeois society. The slave can even have a better existence than the proletarian, but the proletarian belongs to a higher evolutionary stage of society and stands on a higher level than the slave. The slave can free himself since he need only remove that single relationship of slavery among all the aspects of private property and so a slave first becomes a proletarian. But the proletarian can only free himself by destroying private ownership itself.

Engel's catechism of revolt continues in this vein through 25 questions and answers. It is an excellent polemical weapon skillfully composed as a fighting instrument on the economic front, but, like so many eclectic attacks of partisans, is a mixture of selected truths half stated and much falsehood wholly accepted. It is a forecast of the one-sidedness of the *Communist Manifesto* and of the entire Marxian development. Engel's answer to Question No. 7 is a powerful piece of propaganda — until it comes to the last four words, which constitute the objective and purpose of his entire argument. The alternative there proposed is not the only means of solving the problem. The insecurity can be relieved in several other ways, e.g., by the worker acquiring some private property of his own, as frequently happens in the United States; or by social-security legislation; or by old age pensions and profit sharing; or by similar alternatives ignored or unforeseen by Engels.

Marx, like Hegel, did his best work in the field of research, in contemporary observation, in synthesis, and in marshaling an encyclopedic armory of social data and industrial statistics. Witness his factual analysis of the English factory system of the nineteenth century, an indictment of abuses which is impressive and undeniable. But it was in the practical adaptation of workable means to desirable ends, in formulating concrete proposals for an industrial organization of society which would remedy the admitted inequities without destroying human nature that he was deficient — as was the Third International. Both were strongest in exposing the defects of opposing systems, weakest in constructive responsibility. The only place where Marx included some fragments of constructive planning is found in his *Criticism of the Gotha Program.*

In the case of Marx, this psychology of attack was augmented by certain personal characteristics. His private life had been embittered by four influences which cannot be disassociated from his mental processes and from the quality of the power he exerted over succeeding revolutionists. One was spiritual, another emotional, the third economic, and the last gastronomic. They all became fused and sublimated in a cold, organized hatred against bourgeois society. There is no more revealing expression of this permanent spleen than his counsel to Lassalle: "To instill poison wherever possible is now the thing to do."[4]

Marx's father was a Jew descended from a line of rabbis, though himself a lawyer; he was constrained to accept Protestant Christianity, however, as a measure of expediency advisable for a peace-loving inhabitant of Treves in 1824. His son Karl, in consequence, became a titular Christian, rebellious in heart and ultimately despising both Jews and Gentiles for the hypocrisy of the position he was obliged to sustain. The young man's emotional life was further soured by the obstacles encountered in his love for the beautiful Jenny von Westphalen, daughter of a government official of noble extraction. In spite of the intrigues, obstructions, and hostility of her family, lasting seven years, the marriage finally took place, but this early contact with upper-class snobbishness left its residue of class-conscious cynicism in Marx's outlook on society. This bad temper was further sharpened by his failure to achieve professional standing in academic circles. He had cherished an early ambition to embark on a teaching profession. But, though awarded his doctorate at the University of Jena, at the age of 23, his road to a professor's chair was blocked by a new Minister of Education who frowned on the radicalism

---

[4] *Gift infiltrieren wo immer ist nun ratsam* (Briefwechsel zwischen Lassalle und Marx, p. 170).

of the candidate. The frustrated professor thereupon became a caustic critic and a jaundiced journalist.

The third conditioning factor derived from his drab experience as a political refugee in London and elsewhere in Europe. Always in need of money, living on borrowed funds or subsidies from Engels, harassed by importunate landladies and suspicious tradesmen, he developed a wholly understandable personal resentment against capital, interest, profit, prices, and private property. His lodgings were in perpetual disorder, with unpaid bills their chief adornment. Unable to manage a two-room flat, Marx practically lived in the great reading room of the British Museum elaborating a system for the economic management of all mankind. His wife, the former belle of Treves, grew exhausted and melancholy. At Easter, 1852, one child died and the two pounds sterling required for the coffin were advanced by a charitable French refugee neighbor. At the age of nine, Marx's favorite boy, Edgar, died of inadequate nourishment. Another infant died almost immediately after birth.

A typical day in the Marx household is described by Jenny, his wife, in a letter to Herr Weydemeyer. Since wet nurses were extremely expensive, she records her efforts to nurse her own child, but the half-starved infant "sucked so vigorously that my nipple became sore and bled; often the blood streamed into his little mouth." One day while thus engaged, the self-sacrificing mother is faced with another disaster. The importunate landlady appears at the door and demands payment of the five pounds owing on rent. Unable to pay, Frau Marx, with the infant still at her breast, was put to the agony of seeing two brokers enter and put a lien on all her possessions as prelude to selling them. "They threatened to take everything away in two hours. If this had happened, I should have had to lie on the floor, with my freezing children beside me, and with my aching breast. Our friend Schramm hastened forthwith to seek help. He took a cab, the horse fell down, he jumped out, and was brought back into the house bleeding, the house where I was lamenting and my poor children were trembling.

"Next day we had to leave. It was cold and rainy. My husband tried to find a lodging, but as soon as he said we had four children no one would take us in. At length a friend helped us. We paid what was owing, and I quickly sold all my beds and bedding, in order to settle accounts with the chemist, the baker, the butcher, and the milkman, who had heard that the brokers had been put in, and had hastened to send in their bills. The beds and bedding that had been sold were loaded on to a handcart at the street door — and what do you think happened then? It was late in the evening, after sunset; the English law forbids this; the landlord arrived with policemen, saying that some of his goods might be on the cart. . . . Within five minutes, there was a crowd of two or three hundred people in front of the door, the whole mob of Chelsea. The beds had to be brought in again, and could not be sent to the purchaser until after sunrise next morning. Now that the sale of all our possessions had enabled us to pay our debts to the last penny, I removed with my little darlings to our present address, two tiny rooms in the German Hotel, Leicester Street, Leicester Square, where they were good enough to take us in for five pounds ten a week."[5]

Added to these household disturbances, a fourth circumstance contributed to Marx's Homeric rage against the existing order. His health, naturally enough, suffered under a perpetual nervous tension caused by the flight from Germany to France and England, by the wearisome search for an apartment, by the drudgery of writing potboilers for the press, and by the frequent pilgrimages to pawn shops. Suffering from indigestion and a liver complaint, he became a depressed, discontented, capricious, and petulant pedant. He groaned at his stomach and at humanity; eating irregularly and mostly mixed pickles, spices, vinegar, and caviar, he became a victim of a jaundiced disorder which reflected itself psychologically in his theories of universal reform. Even his wholly sympathetic biographer, Otto Rühle, is frank and in places devastating when discussing these unpleasant personal defects of Marx. But, he adds:

Inferiority seeks compensation. The sense of inferiority, stimulated ever and again by recurrent ill-success, failure, and defeat, gives no rest until the minus has been compensated by a plus. If the minus be an inherited defect, the

---

[5] Rühle, Otto, *Karl Marx*, pp. 202–203.

plus becomes a matter of personal achievement. Thus only was it that Demosthenes the stammerer could become the greatest orator of antiquity, that the deaf Beethoven proved the most famous of all musicians, that the hideous Michelangelo was able to hand down to posterity the most marvellous of all depiction of human beauty. . . . The man who had a poor appetite and a difficult digestion propounded a plan for the reorganization of the economic structure of society whose result was to be that every one was to have plenty to eat and an adequate supply of all the conveniences of life. The man who had always been short of money, perpetually in debt, announced and fought for the establishment of a world order in which everyone was to have a sufficient share in the world's goods. The man who was a master of unsociability, and was incapable of true friendship, issued as a watchword that all men were to be brothers. The man who did not know how to spend a shilling wisely, elaborated in his own mind the most profound of all the theories of money; and created imaginatively the splendid thought edifice of a revolutionized economic system, established upon new and communal foundations. As compensation for his sense of inferiority, he made it his life work to be the scientific founder of an economic and social order in which all were to be able to do what he could not do, and all were to have what he lacked.[6]

It does not fall within the scope of the present volume to separate the true from the false in Rühle's encomium nor to institute a detailed study of the economics implicit in Marxism. We are concerned primarily with the power of his teachings as a revolutionary force in modern history. Certain of his leading economic postulates, however, are notably false and have been proved so by time and experience, but only after attempts at enforcing them resulted in more disaster than benefit to the working classes. The labor theory of value, though virtually abandoned in the third volume of *Das Kapital* in favor of a nebulous formula, "socially necessary hours of labor," was actually adopted in its literal and arithmetic form by Lenin during the early years of integral Communism in Soviet Russia. Labor was compensated, not by money, but by ration coupons, each hour of labor being rewarded by a definite piece of paper entitling the holder to a specified equivalent of bread, dried fish, sugar, tea, candles, matches, and similar commodities. The results were catastrophic as a hastily assembled and amateur bureaucracy attempted to keep the books and time sheets of this colossal employment

---

[6] Rühle, *op. cit.*, pp. 385–386.

agency. Crowds of hungry people stormed the doors of the distribution centers, waiting long hours to be served and frequently finding no food available when they reached the head of the line; a laconic sign informed them: "Supplies exhausted; come back tomorrow."

Ending in complete chaos and incipient rebellion, the bizarre and unrealistic system had to be repudiated as famine approached in 1921. Money in the form of currency was restored and the spiral of inflation immediately set in because of a scarcity of consumers' goods, a vacuum which had been induced partly by the breakdown of production and transportation, partly by the incidence of drought, but largely by the reckless requisitioning of foodstuffs by the government. What saved the Communist State in the subsequent famine of 1921–1923 was the accursed money freely contributed by the scorned bourgeoisie of the west and the heroic efficiency of the American Relief Administration.

What Marx meant to say, and what every conscientious reformer is bound to say, is that a money economy becomes good or evil in the hands of good or evil men. The solution lies not in the abolition of currency as a medium of exchange nor in the prohibition of private property but in control of the men who create and acquire them. What Marx analyzed so thoroughly and trenchantly was the observed function of money in an advanced stage of *laisser-faire* and finance capitalism, not an integrated program to restore and preserve social equilibrium. The evils which Marx attacked were equally assailed by Pius XI in the encyclical on the Social Order, 1931:

The immense number of proletarians on the one hand, and the immense wealth of certain very rich people on the other, are an unanswerable argument that the earthly goods so abundantly produced in this age of industrialism are far from rightly distributed and equitably shared among the various classes of men. . . . In our days not only is wealth concentrated, but immense power and economic domination are concentrated in the hands of a few, and those few are frequently not the owners, but only the trustees and directors of invested funds. . . . Some have become so hardened against the stings of conscience as to hold all means good which enable them to increase their profits. . . . The regulations legally enacted for joint-stock companies have given occasion to abominable abuses.

FRIEDRICH ENGELS LEON TROTSKY (*Bronstein*)

V. I. LENIN (*Ulianov*) JOSEPH STALIN (*Djugashvili*)

KARL MARX

The difference between Marxism and the social reforms advocated by Leo XIII and Pius XI lay in the type of remedies proposed. The abuses and defects of capitalism furnish abundant arguments for correction and control, not for abolition of necessary institutions. The baby should not be poured down the drain together with the dirty water.

The materialistic interpretation of history was overstated and overemphasized by both Marx and Lenin. It is expounded by Marx in his *Critique of Political Economy* published in 1859:

> The method prevailing in any society of producing the material livelihood determines the social, political and intellectual life of men in general. It is not men's consciousness which determines their mode of life; on the contrary, it is their social life which determines their consciousness. When the material productive forces of society have advanced to a certain stage of their development they come into opposition with the old conditions of production, or, to use a legal expression, with the old property relations. . . . These antiquated property relations now become hindrances. Then begins an epoch of social revolution. With the change of the economic basis the whole vast superstructure (i.e., of social, political and intellectual life) undergoes, sooner or later, a revolution.

The underlying cause, then, the most potent factor in determining the variations, the advances and recessions, sharp deviations and conflicts in the stream of history must, according to Marx, be sought in the method of producing material goods at the stated period. This relationship, he admits, may not be consciously recognized by men; the changes may occur "unconsciously, according to the laws of natural science." When they do take place, Marx affirms, men become conscious of the antagonism between the new methods of production and the old "legal, political, religious, artistic or philosophical, in short, ideological superstructure: it is with reference to these that men fight out this conflict as a revolution, conscious of their opposing interest. This conflict takes the form of a class struggle." In the *Communist Manifesto* of 1848 the whole course of history from the disappearance of the tribal organization of society to modern times is simplified down to a succession of class struggles between exploiters and exploited, bourgeoisie and proletariat. Marx declared

expressly, in the Preface to *Das Kapital*, that the economic formation of society is a process of natural history.

Now, no realistic reading of human vicissitudes can fail to
find frequent economic influences underlying great events such
as wars, epochal discoveries, and social upheavals. But it is a
mark of dangerous fanaticism and oversimplification to reduce the
complex process of human conduct to a single, inflexible motivation. Events, to be sure, revolve about some concrete issue which
may be tangible, material, and economic, but just as frequently
these *prima facie* occasions are based on some spiritual or cultural
or social complexity. The discovery of America was an accidental
by-product of an economic urge to find a new passage to India;
but a deeper study of the antecedent negotiations of Columbus
with the Spanish Court will reveal how large a measure of motivation was contributed by the piety of Queen Isabella desirous of
opening up new fields for the propagation of Christianity. The
genius of the Renaissance, surely a decisive epoch in European
history, found expression in the desire for and the importation of
precious objects accruing to the Medicis and other princely patrons
partly from foreign commerce and partly from financial transactions at home; but the fascination, the spirit, the stimulation
and progress of the Renaissance was a cultural phenomenon
deriving from a revival of classicism which can with difficulty
be reduced to an economic relationship.

And what economic motive presided over the revolutionary
transformation introduced into the habits of men by the birth of
Christianity? Its Founder was a carpenter who never attacked
the prevailing system, though He often counseled moderation,
equity, and charity in its daily operations. His Apostles were not
doctors of philosophy nor critics of the wage system nor agitators
for industrial reform, but mostly unlettered fishermen, middle-class
bourgeois, artisans, and one banker. His kingdom was specifically
defined as not of this world nor to be won by economic and social
reform. His beatitudes were spiritual, not material consummations;
even Caesar had political and economic rights which were to be
honored by payment of the imperial tax. Christ's Golden Rule of
human felicity bore no reference to economic relations but to

spiritual fellowship. His wrestling was with the powers of darkness and the bondage of sin. His entire preachment was directed to the individual soul through whose personal redemption and sanctification the world was to be elevated to a new vision of freedom. Man was exhorted to multiply his inner spiritual activities, not to lose himself in the multiplication of exchangeable commodities or limit himself to socially necessary hours of labor.

Christ's supreme act of indignation was directed at money-changers not because they *were* money-changers but because they had located their tables too near the sanctuary and turned a house of prayer into a den of thieves. And even a thief was not to be excluded from His salvation, for did He not address to an outcast Jew that tremendous promise, never before or since vouchsafed in such categoric language by the Son of God directly to any living human being: "This day thou shalt be with Me in Paradise"? And what economic motive sustained Him during those three hours of agony on Calvary? What economic compulsion fortified the martyrs whose blood reddened the sands of the Colosseum and induced whole generations to prefer the catacombs to Roman carnivals?

Marx's prophecy that the poor would get poorer, the rich richer, and the workers more enslaved as capitalism evolved was two thirds untrue and one third partly correct. The fortunes of a very small monied minority did indeed increase to proportions undreamed of by the Medicis and the Fuggers of medieval times or by the Rothschilds of the nineteenth century; but it is historically untrue that the condition of the working classes and the power of labor have worsened since 1848, the date of the *Communist Manifesto*. On the contrary, there has been a steady increase both in real wages and in the strength of organized laborers — except in the Communist State, where a situation of peonage resulted from the adoption of Marxist theories.

Real wages in Soviet Russia are notoriously inferior to the average prevailing in other industrial communities of the West where free enterprise still rules. Taking a typical year, in the normal atmosphere of peace, before the dislocations of war occurred, we find, in 1939, that the average wage of a Russian worker, fixed by the State, was $32 a month, the minimum not more than $14 per month. In terms of Russian currency this average wage was approximately 290 rubles. But wages are meaningless unless measured by what they can buy for the sustenance of life in the economic order in which they are expended. In 1937–1939 a pair of shoes in Soviet Russia cost from 150 to 300 rubles, a suit of clothes from 700 to 1200 rubles. Hence a pair of the cheapest shoes would cost a worker more than 50 per cent of his month's income while the best grade would exhaust his entire revenue. A good suit of clothes would require his entire income for over two months, no margin left for housing, food, and other necessities of existence. Certain benefits in rentals and services other than wages, are accorded workers, but the value of these, according to the study made by Sir Walter Citrine, was not more than one third of the stipulated wage. Including these subsidies, the average wage may be computed as ranging from 350–400 rubles per month at that period, still leaving a yawning chasm between wages and prices.

In his authoritative and well-documented study, *Soviet Trade and Distribution*, L. E. Hubbard comes to the conclusion that the market price received by a peasant for his grain in 1913 would buy, on the average, about eight times the quantity of the basic necessities of life which he could buy under the price paid him by Soviet trusts. Furthermore, he points out, the average wage paid to industrial workers under Soviet economy was about eight times the wages paid under the Tzarist regime in 1913, but the retail price of the common necessities of life had increased from fifteen to twenty times. A cabled report from Moscow, on February 14, 1944, stated that Mr. Stettinius on his visit to the Moscow Ballet after the Yalta Conference purchased a bouquet of flowers for the leading ballerina. The price was quoted at 3000 rubles which meant, under the rate of exchange for diplomats, approximately $250.[7]

---

[7] A recent computation, made in terms of hours of work required to earn the price of the same basic necessities of life in *U.S.A.* and in *U.S.S.R.*, points the contrast for average wage earners. See specimens at foot of next page.

The independence of the Russian trade unions is so much a legend that no strike is ever tolerated for the purpose of effecting a higher level of workmen's compensation. On the other hand, in the classical capitalistic civilization — the United States — not only is found the highest scale of real wages, but the power of organized labor is such that unions have often defied the Federal Government and ceased production even at the moment of acute national emergency.

Despite its manifold defects and weaknesses, free enterprise of democracy has made the average American worker the envy of the world in the matter of real wages. In thirty years his average compensation has increased fourfold, sanitary and protective conditions have vastly improved, and his working time has progressively been limited by social legislation. The number of American laborers who arrive at their place of work in motorcars — a form of luxury unknown to the vast body of Soviet workers — is a significant commentary on consumers' income and an index of economic status which, by and large, implies a standard of living unknown elsewhere, and assuredly never approached by the collectivism of the Communist State. This true test of wages was wholly ignored in an amazing article, "Stalin Pays Them What They're Worth," published in *The Saturday Evening Post*, July 21, 1945, by Peter F. Drucker. Eulogistic of the Soviet industrial system and emphasizing the relatively high wages now prevalent, the article nowhere mentions the elementary economic factor: *What can they buy for a workman under the prevailing price level?* This total missing of the point was not committed by another commentator, Edgar Snow, who

Article	Average hours of labor, U.S.A.	Average hours of labor, U.S.S.R.
Man's woolen suit	32 hours	317 hours
Simple cotton dress	{ 2 hours { 14 minutes	43 hours
1 pound of sugar	5 minutes	1 hour, 59 minutes
1 pound of coffee	37½ minutes	27 hours

seemed definitely sympathetic to the Soviet experiment and whose book, *The Pattern of Soviet Power,* appeared at about the same time. Comparing the cost of living, he refers to the "fantastically high" prices he encountered in Moscow in 1944: a pound of white bread cost $10; sugar $70 a pound; butter about the same in the commercial stores, although in the "limited" or rationed-goods shops the prices were not exorbitant — for Americans. One meager snack of tea and pastry for two in the restaurant of the Bolshoi Theatre cost him $48; a Russian "Eskimo Pie" cost civilians outside the theater $6 apiece. Although Mr. Snow's figures refer to what may be termed luxury goods, the same yawning discrepancy is found between the average wages of Soviet workmen and the prices demanded for the necessities of daily life.

The vigor and hardihood manifested by the Soviet population and the Red Army during their conflict with Nazi Germany is tribute to the innate toughness of their physical constitution, to their traditional, often mystical patriotism, and cannot be cited as argument for the success of Marxian economic postulates. Russia survived in spite of Marxism and because Marxism has been quietly abandoned in many important respects. What is here under discussion is the specific Marxian contention that workmen would become more enslaved as capitalism evolved and, *per contra,* that Communism would increase their participation in the profits of collective enterprises. Since wages and agricultural income constitute the norm of judgment for the vast majority of the Russian population, and since neither true wages nor true income from agricultural labor in Russia have yet, after thirty-two years of Communism, approached the standards achieved in representative countries of free enterprise, it can only follow that Marx was a false prophet. What the Russian Army fought for in 1941–1945 was not the Communist Manifesto, but for Holy Russia and for the defeat of a hated invader. They would have done the same for a Tzarist Russia, as they often did in their long and tempestuous history. By the pragmatic test of established fact, therefore, one of the basic contentions of Marxism, to the effect that the seizure of power by proletarians under Communism will improve the lot of exploited workmen, is contradicted and refuted. What the Russian Revolution achieved for the personal economy of workers was to liberate them from the dispersed control of many masters and put the entire proletariat under the Spartan control of one master and on a reduced wage scale in terms of actual buying power.

Marx also promised the proletariat greater efficiency and more evenhanded justice in distribution than was possible under the capitalistic form. The per capita possessions and consumptive record of Communism in Soviet Russia prove the direct opposite. He further foretold the "withering away" of the State as a police agency. No citizen of the parent Communist State and its satellites has observed the slightest indication of such a process.

Marx committed another error, the ramifications of which are discernible everywhere. He left out of his calculations two important social developments — or at best he failed to foresee them; the rise of a salaried class and the growth of the managerial class. His polarizing of society into two antipodes, the bourgeoisie and the proletariat, was too narrow and oversimplified. History added the salariat and the manageriat.

The Communist World Revolution resulting in seizure of power by the proletariat was further justified by Marx and Lenin on the appealing ground that capitalism leads inexorably to war through enhanced competition and colonial imperialism. The Marxian assumption of class conflict and the dialectics of the debaters tend to create the impression that war is a special, inherent consequence and monopoly of capitalism. Discussing that contention, Henry Bamford Parks says, much to the point, in his *Marxism — An Autopsy:*

History does not, however, support this supposition. War has existed since the dawn of history, whereas capitalism is a comparatively recent invention. The epoch of capitalism, instead of being more warlike, has on the contrary been more peaceful than the epochs which preceded it. If it has increased the menace of war, it has done so, not by making wars more frequent, but by increasing so enormously the wealth and power of mankind that war, when it does occur, is incomparably more destructive. During the golden age of capitalism — the century from 1815 to 1914 — there were two periods, from 1815 until 1854 and from 1871 until 1914, without any major war between European powers. These were the two longest periods of peace which Europe has enjoyed since the fall of the Roman Empire. The wars which occurred between 1854 and 1871 were, moreover, caused, not by the capitalistic classes but by the policies of Napoleon III and of Bismarck, neither of whom can be identified with the interest of capitalism; while even the World War of 1914–18, however much the imperialist rivalries of Great Britain, France and Germany may have contributed to it, was not directly provoked by those rivalries, but by a conflict between two powers — Russia and Austria — which were still, to a large degree, in a precapitalist stage of development.

Marx was a bad prophet in another important respect. Socialism, he concluded, could only result from a highly developed capitalistic society where social relations of such a malevolent nature would develop from the contradictions and complexities of mechanized production that proletarian revolt and ultimate elimination of the profit motive would ensue. As Russia in 1917 was a predominantly agricultural country with but a very small percentage of its population engaged in industrial production, the success of the proletarian revolution there suggests that either Marx was wrong or Lenin was not a Marxist — or that the description, Union of Soviet Socialist Republics, is wholly misleading.

Like Hitler, Marx found much ammunition ready to hand in the writings of predecessors in the field of economic history. He borrowed freely from many sources. His genius lay not so much in novelty or originality as in the accumulation, synthesis, and deployment of an imposing array of polemical material. The Labor Theory of Value had already been advanced by Ricardo; Saint-Simon had elaborated the economic and materialistic interpretation of history; Sismondi composed a technical criticism of crises, overproduction and competition, with its celebrated "winch" argument; Louis Blanc canonized the power of the State in the initiation and execution of reforms; Proudhon analyzed the contradictions of the prevailing system, the "philosophy of destitution"; class distinctions and class struggle were commonplaces with Pecqueur, Rodbertus, Babeuf, and the Chartists; Considérant, a contemporary of Marx, provided many a vigorous argument for Socialism; dialectical materialism was the core of the philosophic system of Democritus (*circa* 460 B.C.) who conceived the entire universe as an unending whirlwind of atoms resulting in perpetual movement characterized by stages of growth and decay.

The deficiencies of Marxism should not, however, lead to the conclusion that Marx is not an imposing figure in the history of economic thought and social revolutions. Measured by influence on succeeding generations, he ranks as one of the giants among political forces. It has been rightfully said of him that he found Socialism a conspiracy and left it a movement destined to spread faster and farther than even he foresaw. His creed and his prophecies — though demonstrably false in many respects — furnished a system of attack and an arsenal of revolutionary slogans that lighted fires of revolt in many quarters of the globe.

*   *   *   *

The pattern broadly sketched by Marx and cut to the needs of the hour by Lenin is recognizable in the sequence of events as they unfolded since 1945 under Stalin's dictation in each of the countries now behind the Iron Curtain. By the fortunes of war and not without the assistance of lend lease, the Red Army penetrated far into eastern and central Europe. Against the background of force held in reserve, the technicians of infiltration performed their allotted tasks. It remains one of the melancholy "ifs" of history to speculate on what might have happened had Winston Churchill's proposal for invasion by "the soft underbelly" of the Balkans been accepted and executed. What man can say how far present developments might have been forestalled if Allied Forces were present there as the occupying power? Or if Patton had been allowed to liberate Prague? He was within forty miles of that capital. But that strategic prize had been allocated to Soviet Russia, as was Berlin. What Moscow had in mind was soon to appear.

The process of absorption into the Communist orbit followed a uniform course in all the areas occupied by Soviet military forces, though the tempo might vary. Two types of instruments were utilized, one domestic, the other alien. Together with the Red Army came the schooled agents from Moscow to direct local Communist groups and manipulate them as spearhead for the Kremlin. Under cover of a seductive show of friendly co-operation, particularly in Czechoslovakia, strategic points were occupied in the governmental structure. The secret police began their nocturnal visits; potential political opponents quietly disappeared or fled in time. Men of brains, initiative, and suspected courage vanished into the dragnet. The public police was gradually transformed into a compact body of disciplined, Communist-controlled militia. Places were demanded for Communists in the Cabinet under the soothing pretense of a coalition government; invariably the key posts of Interior, Education, National Defense, and Communications were marked for immediate capture. Rigged and maneuvered elections were held — under military supervision. Decrees and legislative acts then tightened the noose.

When the trap was ready to be sprung, sudden charges of treason and espionage were leveled against selected public officials suspected of "unreliability." The reign of terror was on. Prominent ecclesiastics were imprisoned, business enterprises confiscated, and education reduced to servitude. Fictitious plots were discovered and forged documents appeared. It all proceeded by the book, page by page, but with slight modifications responsive to circumstances prevailing in different countries. Lenin once counseled his followers: "A rebellion can only be successful if carried on not by a conspiracy, not by a party, but by the most advanced class backed by the revolutionary fervor of the masses. One has to look for a turning point in history where the vanguard has reached the climax of activity concurrent with a low in the ranks of the enemies and the wavering rows of the uncertain friends of the Revolution. Time is ripe for action when these rational conditions have been ascertained." He exhorts his numerically small Bolshevik faction not to rely on mere numbers but on organization and strength of will: revolutionists should not ". . . be afraid to leave the wavering to the wavering. They are more valuable to the cause of the Revolution in the other camp than in our own which can only use unconditionally devoted men."

This general pattern was applied to satellite states after 1945 under the alluring guise of a "People's Republic." Stigmatizing certain political institutions as obsolete relics of a discredited past and evil attempts to retain bourgeois forms of state apparatus, the new masters introduced constitutional changes by controlled parliamentary devices. Roumania went so far as to invalidate all legislation enacted by past parliaments. Poland was forced to accept a Soviet general as chief commander of its army and began a "reform" of the office of Public Prosecutor. A sweeping alteration of its entire legal system was introduced in Czechoslovakia. And in all the satellites social and economic collectivization became the prevailing pattern of administrative thought and the obligatory norm for the planning of programs.

These internal transformations were accelerated by the presence of Soviet troops remaining in the "liberated" areas as an army of occupation. How directly this element of force influenced the tempo of revolutionary change and facilitated subjection to Moscow may be judged from the exception that developed in Yugoslavia where no Soviet army had penetrated. Claiming to be a better Marxist and Leninist than Stalin was showing himself to be, Tito followed the broad pattern for communizing a state, but only up to a crucial point. He balked at the final and complete surrender required by the Kremlin and had a national army to support the heresy. Hence, the public denunciations from Moscow, the excommunication from the Cominform, and the secret rage of the Politburo.

The manipulation of parliamentary processes so enmeshed the wavering and unhappy Jan Masaryk in Czechoslovakia that death offered the only escape. His body lying cold, broken, and solitary in the courtyard of his Prague apartment, followed by the progressive hounding of Beneš to the lonely grave where he now lies, testify to the futility of compromising with power uncontrolled by conscience and fortified by a precise philosophy of World Revolution. Mr. Beneš chose a policy of making his country "a bridge" between Soviet Russia and Western culture. He thought he could hold the bridge. What he accomplished, to his dismay, was the opening of a gate permitting Communism to advance westward to one of its most strategic outposts in Christendom. By manipulation of its position in North Korea, the Revolution prepared the assault on South Korea. Conquest of the entire peninsula would give the Kremlin a dagger pointed at Japan and furnish a new jumping-off base for challenging America in the Far East. Only Japan and Formosa would then remain to be dealt with when the Revolution decides to head across the Pacific toward California, or drops unexpectedly out of the skies over the Arctic regions.

It has been asserted in some quarters that the Politburo has even set an approximate date for the inception of direct war against its last great target with the richest booty of all time in the balance. Admiral Ellis S. Zacharias (retired), former Deputy Chief of U. S. Naval Intelligence, asserts that the Russian High Command came to their vital decision on the night of January 28, 1949: an attack on the United States would be launched not later than 1956.[8] The calculation was based on two assumptions: (*a*) a major depression would ensue in the United States sometime between 1954–1956; (*b*) to offset internal disaster and demoralization the Americans would launch a war about that time. Hence the Communist government would forestall the event by taking the initiative and luring the United States into a land war on some distant territory where forces and supplies would first have to cross a dangerous expanse of water.

---

[8] *Behind Closed Doors*, G. P. Putnam's Sons, 1950.

CHAPTER IV

Soviet Conduct No Enigma

THE most critical and searching test of a revolution comes after its initial military victory. The classical enemy has been defeated in the field or at the barricades but other enemies remain. The very nature and definition of a continuing revolution imply opposition. Its life depends on its power of denial. It must continue to attack somebody or something — particularly when it claims to be a permanent revolution, and doubly so if it assumed leadership of a world revolution. A new devil and a fresh whipping boy must be continuously provided if the managers are to offer a dynamic and positive program. The humdrum necessity of social and economic reform on the domestic front, industrial productivity and similar chores of national housekeeping, though vital and challenging to a new government, can rarely be dramatized as heroic postures. There must be legends. There must be a mythology. There must be a villain some place in the offing to serve as target for sustaining the revolutionary spirit and assuring popular support for the transfer of power to new masters.

Perhaps the most brilliant achievement in that field was the propaganda attending the first Five-Year Plan launched by Stalin in 1928. After careful preparation on the part of the economists and statisticians respecting the need of electrification, the exploitation of natural resources, and the dearth of manufactured commodities, a psychological campaign was inaugurated on vast proportions. The land was deluged with alluring posters, literature, and oratory; every kopeck was mobilized to achieve what was described as "a leap across centuries" in the industrialization of Soviet Russia. But, mark you, there was an international villain on the stage of that colossal spectacle, a foreign enemy to justify the crushing effort demanded of the Russian people. It was the old devil, Capitalism, who was now to be attacked with his own weapons and on the international level since he showed signs of re-entering the arena.

In the official pronouncements accompanying that crusade we find renewed warnings and stylized slogans describing the imminent danger. On August 29, 1929, *Pravda*, the official Party organ, declared:

The Five Year Plan is an important part of the offensive of the proletariat of the whole world against Capitalism; it is a plan tending to undermine capitalist stabilization; it is a great plan of World Revolution.

The naming of a specific enemy at that stage was in accord with tactical necessity and revolutionary custom. In numerous directives, Lenin counsels his followers never to play with revolution; having begun one you must go on to the end.[1] A defensive attitude is fatal. Day by day, hour by hour the Revolution must take the offensive.[2] Revolutionary parties must continue to learn.[3] In waging war against the international bourgeoisie, it would be folly to renounce the advantage of making temporary compromises and entering on formal agreements — but only as maneuvers in a zigzag advance toward one's objective.[4] After victory in one land, reforms may be initiated but only as a by-product of the revolution's progress to the international arena. Reforms then take on a new relationship, i.e., they are only breathing spaces.[5] Stalin later emphasized the need of a conscious leadership obedient to an infallible scientific program. Reforms, he pointed out, are to be advocated as "a meshing of the legal work with the illegal purposes

---

[1] Borrowed from Saint Just, one of the protagonists of the French Revolution: *He who stops half way in a revolution, digs his own grave.*

[2] *Collected Works*, Russian Edition, Vol. XIV, Part II, p. 270.

[3] *Ibid.*, Vol. XVII, p. 121.

[4] *Ibid.*, Vol. XVII, p. 158.

[5] *Ibid.*, Vol. XVIII, Part I, pp. 114–115.

. . . as a cover for the illegal work which aims at revolutionary preparation of the masses for the overthrow of the bourgeoisie."[6] A sense of timing is extremely important: aggressive tactics are for a rising tide of opportunity, compromise and even retreat must accompany an ebbing tide.[7] Fear of an imminent attack by capitalist powers must be kept alive and vigorous at all times: "It must be remembered that all the time it is only the breadth of a hair that divides us from invasion."[8]

The first enemy in 1917 had been the Romanov dynasty with its attendant aristocracy. The Tzar and the Grand Dukes furnished prominent and shining targets. Hence, the entire Imperial family was murdered at Ekaterinburg; the various Grand Dukes were either slaughtered or driven into exile. The Provisional Government in its turn was an easy mark and furnished the alert propagandists of the left with pretexts for identifying it with the old regime — "same old exploiters." The ensuing civil wars gave the Revolution clear and visible opposition in the persons of Kolchak, Petlura, Wrangel, and Denikin. These eliminated, the Revolution turned on the bourgeoisie of Russia in a campaign which opened up an excellent field of operations during the next five years. The Church, too, was dramatized as a constant menace, and religious persecution kept the people aware of the Revolution's vitality. During the five-year plans, the kulak served as whipping boy on the domestic front and he was suppressed with vigor and appropriate publicity.

Then came the period of sensational State trials of foreigners accused of espionage and sabotage, followed in due order by the purging of old-line Bolsheviks, former high officials of the Party, and prominent military figures — all accused of treason and conspiracy. In the early thirties the rise of Hitler, the expansion of Japan onto the Asiatic mainland, the empire building of Mussolini, and the revolt of Franco furnished ample motivation for rekindling the fires of revolutionary vigilance. Mobilization against Fascism became the catchword of the times. That device served for four

---

[6] *Problems of Leninism,* Russian Edition, 1945, p. 63.
[7] *Ibid.,* p. 55.
[8] Stalin, *Reply to Comrade Ivanov,* 1938, citing Lenin's previous dogma.

years. With the ease of an acrobat the Kremlin swung over to an alliance with Hitler in 1939, explaining that the danger then consisted in not doing so. But the invasion of Soviet territory by Hitler in 1941 gave the Russian Revolution its greatest challenge — and its greatest fright.

This spectacular assault might be used, superficially, as an argument to prove that Lenin and Stalin were right in their doctrine that only a hair separated Soviet security from capitalist invasion. The cold facts of record, however, preclude such sophistry. It was Soviet Russia who wantonly invaded Poland, Latvia, Lithuania, Estonia, and Finland in 1939, profiting by the confusion induced by Hitler's launching World War II on September 1, 1939. The two aggressors had moved simultaneously on their victims in accordance with the secret agreement included in the Nazi-Soviet Pact of August, 1939. The gamble failed, at least temporarily, when Hitler turned on his partner and drove the competing Russian Revolution back to Petrograd, Moscow, and Stalingrad.

By 1945 all these forms of organized opposition were eliminated or discounted and a new peril had to be found — or created. Nothing is more dangerous for a permanent revolution than lack of an adversary. Even in peacetime such a stimulus is vitally necessary for the survival of militant Marxism; otherwise the plant would die at the roots and the leaves wither on the vine. The answer to the newest urge for fulfilling a messianic mission was provided by the circumstances and opportunities of the postwar period.

Strengthened by military success and with its area of operation increased by some 273,947 square miles of newly acquired or dominated territory,[9] the Soviet government then openly declared all bourgeois society, including its late allies, to be in conspiracy against the Soviet homeland. The Western powers suddenly became warmongers, capitalist exploiters, encirclers of Soviet Russia, etc., etc. In an order of the day on May 1, 1946, Stalin warned the Russian people "not to forget for a single minute the intrigues of international reaction which are hatching plans for a new war . . .

---

[9] By 1951 the controlled areas in Europe exceeded 500,000 square miles. To this must be added several million more in Asia.

to be constantly vigilant . . . to protect as the apple of one's eye the armed forces and the defensive power of the country." On October 6, 1947, came the announcement from Moscow that the Communist parties of nine states had united for consolidated ideological warfare against "United States aggression." This country was singled out and denounced in the manifesto of the Cominform as the "leading force" in an antidemocratic imperialism, precisely at the moment when we were demobilizing the greatest armed force in our history.

The United Nations then furnished an open and privileged forum on American soil for continued assaults in vitriolic language on the motives and conduct of the American government. The stereotyped incriminations of Molotov, Vyshinski, Gromyko, and their successors were designed to supply renewed justification for keeping the Revolution actively prepared to repel a fictitious invasion by "international brigands" operating under a Marshall Plan. "Crazy idea of world domination . . . vicious fabrications . . . poorly camouflaged preparation for war . . . , " declared Vyshinski before the General Assembly on September 18, 1947. He repeated and enlarged the pattern during the Korean war.

One of the most incendiary and hate-provoking attacks against the United States was launched on January 21, 1951, at the ceremonies commemorating the 27th anniversary of Lenin's death. The speech of Peter Pospelov, a leading figure in the Russian Communist Party, delivered in the Bolshoi Theatre, Moscow, under the approving eyes and ears of Generalissimo Stalin, outdistanced all previous diatribes in viciousness and colossal falsehoods. Pospelov described American leaders as "political madmen . . . hands of American imperialists are red with the blood of the Russian people . . . bloody crimes. . . ." The American government is described as a "rampant beast . . . with mad rapidity" pushing the American people to "the precipice of a third world war." This conventional attitude received the personal and official benediction of Stalin himself by his repetition of similar accusations in his interview published in Pravda, February 16, 1951.

By manufactured fears and violent distortions of truth the Politburo has given the longest demonstration in modern history of revolutionary continuity. If there cannot be one Rome, they will see to it that there are two Carthages. Such sustained crusading must repose on a great love or a great hatred. Probably both.

The coexistence of these two motives in the Soviet mind reflects the antagonisms of the age into which the Russian Revolution was born. It appeared at the end of a definite, recognizable phase of social disintegration throughout the world, particularly in the West. The divisive tendencies of the Industrial Revolution culminated in an increase of class consciousness based on the disproportionate sharing of benefits created by the increased productivity of machinery and technological inventions. This inner schism of society was growing and observable to thoughtful men long before the Soviets dramatized the conflict. Leo XIII, with remarkable acumen, laid his finger on the mounting tension in his celebrated encyclical of 1891, *The Condition of the Working Classes.* Forty years later, in 1931, Pius XI repeated the warning and cried alarm with renewed intensity. Lenin did not create the crisis in 1917; he and his successors merely seized it, deepened it, and capitalized on it mightily.

Coming, as it did, in the course of a mounting degeneration in the moral and spiritual vitality which had once created a Christian culture, the anti-Christian and illiberal Russian Revolution added the cult of power to supply the affirmative incentive. It struck at the end of an epoch, when the ethical resources of a secularized Europe were at their lowest ebb, and when the hierarchy of values created by a once united Christendom had given place in many quarters to the cultivated perplexity of the skeptics playing with the meaning and the content of life. The currency of thought had been debased by eighteenth-century rationalism and the treason of countless intellectuals had undermined man's faith in his own spirituality and destiny. Long before Stalin was to harness hatred to power, Dostoevski, in *Brothers Karamazov,* foresaw the progressive dehumanization of man and how disbelief in God would end with the strangling of belief in the dignity of man. Then would arise the demons who tormented the fictitious characters of his terrifying novel *The Possessed.* They would come in legions and humanity would immolate itself on the altar of its own negations. Nazi Germany supplied the *entre acte* — a sort of parenthesis in the text, as Hitler made supreme efforts to play the role of

Nietzsche's superman endowed with the will to universal power. He failed and passed from the stage. The mantle then reverted to one of Dostoevski's countrymen from Georgia and the crisis now continues in the same direction but under more skillful leadership.

By measure of its extent and objectives, the resultant international conspiracy has become an international reality which historians of future generations may well record as the most formidable and far-reaching challenge to Christendom since the Moslem invasion of Europe was checked by Charles Martel at the battle of Poitiers in the year 732. But a new element has been introduced, a subtlety eminently characteristic of the modern mind. The invaders of the Christian West in the eighth century, like the Mongolian hordes of a later age, relied on their own prowess and their own resources. Their adventure stood or fell without the aid of auxiliaries recruited from inside the opposing camp. They could not count on organized treason within the very stronghold of their prospective victims. Not so in the present crisis. The latest aggressor has a well-organized and waiting fifth column at his command, an international brigade, stationed at strategic points in every capital of the bourgeois world.

The groomers of Moscow's Trojan Horse have found the way to invoke legalisms and the guarantees of the Constitution to assassinate freedom at the foot of the Statue of Liberty. Under cover of the Bill of Rights, they have solved the great riddle of how to destroy an organism legally, by the very processes which were devised to safeguard its vitality. How did they develop their program?

The evolution of the technique shows an amalgam of planned policy and fluid opportunism. The former is constant and fixed both in method and objectives, the latter extremely adaptable to local circumstances and international tensions as they developed during the three decades following World War I. The fortunes of war and the fall of the Russian Empire in 1917 put the entire machinery of the Russian State under the control of a general idea — the concept of man in the mass as opposed to the metaphysics of personality and individual responsibility. The conception of a world inhabited and cultivated by men each of whom is a responsible person was displaced by the vision of a class

Leviathan called the proletariat. What counts for the new iconoclasts is the impersonal man without soul or individual conscience
and valuable only as a cog of a great wheel in a mechanized
humanity. The blueprints dealt with types, not individuals. The
ideal was the collective impersonal, not the "rickety little ego"
whom Bednyi, an early Soviet poet, lampooned in his verses.

The new Monism was to express itself primarily as economic
productivity:

> Million-footed: a body. The pavement cracks.
> A million mass: one heart, one will, one tread.
> Keeping step, keeping step.
> On they march. On they march.
> March, march.
> Out of the factory quarters, smoke-wreathed,
> Out of the black dungeous, filthy rat holes,
> He came — his fingers bent like pincers —
> Burst the thousand-year-old chains rattling about him —
> Came now the new ruler on to the street. . .
>
> The houses thunder back. The highway clamors.
> The giant stands fast.

It will be noted that in Bednyi's heavy lyric, as in all Communist
thought, the emphasis is on the body, the material, and the
physical. Spirit and mind and ideals are incidental. Man, in Stalin's
frigid language, weighs no heavier on the scale of values than
a tool; at best he is "the most precious capital." This vast reservoir
of man power within Russia itself is under the complete control
and iron discipline of a Party which numbers approximately 3 per
cent of the population. It is a self-perpetuating monopoly, dedicated
not to a dictatorship of the proletariat but to dictatorship *over* it.
A similar debasement is being rapidly affected in all satellite lands
whose sovereignty has been transformed into the status of fief
to Moscow.

The capture of the proletarians of the world was planned in
a manner to harmonize with the diversity of culture and the
measure of control available over those against whom it was
progressively directed. On Soviet territory it was mandatory and
applied by force through five-year plans, by collectivized agri-
culture and organized terrorism. Outside the Soviet Union, the

program was entrusted to local Communist Parties under the direction of Moscow-trained leaders and applied first to such masses as were most capable of being manipulated. Lenin's shrewd directives had warned against premature plucking of fruit; the situation had to be "ripe," and if the plum was not soft enough, further cultivation was indicated as guarantee of smooth swallowing. Recognition of the right moment, coupled with a correct estimate of the enemy's powers of resistance, was his criterion for a successful revolutionist. In China, eastern Europe — and to a less degree in central Europe — a semifeudal form of land holding provided an excellent seed bed for the organization of discontent among peasant populations, while concentrations of industrial power and the social abuses of finance capital encouraged class consciousness among urban workers.

This organization of Communism on world proportions proceeded steadily and systematically, particularly after 1945; from its beginning, however, even before 1917, it followed a military pattern not only in its slogans but in the intellectual formation of its personnel. After 1917 the Party considered itself as engaged in an active global war, a militant crusade; members of the Party constituted an army with a clearly defined top command, a general staff, field officers, regiments, companies, commanders, echelons, cadres, sergeants, corporals, and privates. The Table of Organization paralleled the structure of the Red Army. The factory cell and the block leader continued the chain of command down to the lowest levels, while couriers, inspectors, finance officers, and control agents journeyed crisscross from Moscow to every theater of operations. Once in power and ready for full-blown action the Party, both outside and inside Soviet Russia, duplicated a military force in every organizational respect: recruitment of new members, induction, boot training, indoctrination, advanced shock troops, establishment of courts martial, sentencing and execution of serious offenders, counterintelligence service and attachés in embassies with diplomatic immunity. It adopted all the characteristics and paraphernalia of a military component — except uniforms, weapons openly displayed, and a chaplains' corps.[10]

---

[10] The internal organization and military character of a Communist Party wherever located is described in great detail and with copious documentation

This militarization of the Communist Party on its road to total empire responded to the will-to-power psychology of its founders. But Clausewitz's classic *On War* had much to do with it as well. The German general's celebrated axioms: *war is an act of social life* and *war is a continuation of policy by violent means,* were accepted by Lenin and copied down as guiding principles in his notebooks. On war as a continuation of political ends, he wrote: "The Marxists have always considered this axiom as the theoretical foundation for the meaning of every war."[11]

The windfall occasioned by the collapse of Nazi Germany and Japan opened new perspectives both in geography and power potential. Firmly entrenched in occupied lands, and with Latvia, Lithuania, and Estonia already absorbed through military conquest, the Politburo unfolded its next series of blueprints for consolidating the expanding empire. Maneuvering for position under local conditions the Revolution effected its progressive seizure of power by a pattern adapted to the legal institutions and social environment of Poland, Czechoslovakia, Hungary, Roumania, Bulgaria, Albania, and China. The tactics and the tempo of events varied in step with the risk; the progress was not always so plunging as was the conquest of the Baltic States. In Roumania and Bulgaria the seizure of power, though gradual, was direct, open, and ruthless. Vyshinski finally came in person to Bucharest and delivered Moscow's ultimatum; in Sofia, Dimitrov simply "liquidated" the opposition, which meant persuasion by firing squad, by gallows, or by total disappearance of designated victims under unknown circumstances. But in proportion as the Revolution moved westward into areas of more stabilized democracies and greater political maturity, it deployed its forces in slightly different guises and by the slower stages of controlled parliamentary processes. That is the current phase of the conflict in France and Italy. In East Germany the pattern is mixed — partly parliamentary, partly direct seizure of

---

in W. R. Kintner's *The Front Is Everywhere* (University of Oklahoma Press, 1950). Its international ramifications are catalogued in a comprehensive survey, country by country, in *World Communism Today,* by Martin Ebon (Whittlesly House, 1950).

[11] See "Clausewitz and Soviet Strategy," by Byron Dexter, in *Foreign Affairs,* October, 1950, pp. 41–55.

power by preponderant force, with the Red Army massed, a quarter of a million strong, on the sidelines.

*   *   *   *

As the Revolution has not as yet launched a direct and overt military assault against the United States and since there is no Communist bloc in the Congress, the tactics here are still confined to prerevolutionary devices. The psychological-warfare phase includes among its primary weapons the seducing of chosen dupes into the net of treasonable co-operation. The tragedy of Alger Hiss, the case of Judith Coplon, the mystery surrounding the violent death of Laurence Duggan after his name had been mentioned during an inquiry into subversive activities, the confessions of Whittaker Chambers, Miss Bentley, Louis Budenz, and Julian Wadleigh furnish disturbing reminders that the Russian Revolution is not merely an echo of things far off and un-American but a tangible reality that has taken its place on American soil as the main issue and greatest challenge of the times.

The culmination of understanding and final acceptance of the domestic menace came on September 23, 1950, when Congress by an overwhelming majority overrode the veto of the President and enacted a Communist Control Law which outdid the Alien and Sedition Acts of 1798. Already at grips with the empire builder in Korea, the public conscience demanded expression in legal form of its determination to cope with his agents in America. Open to technical criticism in some of its provisions and probably needing revision of its too broad language, the Act represented an awakening long overdue.

But neither law now tightened security measures will solve the conundrum: how was it possible for Stalin to enlist so many apparently intelligent Americans in his foreign legion?

Limiting our inquiry to Americans who openly espouse the Soviet cause or else support it without taking the ultimate step of becoming registered members of the Communist Party, we find a variety of types corresponding to the quality and extent of their collaboration. At the outset, the Revolution of March, 1917, was very properly eulogized by Americans both in private and public life. Woodrow Wilson welcomed the new freedom as a "fit partner in a league of honor"; he promptly recognized the provisional government and accorded diplomatic status to its ambassador at Washington. Public feeling, in mass volume, flowed steadily toward the infant democracy. But the advent of a new element — Marxian Communism with its declared objective of world domination — soon created disillusionment and eventual estrangement between official Washington and the regime which seized the government of Russia on November 7, 1917. It was then that confusion entered the thought of many Americans and created the first schism among the intellectuals. The infection ranged from simple muddle-headedness to calculated chicanery. Senator Borah was pre-eminent among this first group of Soviet advocates and his public attitude for many years demonstrated how difficult it is for a professional liberal to abandon a position once taken and confess either to ignorance of the facts or gullibility in having accepted manufactured evidence.

Others in this category — and I assume a basic sincerity in their souls — succumbed to wishful thinking and clung to the hope that Soviet Russia would eventually evolve into a true democracy and would renounce her grandiose ambition to communize all humanity. Still others attempted to draw a distinction between the Third International and the Soviet government; they accepted Moscow's preposterous claim that the Comintern was a private organization of hotheads not to be equated with official Russia. In so doing they did great violence to the rules of evidence and permitted an emotion for freedom *per se* to control their will, their intellect, and their eyesight.

It was a curious paradox in those early days to hear passionate appeals for "tolerance toward Soviet Russia" on the lips of men quick to denounce the government of the United States engaged in punishing common-law criminality at home. By a sort of habit induced, possibly, by original sincerity and the exhilaration of being considered an advanced thinker, this type of seduced liberal was often sucked into the romantic attitude of crusading for what was described as the "underdog"; the dilettanti never adverted to the possibility that an underdog small or large may have rabies.

A more sinister type of aid and solace to Lenin's cause was provided by certain professors and instructors of youth who utilized their chairs to sow the seeds of doubt in the immature minds of students still in their salad days and not yet capable of discriminating between cynicism and constructive criticism of political institutions. The two favorite targets in the decade following World War I were patriotism and religious conviction. Soviet Russia was frequently held up as a pattern of rationality; agnosticism and skepticism were canonized as the only intelligent attitudes toward life and its problems, an orientation which led subtly to the atheistic materialism of Marx, Lenin, and Stalin. It was not without logicality that such pedagogues found themselves in sympathy with the Marx-Lenin principle that religion is opium for the people. The result was an adolescent worship of empiricism, pragmatism, and the amoralism of that frigid evasion: "Science is not concerned with values."

There was much poisoning of the wells of loyalty by sniping at the principle of authority whether embodied in the Constitution or in the relation of sons and daughters to parents. National defense was denounced as disguised militarism and patriotism derided as political superstition. It required steady nerves and great faith for a student in too many universities to join the ROTC unit or attend chapel with regularity. He ran the risk of withering sarcasm leveled in his direction from professorial coteries which, though not avowedly members of the Party, were the darlings of the campus Communists.

It is to the credit of the generation of American students who were subjected so widely to that barrage during the years between World Wars I and II that they proved better judges of values than the mentors who sought to undermine their patriotism and faith in the American system under the cloak of academic freedom. When the hour of testing came in December, 1941, their pupils rallied to the colors by millions, while the academic termites relapsed into the silence of frustration — or slipped into a comfortable berth in some government department.

The question arises: what is the motive and what are the thought processes of an American who will work for the cause of Lenin and Stalin while still enjoying the freedoms guaranteed by the Constitution of the United States? In the case of the 54,174 card-bearing members of the Communist Party in this country the answer is ready to hand. They do not consider themselves primarily as citizens of the United States; the conditions and requirements for formal admission into the Party stipulate that they are citizens of an international community, whose capital is Moscow and to which they owe moral and intellectual allegiance. The leader of the Party, Mr. Foster, explained to a Congressional Committee on May 29, 1948, that, in the event of war with the Soviet Union, American Communists would not fight against Russia. We know, then, where they will stand, what they think, and what they will attempt to do if the people of the United States ever find themselves in such an armed conflict.

It is with the outer fringe, the sympathizers, the fellow travelers and secret operators, particularly with those who may occupy influential positions in public life, that we are here concerned. This category has been estimated by Mr. J. Edgar Hoover at something like 500,000 in number. We may again narrow the field and exclude such aliens or newly arrived citizens as still retain a hidden psychology of inherited resentment and regard their sojourn in America as temporary and for revolutionary purposes. They, too, present little difficulty for the analyst of motivation. Our inquiry is directed, consequently, to the remaining group of native Americans, born into the American scene, enjoying the high standard of living and the palpable benefits of a prosperous, free, and democratic society which is still developing the field of individual opportunity and progressing rapidly in its task of removing social injustices, racial segregation, and all similar obstacles to legitimate human freedom.

There are no concentration camps here for political opponents; there is no NKVD to hound us out of bed at 2 a.m. for extrajudicial trial before a secret tribunal with sudden death or exile to Siberia in the uncontrolled discretion of its inquisitors; there is no confiscation of property or molestation of the person without due process of law; there is freedom of occupation, of the right to strike, of religion, and of education. There is freedom of the press to an extent undreamed of in Soviet Russia. Representatives of the Moscow press are admitted freely to the halls of Congress and to the President's press conferences; they are free to cable to Moscow their mendacious and twisted interpretations of the American democracy. There is a salary scale for organized labor in this country which is the highest in the world; there is full participation by the people in every election, with universal suffrage and secret ballot. There are provisions for health, recreation, and general social welfare that dot the land with public facilities. There is unemployment insurance and old-age assistance from the treasury of state and federal governments, with pension plans on the increase in private industry. There is a mounting productivity of manufactures to meet both the necessities and amenities of civilized living. There is a system of free care for wounded veterans and free education at college level for servicemen on a scale never yet attempted by any other country in the world. In a word, there is here, in being, a measure of social welfare such as Marx never conceived and which, far from constituting oppression of the proletariat, has approached a point deemed by many to be the very definition of prodigality and destructive of initiative.

Turning to international welfare the record is equally impressive. After World War I American charity poured relief supplies, food, medicine, books, libraries, clothes, and good will into every afflicted country, Russia not excluded. In recent years *Care* packages are bringing solace to every European country where governments have not prohibited them; loans and financial assistance have been generously extended. Exchange of students brings thousands of foreign youths to America for education and scientific training under the Fulbright Act supplemented by the generosity of private endowments. Finally, the Marshall Plan stands behind reconstruction in Europe under terms which provide a breathing space for the shattered economy of war-torn lands. Simultaneously, help is extended to Greece, to Turkey, and numerous other peoples of the old and the new world. It was offered even to the satellite countries. All in all, it has been estimated by the Director of the Budget, Frank C. Pace, Jr., that the final cost of the war to the United States of America, including both war activities and postwar rehabilitation at home and abroad, will reach three trillion dollars. The estimate was made before the total rearmament program of 1950.

These contributions to human welfare and the cost to the American people are not cited in any spirit of boastfulness or vulgar complacency. For thoughtful men they rather engender a sense of humility and responsibility, tempered by apprehension at the staggering load imposed on the national economy and the individual taxpayer. They have been catalogued — imperfectly and probably not in their entirety — in order to lay them on the balance with a great paradox. The country and the system which could produce such tangible achievements is to be weighed against the public record of Soviet Russia, too well known to require detailed description. In the occupied zones of Germany, Austria, and Korea, as well as in the satellite lands, the inhabitants furnish melancholy evidence of the contrast. American occupation forces, despite the occasional lapses of individuals succumbing to temptation or to the pull of the old Adam in every man when released from discipline, have not lived off the land or reduced the inhabitants to hewers of wood or drawers of water; they have not made the name of America synonymous with organized rape, wholesale looting, and recruiting of slave gangs for concentration camps. One has only to tabulate the authentic experiences of those who have lived in occupied territories in order to understand the meaning of Soviet "liberation" and Soviet practices on foreign ground. Their external conduct was uniform with domestic practices. Mr. John D. Littlepage, an American mining engineer, who resided in Soviet Russia from 1928 to 1937, describes the entire population as "prisoners on parole."[12]

Why should any American wish, much less conspire, to betray the United States to the wardens who control the prison house that Russia is and the satellites have become? Is the motive to be sought in a lust for power thirsting to advance some private ambition at any cost? Is it that perverted sense of frustration and wounded vanity which makes some introverts imagine that their abilities have not been properly recognized by fellow Americans but would be appreciated and rewarded by the rulers of Soviet Russia? Is it sheer exhibitionism in the grand manner? Is it a manifestation of what Goethe described as "the malignancy of littleness"? Can it be due to a blind spot in the brain which shuts out the facts of America and leaves the mind susceptible only to the falsities of

---

[12] *In Search of Soviet Gold* (Harcourt, Brace & Co., 1938), pp. 140–141.

Soviet propaganda? Is it the fanaticism of zealots who — to recall Santayana's perceptive thought — continue their momentum even after they have forgotten their purposes? Is it the naïveté of Utopians mistaking Communism as the nearest approach to their cravings? Is it the thrashing about of neurotics whose case history will reveal the scars of some previous conflict with family or society? Is it a transfer complex of those enemies of Fascism and Nazism who imagined that opposition to those two totalitarians required adherence to Communism? This narrow concept of alternatives led many an immature liberal astray, particularly during and immediately after the Spanish Civil War. Their emotional hysteria gave a distinct coloration to the Pink Decade.

There is renewed need of clear and accurate thinking at this point. We are still not inquiring what produces a Communist in a poverty-stricken country or among men driven to desperation by economic injustice, vicious exploitation, peonage, or the political absolutism of a privileged caste. Under such circumstances Communism is at once an understandable social consequence of an intolerable regime — and the judgment of history against it. Our question asks: what makes a Communist or a sympathizer out of an American comfortably placed, sometimes a millionaire, often a successful author, a playwright, a Hollywood figure, a schoolteacher, a government employee, a well-paid labor leader, a lawyer, or a city councilor? Specifically we are seeking to understand why he would transform this country — to which 249,187 persons recently emigrated as to a haven of refuge[13] — into a replica of the servile state with the inhumanity and the terrorism which prevail in every land where Communism triumphs.

To continue our probing into the roots of motivation: is the mainspring naked treason — not unknown in American history — treason not yet of hand, but a covert surrender of heart and head to the seduction of cold cash or the promise of it? Is it the craving for revenge which pride can engender in minds embittered by some real or imagined personal affront from society? The most dangerous and incurable pride is the conceit that argues itself into a secret conviction of personal infallibility. The most dangerous truth to

---

[13] Immigration figures covering period June 30, 1949–June 30, 1950.

be ignorant of is one's own ignorance. Is it some twisted pacifism that would save America from the horrors of a third World War by rendering her people incapable of waging one should Soviet Russia decide to transform the cold war into a shooting contest? Is it the moral schizophrenia by which Fuchs, the British scientist, justified his transmission of atomic information to the Kremlin? He had two consciences, he explained, one as an Englishman, one as a scientist with an international outlook which impelled him to share the secret with Soviet Russia. Why Russia was thus favored, instead of science in the Argentine or Belgium or Norway, he did not elucidate.

One explanation derives from the urge some minds feel for being different and for exercising what ecstatic pedagogues in progressive schools for children extol as the right to self-expression. Mr. Henry Julian Wadleigh, the former State Department official who confessed to having acted as a spy for Soviet Russia while serving as economist in the Trade Agreements Division in 1936, published an illuminating analysis of his double life.[14] After explaining his method of abstracting important documents from papers which passed over his desk and slipping them surreptitiously to his Moscow "contact" he speaks of his "psychopathic aversion to being conventional." This secret obsession for rebelling against "a pattern set by convention or public opinion" influenced his manner of dress and personal appearance even to "wearing no garters and sometimes letting my hair grow for six weeks without a visit to the barber." This self-consciousness expressed itself in his frequent sending of secret information to be microfilmed by the Soviet agent awaiting him at Washington street corners or in obscure restaurants. "Had it not been for my underground work with the Communists and my belief in its importance, I would probably have decided to leave the State Department after the first two weeks — as soon as I could find a satisfactory job elsewhere."

Is the motive perhaps the megalomania of liberalism gone mad with egotism? Or on the other hand is it a naïve idealism innocent of evil intent, but too inexperienced to separate the counterfeit from the real? Is it a secret passion for excitement and dangerous living

---

[14] *Washington Post*, "Julian Wadleigh's Own Story," second installment, July 31, 1949.

such as torments the pyromaniac and drives him to seek satiation in the spectacle of fire? Is it plain, unadulterated demonism taking possession of an unwary victim and seducing him to unexpected crime on his leaning side? Is it a calculating self-interest, an insurance policy, as it were, to guarantee safety for cowards prepared to accommodate themselves to "the wave of the future"? . . . Is it a combination of several or all of these paranoiac aberrations of the mind?

Whatever motive may lurk in the subterranean recesses of the subconscious ego, one fact is patent in the light of facts. Lenin has left to the world more of his personality than is revealed by his embalmed corpse just outside the Kremlin wall. On a wintry afternoon in 1922 the writer of these lines spent some time wandering through the Red Square and searching for the grave of an American who had been buried in the same locality. There it was, the last earthly resting place of John Reed, the brilliant but erratic Harvard graduate who had cast his lot with Lenin's cause as early as 1917, and left an authentic, factual account of the Revolution in his book: *Ten Days That Shook the World.* He was one of the few Americans who adhered to the cause of Lenin in those days. Today, if Mr. J. Edgar Hoover is correct, there are 500,000 John Reeds walking the streets of the United States.

The tactical role and combat station of these domestic allies have been systematically defined and reliable personnel allocated to specific tasks. Approximately one half the strength of the Party in the United States is concentrated in major industrial areas where, in the words of the Director of the Federal Bureau of Investigation to a Senate subcommittee in 1950, " . . . they would be able to sabotage essential industry in vital defense areas in the event of a national emergency." Mr. Hoover specified the sensitive spots: "steel, heavy machinery, mining, communications, transportation, electrical and maritime industries."

According to *Newsweek* in its edition of January 8, 1951, the Party held a secret conclave shortly before that date at which the organization secretary, Henry Winston, boasted that 22,000 reliable members were stationed in basic industries, ready for sabotage of defense mobilization. The distribution of these selected saboteurs was claimed to be:

Food processing	5700	(28%)
Auto and aviation	4200	(19%)
Electrical and machine	3800	(17%)
Steel and fabricating	3100	(14%)
Transportation and maritime	1900	(8%)
Mining, all types	1700	(7%)
Rubber, chemicals, and petroleum . .	1700	(7%)

Since every reliable Communist is the focal point of a small group of secret sympathizers on whom he can count and to whom he transmits the Party Line, it has been estimated that there is a guerrilla force behind the domestic defense lines of America to a strength of something like twenty divisions.

Like the iceberg which has seven eighths of its bulk under water, with only one eighth visible, the forces of Mr. Stalin's World Revolution in this country are mainly underground and out of sight. The Politburo some 20 years ago took steps to provide for just such an upsurge of American vigilance as is now in full development. The official organ of the Comintern, *The Communist International,* on September 1, 1931, published detailed instructions on the measures to be taken in a country where opposition to Communism rises to the stage of restrictive legislation. The master plan, entitled *Organizational Problems in Underground Revolutionary Work,* was signed by B. Vassiliev, a prominent figure at the Moscow headquarters of the World Revolution. His directives are based on an observed strengthening of resistance among enemy, i.e., capitalist, States. "Thus," he wrote, "the increasing artfulness of the police apparatus of the bourgeois governments in the struggle against the Communist movement makes it essential for the latter to have a more complicated, flexible and accurately functioning organization. This organization will inevitably have to rely on a strong conspirative apparatus, supplemented by widely adopted methods of legal Party work."

On that supposition, certain concrete measures were then set forth in the Vassiliev document. Among the more important directives may be noted:

1. The Party will have to rely on a strong conspirative apparatus

which will be supplemented by such open activities as may still be legal in some countries.

2. Although police pressure may increase, the legal position must not be abandoned wherever it still exists.

3. Alongside the still legally functioning Party, an underground apparatus must be created, if it does not already exist, parallel to the legal organization. This will enable the clandestine group to take over immediately and without interruption when the legal work becomes illegal.

4. But the underground should not be so perfectly hidden that it loses contact with the toiling masses and degenerates into an academic conspiracy. Hence, contact must be maintained by means of the legal Party newspaper, by village correspondents, by the Communist fractions in Parliaments, in municipal bodies, musical clubs, mathematical societies, sports clubs, Freethinker groups, etc. A new name must be ready for the Party newspaper in case it is suppressed.

5. All members of the Party engaged in this conspiratorial work must act as if they were not members of the Party; in secret meetings of the nuclei the real names of members should not be used, only pseudonyms.

6. In anticipation of bourgeois resistance leading to possible arrest of known leaders of the Communist Party, a second string of secret officials must be prepared for the underground work; safe buildings must be chosen for storing the Party archives and to house illegal printing presses; secret meeting places must be chosen, codes worked out, and a chain of effective stations for delivery of correspondence [letter drops].

Promulgated nearly twenty years ago, this blueprint of a hidden empire throughout the world came vividly to life in recent times. From the evidence presented in the trial of the eleven American Communists in New York and from authentic documentation gathered by the FBI (which is not inclined to hysteria), we may observe the continuity and integration of the conspiracy up to the present hour. Performance coincides substantially and point for point with the directives.

It has now been established by competent information that Communists no longer carry cards of membership in the Party; records attesting to membership and payment of dues are no longer kept, while previous rolls have probably been destroyed. On April 3, 1950, Mr. J. Edgar Hoover informed a Senate subcommittee that orders to that effect had been issued almost two years previously. The frequent passage of Communist couriers to Cuba and Mexico gives rise to the belief that certain basic and essential records may be hidden in secret depositories in those countries. Secret printing presses were purchased and stored in basements and attics many years ago; lists of substitute editors are ready on a moment's notice to take the places of editors who may be arrested. Secret committees have been trained for the surreptitious distribution of illegal papers and pamphlets; secret buildings have been designated for illegal correspondence and conspiratorial meeting places. Well-trained substitute leaders are ready to step into the shoes of Communist Party leaders as fast as they may be taken into custody. Codes to be used in written and personal contacts between conspirators have been contrived; designated personnel is ready to act as intermediaries between Communist leaders-in-hiding and leaders of still legal organizations. An array of front organizations through which the outlawed conspirators may appeal to public opinion has been cultivated. A corps of lawyers has been trained to exploit every legal loophole for traitors. A sprinkling of professors has been recruited — and even some clergymen posing as liberals — for the sole purpose of bending public opinion to the ends of treason. Planted agents and spokesmen in legislative and other governmental bodies have been alerted; riot leaders have been carefully coached for defiance of police authorities and for incitement to mass violence. Sabotage squads, known in Communist jargon as "factory nuclei," have been placed in all the large industrial plants of the country.

To be sure, such an elaborate underground apparatus was not created in this country in the short period that has elapsed since 1945 nor with a view solely to the present emergency. The process is world-wide and dates from the very inception of the Communist movement. But it assumes new national importance and becomes a paramount international issue in the light of what has happened in the world since 1945. It constitutes the bridgehead over which the Red Army expects to pass at the appointed hour.

CHAPTER V

Dialectical Materialism in Arms

RECOGNITION of the constant factors among the variables of the Russian Revolution is the essential key to an understanding of its outward success and its continuity. The timing of zigzags and recognition of opportunities in the general postwar demoralization were all present, to be sure, but the cornerstone of the Communist faith remains unaltered. It is known as Dialectical Materialism. By that infusion of secular revelation the empire of Lenin lives, moves, and preserves its being.

Neither time nor space will permit an extended review of the antecedents and genesis of Hegel's celebrated hypothesis: that life and social evolution proceed through contradictions, negations, and the emergence of new forms through death of the old. It must suffice to say that such a concept fascinated Lenin and gave him a starting point for a systemized offensive against all non-Communist cultures. He had found at last an over-all explanation of history which satisfied and supported his revolutionary instincts. His subsequent directions for organizing a revolution included, as we have already noted, the basic canon: "without a revolutionary theory, there cannot be a revolutionary movement. . . . Only a party guided by an advanced theory can act as vanguard in the fight." For purposes of practical understanding of the forces now aligned against us, at least a brief review of the Marxist adaptation of Hegel's triadic process would seem to be imperative — that is, if our policy toward Russia is to remain something better than continuous improvisation and reliance on the ingenuity of each new quarterback rushed into the diplomatic fray.

Dialectical materialism is perhaps the most mystical and esoteric dogma in the Marxian interpretation of economic history. Nevertheless it is explicit in all their revolutionary strategy and implicit in their tactics. A special brand of metaphysics thus entered, for the first time, into the practical politics of a modern State, becoming the official language of its governmental intelligentsia and a permanent force in their campaigns for the conquest of power on a world-wide scale. Each term should be clarified. Materialism defines itself as the doctrine which explains all human phenomena, physical, mental, and moral, by the activities, combinations, and reactions of matter, to the exclusion of spirit and ideals. It exalts matter to the prerogative of mind, and limits mind to the unexplored capacities of sentient matter. By so doing, and by thus seeking to explain the manifold activities of life and intellect by physics, chemistry, and motion, materialism demands more miracles than faith has ever required. Chief among the postulates which materialism assumes is the sweeping requirement to attribute exclusively to unaided matter the phenomena of thought, volition, knowledge of the abstract, universal ideas, and the powers of deduction and induction.

Dialectical materialism means the establishment and defense of such materialism in the field of social relations by a specific process of argumentation called dialectics, which Marx derived from Hegel and adapted to everyday economics. This form of reasoning approaches the subject which it is investigating by first regarding the object — or the process, or the fact — primarily for the purpose of discovering what its opposite or contradictory would be, is, or will be. Then, by comparison with the opposing form thus discovered, one arrives at a satisfying knowledge of the nature of things. Lenin writes in one of his philosophical notebooks: "The division of the one and the knowledge of its contradictory parts . . . is the essence of dialectics."[1] In a letter

---

[1] *Collected Works,* Vol. XIII, p. 320.

to Maksim Gorki, November 29, 1909, Lenin further wrote: "By gad, the philosopher Hegel was right — life does progress by contradictions."

The dialectical method was popularized by Plato four centuries before Christ and is developed to its classic perfection in his Dialogues. In the Platonic form, it was essentially a philosophic conversation, a debate, in which one participant made an assertion, however broad and tentative, as a starting point on the road to the discovery of truth. Another member of the symposium would question the proposition, by endeavoring to demonstrate some contradiction attaching to it or allege a difficulty growing out of the statement. This contradictory attitude would lead to a more focused definition of terms, create greater accuracy, and result in better expression of ideas so that, finally, a conclusion is reached by such a process of affirmation, followed by contradiction and ending in reconciliation or synthesis of divergent ideas. It sought to find truth by knowledge of its opposites and by a kind of assumed skepticism which forced the defender of a doctrine to exclude falsity and assert only the naked truth. By this methodology, which he called the dialectic, Plato arrives at his ideal utopian State in the *Republic*, sets Socrates on a search for honesty of philosophic inquiry in the *Apology*, establishes the nature of Law in the *Crito*, examines the soul and immortality in the *Phaedo*, discourses on virtue in the *Protagoras*, on eternity in *Timaeus*, and so following.

Hegel's sweeping panorama of history and his analysis of the inner processes of the human intellect resulted in conclusions which dominated and shaped his whole philosophic system. Motion fulfilling itself in affirmation, negation, and synthesis became for him the very core of being, of intellect and history. It would be tedious and irrelevant, requiring much more time than is now at our disposal, to rehearse here how Hegel applied this method to ideas, to being, to the mind, and to social categories. The result was a highly complicated and subtle metaphysics, now somewhat shopworn. The usable element that was drafted to the service of social revolution by Marx is precisely the claim that all things pass through successive contradictory stages, tend to their opposite, and finally emerge in some final and more perfect form which is, in essence, the negation of the form that immediately preceded it. Hence, reality is best understood by the negation of negatives; light is best understood by contrast with darkness and truth ascertained by experience of falsehood. But Marx did not accept this Hegelian machinery in its entirèty. He combined it — or better, modified it to his revolutionary purposes by adding ideas derived from another German philosopher, Ludwig Feuerbach, who had revolted against Hegel's idealism, particularly against his apparent acceptance of a divine personality. Retaining certain Hegelian principles, Feuerbach adopted an atheistic position which coincided with Marx's personal beliefs. Hence, preserving the Hegelian dialectical pattern but turning it upside down and adopting Feuerbach's anti-Christian empiricism, both Marx and Lenin evolved a new dialectical materialism designed for social conflict. In the words of Adoratsky, Director of the Official Institute in Moscow which interprets the thought of Marx, Engels, and Lenin: "Dialectical thinking is the opposite of metaphysics, which regards things and phenomena not in their unity and inter-relationship, but each separate from the other . . . not in motion. . . ."[2]

For Aristotle and his school the important consideration, the very starting point for reasoning about the table on which these lines are being written is the fact that it exists here and now as a wooden substance carpentered to the accidental shape of a flat-topped desk. But still more important for Hegel is the fact that it once was a tree and one day will be dust or ashes. The same destiny, in varying degree, is true of all things. Each of them is a something headed for its contradictory, nothing. This perpetual becoming (*das werden*), not the present mode of being (*das ding an sich*), is the highest expression of reality. Hence, full knowledge of an object, be it thought, life, society, or the State, is attained when we know what it once was, what it now temporarily is, and what it finally will be after its necessary evolution and triadic stages. Lenin, in multitudinous ways throughout his voluminous writings, and in the detailed fashion that has become classic among Communist propagandists, applied this

---

[2] *Dialectical Materialism*, p. 30.

methodology to the economic organization of society, particularly to Capitalism and Communism.

The process of discovering contradictories, he notes, is the most scientific form of knowledge. Thus:

In Mathematics:	we have plus and minus, differential and integral.
In Mechanics:	we have Action and Reaction.
In Physics:	we have Positive and Negative electricity.
In Chemistry:	we have Combination and Disassociation of atoms.
In Astronomy:	we have the attraction and repulsion of nebulae.
In Social Science:	we have the conflict of opposing interests, resulting in Class Struggle and the Dictatorship of the Proletariat.[3]

No knowledge, consequently, no literature, no art, no scientific concept is worth wasting time with, unless it bears on the class struggle and the eventual dictatorship of the indicated class. In fact, the only value of the Hegelian Dialectic for Marx and Lenin lies in its applicability to economic life and its consequent availability as a prop to support Communism. When Hegel permitted his reasoning to arrive even at a vague concept of Deity, Lenin penciled on the margin of the text: *"swine."* The argument of Marx and Lenin would run thus: The primitive form of holding property was assumed to be collectivism, in which there was one sole proprietor, the mass, the community. This would correspond to the *thesis* of the Hegelian cycle. In the course of time, the contradictory form was evolved, just as plant life springs from the corruption of seed life burgeoning into plant and flower and tree. Thus private property arose as a corruption of the collective way of life (*antithesis*). The evolutionary process continues until, inevitably because of the contradictions and abuses of capitalism, an opposite and contradictory social form is evolved, namely, Communism — *synthesis*.

---

[3] Although they appear sporadically throughout Lenin's writings, these conceptions are found in systematic order in his *Philosophical Notebooks* in the section dealing with Hegel's *Science of Logic*.

As projected by Marx and Engels into the future evolution of economic life throughout the entire world, the cycle would begin with the existing social order. Bourgeois society as they observed it in the nineteenth century would be the *thesis,* which itself had emerged from the disintegration of a previous feudalism. The *antithesis* would be the proletariat created by the conflicts and contradictions set in motion by the Industrial Revolution of the eighteenth century. The *synthesis* would be twentieth-century Communism born of the conflict between the owning-employing class and the working class during the nineteenth century. The final triumph of Communism would mean the arrival of a golden age for the general good of all mankind. Wherever you may choose to begin the cycle, one conclusion is predetermined in the Marxist dialectics — you must come out a Communist.

Hence the law of life, as he sees life, and the logic of his dialectic compel the Communist to an act of faith in dynamic change — not only change in ideas but in political institutions, in the manner of producing economic goods, in the marketing of them, and in the concept of property. Knowledge of these inevitable opposites is what constitutes the special inner vision and the infallibility which convinces a Marxist that the decadent political and economic institutions of the bourgeois world are doomed to be cast into "the dustbin of history." What will survive is likewise defined as an article of faith: the dictatorship of the proletariat in a Sovietized World State. The old classical philosophy merely interpreted the world; the new evangel intends to change it. The perpetual motion of matter viewed as self-sufficient in its reproductive energy is the Communist God, no other divinity allowed. And that is all that men need know of the supernatural.

From this prime postulate establishing the basic rhythm of life flow important attitudes governing social relationships. The philosophy of law and the legal institutions of the Soviet system are logical corollaries of the dialectical premise. Hence the role of the judiciary is both a key to understanding of the dialectic and an instrumentality of government for continuing the Revolution. The duty of Soviet courts is not to guarantee or administer justice impartially through independent tribunals but to safeguard the class interests of the new elite. In the words of one of the most authoritative interpreters of Soviet legality (he was authoritative until sometime in the '30's), Krylenko frankly defined justice under Communism:

> The court is . . . a weapon for the safeguarding of the interests of a given ruling class . . . a club is a primitive weapon, a rifle is a more efficient one, the most efficient is the court . . . our judge is above all a politician, a worker in the political field. . . . We look at the court as a class institution, as an organ of government power. . . .

Although the earlier, ruthless power of the Secret Police — which persists unchanged under its various titles, Cheka, OGPU, NKVD, MVD — has been subjected to certain legalistic controls, the psychology of class justice and swift annihilation of political opponents remains unaltered. Certain external forms have been introduced for the purpose of creating appearances of legality. The savageness of Krylenko in his court trials (at one of which I saw him perform as Public Prosecutor) and certain of his doctrines disappeared with himself during one of Stalin's purges. But nothing substantive in Soviet jurisprudence has been abandoned. It is still the practice to deal more leniently with murder, theft, or similar statutory crimes than with political offenders. The State theory and the Communist Revolution — these are the untouchables, not the dignity of human personality or the rights of individuals. Hence judicial decisions follow governmental policy; precedent, however, is not considered as a source of judicial action. There is no constant jurisprudence, except the paramount precedent of the dictatorship of one class and the organized liquidation of all others. *Thesis — antithesis — synthesis.*

Mr. Vyshinski succeeded Krylenko as Attorney General and became one of the contemporary legal authorities in Soviet Russia both by his law textbooks and by public pronouncements. His definition of Soviet courts is found in the section of his work dealing with the nature and organization of the judicial system of the U.S.S.R., second edition, 1936: "The Court of the Soviet State is an inseparable part of the whole of the governmental machinery of the proletarian dictatorship. . . . This also requires that the entire work of the Soviet Court be so construed as to secure an unswerving fulfillment of the general Communist Party Line by the court." And in 1941 he added: "Neither court nor criminal procedure is or could be outside politics. This means that the contents and form of judicial activities cannot avoid being subordinated to political class aims and strivings."[4]

The economic vulnerability and lack of social justice in certain sectors of the non-Communist world is clear gain for the Politburo. But that is incidental in the main account and is merely good luck for the conspirators. Their program is directed against all bourgeois society, good, bad, or indifferent, against all religion, primitive or institutional. They would be bound, by the logic of their position, even to include a Utopia among their enemies, if the Utopians refused to follow the Communist pattern. The only problem in that case would be the timing, the form of the assault, the pretext, and the chances of success. A prosperous, well-balanced, socially just, and economically stable State might turn out to be a harder nut to crack, but the Revolution is directed against it as inevitably as against a government notoriously un-mindful of its underprivileged groups.

That is why moderate Socialism is both hated and feared by Communism. The record will show that Socialists and Agrarians who did not wholly conform to the Marxist line were attacked and liquidated without mercy, wherever and whenever Communism got the upper hand. When no longer needed, they are first vituperated as "revisionists" or "deviationists," then indicted as "agents of imperialism," and finally eliminated as "enemies of the working class" or "warmongers." Witness the case of Marshal Tito in Yugoslavia; the fate of peasant leaders such as Maniu in Roumania, Petkov in Bulgaria, and Mikołajczyk in Poland. A Labor government in England is as much of an abomination to Moscow as a capitalist regime in the Argentine. There is no greater heresy in the Soviet Index of Prohibited Thoughts than partial Communism. That is usually more hated because more dangerous and more knowing than outright capitalism. An American millionaire was much more acceptable as ambassador to Moscow during the

---

[4] The vast subject of law, legality, and jurisprudence in Soviet Russia has been treated *in extenso* by Vladimir Gsovski in his two-volume work, *Soviet Civil Law* (University of Michigan Law School, 1949). The present writer has profited from that scholarly work as well as from many personal conferences with Dr. Gsovski.

honeymoon of Soviet-American relations than Norman Thomas would have been, or a member of the American Federation of Labor would now be.

Communism, therefore, in the Hegelian-Marxian-Lenin dialectics, is the inescapable absolute, the final and most perfect organization of human society. The stages of purgation through which Russia passed and through which all the world must pass, will be accelerated, to be sure, by a revolutionary prod now and then from the Marxists, the Leninists, the Stalinists, and the fifth columnists, all of whom conscientiously believe themselves to be legitimate instruments of destiny, auxiliaries in a predetermined metamorphosis of endlessly evolving dynamic matter. History is interpreted as being on their side and the nemesis of time will inevitably liquidate the bourgeoisie.

Certitude of intellect and fortitude of will combine to produce a kind of theology of history, and Lenin's voluminous writings on the strategy and tactics of class warfare purged of all idealism constitute the most complete handbook ever composed on the art of revolution. The deification of matter and motion leads to the necessary acceptance of economic determinism and the materialistic conception of history. By that is meant that all historical processes, the various types of civilization with their resulting cultures, the moral codes that ensue, even religion, artistic achievements, and the diverse structure of political institutions are determined ultimately by the specific mode of producing commodities prevalent in the successive phases of human development. According to Marx in the Preface to *The Critique of Political Economy*, it is not consciousness or the mental processes of men that determines the social environment of man's existence, but on the contrary it is their social environment that determines his inner life and ethical judgments. Among all the factors influencing a given type of civilization, the economic element is the decisive power. There is a family resemblance in the resulting Marx-Lenin-Stalin collectivism to many another modern offspring of Darwin's *Origin of Species*. For Hegel, the absolute was the Prussian State; for Lenin, it was the Stateless, proletarian dictatorship which will take over after the "withering away" of the State — a process, be it noted, not yet discernible in the Soviet Union.

It is all very comforting for the initiated who have accepted the predestined doom of the existing social order and its inevitable transformation into a pattern agreeable to their conceptions. But it is sometimes embarrassing when Destiny falters or drops asleep at her historic task. In the first place, there is an awkward moment in the early stages of the dialectical process as invoked by Marx and Lenin. The argument assumes that property, by universal custom, was collectively held and administered in the earliest stages of the race. Now, Communism claims to be a scientific process and a rational method based upon facts, not on myths or manifestations of spiritual idealism, both of which are stigmatized as "bourgeois prejudices." Very well. It should itself begin, then, with an historic fact — not with an imaginary condition of unproved incidence. Let us consult the science in question, the science of fact finding which is history. Limiting ourselves — again scientifically — to the recorded facts, we find that private property in land and produced commodities was the normal form of ownership discernible as far back as the records reach. The institutions of the ancient Jews, the Egyptians, the Babylonians, and Sumerians, whether expressed in oral traditions or folklore, on papyri or on cuneiform inscriptions, bear testimony to innumerable business and financial transactions that can only be explained by the fact of private ownership. In no place is this clearer than in the code of Hammurabi. Such is the record of the monuments, the tablets, the inscriptions, and the manuscripts. The opposite assumption does summary violence to that very scientific attitude which Marxism insists on arrogating exclusively to itself.

It has sometimes been argued that such primitive tribes as still exist in remote regions and whose *mores* have been examined by anthropologists actually do practice the collective way of holding property and hence they furnish presumptive proof of the property customs existing at the dawn of organized society. Again the argument falls back on an assumption, on an analogy, on an *ex parte* interpretation of isolated cases which are then hypothetically transformed into demonstrations of an assumed what-must-have-been and universal status. This is not scientific demonstration, nor will it ever be such until the missing first link in the chain of proved facts is revealed to have been collectivism. But as far back as we can go historically the evidence points to private property, to contracts and conventional finance.

The only safe conclusion to be drawn from the primitives is the statement that when certain tribes were first discovered they were addicted to the communal form of economic holding. If it be alleged that their oral traditions run back as far as the elders can remember, the question promptly arises: "How far back is that? Does it run back to the original formation of human societies?" There is no evidence, moreover, that the primitives maintain an unbroken continuity in their social customs. Progress and retrogression, heights of civilization and depths of barbarism are indicated in the great, silent ruins of Java, Cambodia, Mexico, and southern Arabia. The observed collectivism among primitive tribes might just as well be a case of devolution as proof of unbroken communal customs. Obviously, by pursuing this dialectic, one would be lost in a maze of conjecture, obscurities, and unprovable assumptions.

It is more rational and certainly more in accord with the canons of historical research to abide by the earliest obtainable and definitive records. What do they reveal? Communism in tenure of land may have existed when the human family was small and acted as a single family, or in the Garden of Eden; but with the increase of progeny and the rise of separate parental responsibility a division of property resulted as a natural sequel of such multiplication. Thus Abraham and Lot, as related in the Book of Genesis, finding their herds and flocks too large and unwieldy, agreed to separate, Lot choosing the country about the Jordan and Abraham the Land of Chanaan. Communal warehouses sometimes existed for special limited purposes in many social units but they do not cancel out the evidences of general private property. Hence it must be concluded that dialectical materialism starts from an historically false premise, is based on wishful thinking, and ends in a false, prejudged conclusion helpful for class warfare and proletarian revolution. The intervening examples of triadic devolution and evolution may fascinate the imagination, but they furnish no proof of the point where the alleged process began or where it will end. It furthermore assumes that the bare series of events is endowed with a dynamism and purposeful will of its own, distinct from and above human volition. Too intelligent for that, Hegel was forced to identify the processes of history with universal mind: "Spirit is the only moving principle in History." Impelled in a contrary direction by their phobia of divinity, Marx, Engels, and Lenin took refuge in accusations of capitalistic diabolism.

The dogmatism of the Marx-Lenin formula suffers negation also from more recent realities. In Italy, for example, in 1923, everything was moving in strict Marxian grooves, except that, in the hour of synthesis, the State fell, not into Communism, but into the outstretched hands of Signor Mussolini and his Fascists, who were the very antithesis of Communists. Germany, too, in 1933, became dialectically ripe, only to fall into most un-Marxian hands. Such embarrassing contradictions are left unexplained by Soviet dialecticians, as they leave unexplained another extremely annoying paradox.

If this triadic process is inherent to all vital forms, including the State, and if perpetual evolution through contradiction is the dynamic law of life, why should societal evolution stop short at Communism? Who put the stop signal precisely there? Why is Communism the final term in an alleged perpetual motion which is described as inherent and determined by "inner laws"? Does not the argument demand a degeneration, in due time, of the Communist form of social control and a reversion to its opposite, which is private property? Echo still queries — Why? And who? In point of fact, there is already much private property in Soviet Russia today in the shape of investments, bank deposits, insurance policies, and a limited measure of conveying property to heirs. Nature is quietly triumphing over the unnatural.

But your orthodox Bolshevik has an answer for all contradictions; it derives from his love for abusive language, fortified by a richness of expletive and vituperation that was taught him by the master. I once made a catalogue of the favorite epithets used by Lenin to describe those who questioned the Marxian hypothesis. In a very limited number of pages one finds: bootlickers of the capitalists, idlers, drones, loafers, tyrants, bullies, bosses, sweaters, exploiters, traitors, liars, despots, spoilers, grafters, robbers, swindlers, plunderers, thieves, and sneaks. To the unresponsive masses unendowed with a sense of "gradualistic objective" he applied such descriptive terms as: slaves, serfs, bondsmen, cringers, crouchers, boneheads, boobs, goats, dupes, duffers, fools, tools, prisoners, cat's-paws, galley slaves, curs, cravens, dogs, and beasts of burden.

All of which duplicates the finality of the reply given by that mule driver in the artillery regiment in France during World War I. He came from the mountains of Tennessee, and when his caisson stuck in the rich, clinging mud of the Argonne, he urged his mules forward with a Niagara of profanity that made the leaves tremble. A chaplain was hurrying past, and out of sheer curiosity he paused and asked the mule driver: "Son, where *did* you learn it?" Who replied: "Parson, it ain't ever learned: it's a gift!"

Thus armed with a wide choice of weapons adaptable to all circumstances and to all levels of literacy, the Third International embarked on its twenty-four years of international belligerency. It became the avenging sword of dialectical materialism, its hilt in Moscow, its tip everywhere seeking the vitals of the bourgeois world. The record of its activities would require a separate volume devoted to secret conspiracies and open provocation of established governments in every corner of the globe. The fountainhead in the Moscow headquarters was fed from an elaborate subsidiary educational apparatus devoted to the training of agitators both foreign and Russian. The International Division of the Communist University at Leningrad was located in the former palace of the Duma, afterward called the Uritzky Palace, and bore the slogan in stone, *Workers of the World, Unite.* One who attended its instruction, Jan Valtin,[5] records that by the winter of 1925, 6000 students attended this university, the foreign students intended for revolutionary work outside Russia being incorporated in a special division. Chinese, Japanese, Koreans, and Malayans were trained for subversive activities in *The University of the Peoples of the East* at Moscow and in a smaller institution, The Pan Pacific University at Vladivostok. The graduates are now openly active in China and Korea and covertly organizing subversive

[5] *Out of the Night,* p. 136.

elements in Japan and the other unconquered areas of Asia. American Communists were instructed at *The University of the Peoples of the West* in Moscow and in *The Lenin School.* Mr. William C. White, writing in Scribner's for June, 1930, reported that he had found 450 students under training for the revolution in the Moscow branches. Americans undergoing instruction in the technique of overthrowing the government of the United States numbered some 20 whites and 7 negroes; they were paid $35 a month with the usual perquisites — free board, free lodging, medical attention, and travel expenses to and from their homeland.

The curriculum in all these training centers of World Revolution was directed almost exclusively to practical subjects connected with class warfare and the concrete struggle for power. Beginning with Marx's theory of surplus value and economics in theory and practice, the courses covered all aspects of revolutionary activity — the fomenting of strikes, formation of "cells" in factories and in the military forces, sabotage, secret press, illegal work, finger-printing, photography, invisible inks, sabotage, the transformation of strikes into a civil war, and the transformation of imperialist wars into civil strifes. One course treated the "Application of Clausewitz's Rules of Warfare in the Conduct of Strikes." Another dealt with "Mass Psychology and Propaganda." Officers from the Red Army instructed the candidates in street fighting and the scientific conduct of civil war, as well as in the use of small arms and target practice. Valtin relates that one of the physical training exercises consisted in doing gymnastics while standing under icy showers; *severnoe siyanie,* the torture was called — *aurora borealis.* The students arose at six thirty, "awakened by a swarthy house superintendent, a Georgian who ran from room to room shouting hoarsely, 'Arise, ye prisoners of starvation.'"

The same pattern of indoctrination and formation of revolutionary personnel was duplicated by local Communist parties in their homelands under the auspices of the Third International. Many well-organized normal schools after the Russian model were conducted in the United States — at New York, Chicago, Boston, Buffalo, Philadelphia, Cleveland, Los Angeles, and San Francisco. The two most pretentious institutions were located at 35 East Twelfth Street, New York City, with 3000 students in 1934, and at Ruthenberg House, 121 Haight Street, San Francisco. The announcement of the latter school warned the public against un-authorized exponents of Marxism, particularly against "so-called liberal schools." The science of Marxism, it cautioned, "should be distinguished from the shallow vaporings of pedants who hide their bankruptcy and confusion under the title of 'liberalism.'" The curriculum of this Los Angeles training center for the antici-pated revolution in the United States, in addition to the con-ventional courses on Marxian economics, Leninism, and the materialistic interpretation of history, announced an appetizing fare of technical craftsmanship. Thus we find: *Trade Union Strategy and Tactics* which developed the difference between a revolutionary union and a reformist union and emphasized the strategy of strikes; *Youth Movements* — how they may be guided to revolutionary objectives; *Self-Defense in Courts* — a survey of "Capitalist Court Procedure" and methods of proletarian defense; *Agitation and Propaganda Technique* — theory and practice of ef-fective revolutionary agitation by slogans, pamphlets, leaflets, organization of street and mass demonstrations; *Revolutionary Journalism* — workers' correspondence, reporting, shop papers, and contradictions of the capitalist press; *Revolutionary Theater* — function of the theater in society . . . period of radicalization within the bourgeois theater and rise of the revolutionary theater "which is its historical successor." *Hygiene and Diet* — no details of rela-tionship between food, health, and revolution were given, merely place, time, and Dr. H. F. Unsinger, instructor.

The training of leaders, not only the incitement of the masses, was consistently emphasized. In his report to the Ninth National Convention of the Party, Mr. Earl Browder showed himself both a realist and a competent pedagogue when he warned the dele-gates: "The best policy in the world turns out in life to be no better than the people who must execute it, who must apply it to the thousand variable conditions of daily life. Application of policy among the masses is first of all a problem of securing a high quality leading personnel." The criteria for selecting and training such leaders for the World Revolution were formulated by Dimitrov, President of the Third International, at the Seventh World Congress, Moscow, 1935:

First, absolute devotion to the cause of the working class, loyalty to the party tested in the face of the enemy in battle, in prison and in court. *Second,* the closest possible contact with the masses. *Third,* ability independently to find one's bearing and not be afraid of assuming responsibility in taking decisions. . . . *Fourth,* discipline and Bolshevik hardening in the struggle against the class enemy as well as in their irreconcilable opposition to all deviations from the Bolshevik line.

The traditional and official "line," obligatory on all affiliated Communist parties, was radically and dramatically altered in 1935. Communism found itself at that period challenged by a new rival judged more menacing even than the stabilization of capitalist society. The commissars had long recognized that Fascism and Nazism would bear watching; but they were now convinced that the conquest of power by Hitler in 1933 marked the intrusion of an aggressive competitor in a field previously their own. He bulked far larger on their horizon than did Mussolini. Important changes were taking place in Germany, marking the culmination of an historic process in which Soviet Russia was being displaced from leadership of the World Revolution; the Communist State was menaced, too, in its national security by an enemy endowed with formidable military efficiency.

During the years of Hitler's campaign to capture the organs of government in Germany, a veritable race was in progress on the continent of Europe, a race between two ideologies, between two grandiose concepts of power and two practitioners of power. The spectacular Five-Year Plan of Joseph Stalin was being sold — and successfully sold — to the Russian Revolution, while a thousand-year vision of Teutonic supremacy was being unfolded to Germans in revolt. Teuton and Slav, historic rivals, were on the march again while England slept, while France disintegrated and America grappled with her great depression. Lenin's internationalism and Stalin's industrialized soviets supplied the focus of world attention in the first decade of the postwar period; Hitler's meteoric rise to power and the challenge of National Socialism dominated the second. The Teutonic claims were finally climaxed in the third decade by Hitler's order of the day letting loose the dogs of war and affirming that the destiny of Germany was about to be determined for the next thousand years.

The two political concepts which dominated Europe during those years — Communism and Nazism — included an identical objective, World Revolution. They expressed, each in its own language and psychological forms, two potent principles; they were, in fact, the only dynamic forces in the European balance of power. By their content and universalism they were inexorably destined for eventual collision. Two such claimants for universal hegemony could not coexist and simultaneously activate their programs for long on the same continent, a fact which was basically clear to both long before the German attack on Russia in June, 1941. Both, in their own way, accepted the dogma Hitler formulated in *Mein Kampf:*[6] "Political parties are inclined to compromise; world-concepts never. Political parties count on adversaries; world-concepts proclaim their infallibility."

Faced with a new and serious situation the pragmatic Muscovites executed a tactical maneuver dictated by the challenge resulting from the rise of Mussolini and Hitler. The bourgeoisie and democracy were no longer to be ranked as the main enemy. It was now Fascism. Hence the democracies should be cultivated and regarded as potential allies in the inevitable conflict which the Soviets apparently foresaw more clearly than most Western statesmen. In the summer of 1935, after seven years of postponement, the Third International was suddenly convoked for the first World Congress since 1928 and new sailing orders issued. Although the conventional heated oratory against the bourgeoisie and capitalism had free rein and despite the traditional theses published at the close of the meeting in August, 1935, a decided change in practical tactics was observed. Dimitrov, Secretary-General, set the compass in his celebrated figure of speech: "Comrades, you remember the old legend of the conquest of Troy. Troy had protected itself from the attacking army by an insurmountable wall, and the attacking army that had suffered no slight losses could not be victorious until it succeeded in penetrating into the heart of the enemy with the aid of the Trojan Horse. We revolutionary workers should not hesitate to apply the same tactics against our fascist enemy who is protecting himself from the people by means of the living wall

---

[6] Chapter V, page 440.

of his bands of murderers." So was born the United Front phase of the Russian Revolution. A world-wide mobilization of all workers, lovers of peace and enemies of war and Fascism, was decreed; the active and aggressive Communist Party was instructed to "lead the masses from the struggle against Fascism into the struggle for the rule of the Soviets." As executive director of the Third National, though not its controlling hand, Dimitrov made it perfectly clear that no change of ultimate objective was intended. The redeployment of 1935 was merely one of the zigzag movements which Communism often executes in its Machiavellian approach to revolutionary power in every country. Meanwhile, he explained,

> . . . all of the conditions for the unrolling of a real people's anti-fascistic front exist in the fascist countries. This front could be used in the struggle against fascist dictatorship, since the *Social-Democrats, Catholics* and other workers, for example in Germany, can recognize immediately the necessity of a common struggle with the communists against fascist dictatorship. . . .
>
> Comrades: Proletarian internationalism must acclimate itself, so to speak, in every country, in order to send its roots far into the soil of the native land. The *national* forms of the proletarian class-struggle, and of the workers' movements in the individual countries, are not contradictory to proletarian internationalism. On the contrary, in these *forms* one can successfully defend the international interests of the Proletariat as well.

The effects of the new policy became apparent in every affiliate. The Communist Party of the United States began a planned campaign of publications and speeches which developed the idea: *Communism is twentieth-century Americanism;* Jefferson and the founding fathers, though in previous polemics clearly included among exploiters, landlords, slaveholders, and plantation bosses, now became miraculously identified with the democracy of Communism. Even the Catholic Church was courted with ardor and unction. Although all religions are denounced by Mr. Browder in his various works, notably in *What Is Communism?* (1936), he now loyally followed the new line by moving his Trojan Horse close to the battlements of the Catholic Church in the hope of breaching the walls of Communism's most feared international opponent by a show of amiability and conciliation. Nearly one hour of Browder's four and a half hours of report at the National Convention of the Party in 1938 was devoted to the question of Catholic co-operation. "Within the camp of Democracy," he proclaimed, "are included the great majority of the members of the Catholic Church. We Communists extend the hand of brotherly co-operation to them and express our pleasure to find ourselves fighting shoulder to shoulder with them for the same economic and social aims." As the Catholic community was well aware of the unchanged religious aims of Communism and how they are put into effect once the ground is prepared by social and economic conquests, no one was impressed, though all were startled by the new bedfellow. Mr. Browder continued to bite on granite and though the effort may have sharpened his dialectical teeth, it left no impression on the rock. Similarly, the Knights of Columbus were unmoved by the eirenic letter received from the Communist Party of New Haven in February, 1937, in which Mr. Paul C. Wicks, the city secretary of the C. P., assured the Knights: "We note with a great deal of interest in the local newspapers that your organization is conducting a nation-wide educational campaign and that your local council is planning a campaign in this vicinity.

"The Communist Party has the greatest respect and friendship towards the believers of the Catholic faith and we are extremely pleased by the prominent role that the Catholic people played in the recent elections in defeating the reactionary Liberty League-Landon combinations. We Communists are not sectarians or bigots. We strongly opposed such reactionary organizations as the Black League and the Ku Klux Klan who attack Jews, Catholics, trade unionists and all progressive minded people. We are believers and defenders of the American principle of religious freedom. . . . The Communist Party of New Haven, while we hold certain beliefs in common, feels that there is some misunderstanding as to its aims and we therefore suggest that at your forthcoming meetings a Representative of the Communist Party be invited to present our program for our mutual clarification." The Knights, being under no misunderstanding of the militant atheism inseparable from the Communist Credo and being abundantly informed of the program for the "Soviet America" forecast in Communist pronouncements, tabled the unsolicited offer of assistance. Of course Mr. Wicks was only doing his best to implement the United Front and doubtless had read Lenin's frank analysis in Volume XVIII of his *Collected Works:* "To build a Communist Society by the hands of Communists — this is a childish idea. The Communists are a drop in the ocean, a drop in the ocean of the people. They will only be able to lead the people along their path if they correctly define the path in the sense of a world historical direction. We shall be in a position to define economic development if the Communists are able to build up this economic system by other hands, while they themselves will learn of this bourgeoisie and direct it along the path which they wish it to go."

The Trojan Horse was thus zealously nibbling into many inviting pastures around the world — until it encountered an earthquake which shattered the very structure of the Party outside Russia. The Soviet-Nazi Pact of August, 1939 — which virtually allied the Communist State with the hated Nazi regime and enabled Hitler to launch World War II without fear of attack on his eastern flank — stunned and disintegrated the local parties which had been left completely in the dark respecting impending plans in Moscow. The cause of the Communist World Revolution reached the nadir of discredit. American Communists had denounced the European conflict as an "imperialistic war," had fomented strikes in war industries, denounced President Roosevelt as a "warmonger," and assured Europe that "the Yanks are not coming." The August thunderbolt bewildered the Party ideologists — but not for long. Quickly recovering their breath, they executed one of the dialectical somersaults for which they were notorious, and slavishly followed the new line which unfortunately had not been cabled from Moscow in time to allow a decent period for gradual readjustment. As a result the new position of Soviet Russia had to be justified immediately and brazenly. Hence the alliance was simply described as a masterpiece of statesmanship which would contribute to the stability of Europe and remove certain silly misunderstandings between two great peoples. But the effect on American liberals was one of profound disillusionment; regular commuters began quietly to drop off the Moscow local, generally at inconspicuous way stations, or at night in the larger cities.

The Communist World Revolution now entered on a distinctly new phase in Europe while Mr. Browder went to jail in America.

It advanced militarily and, by virtue of its partnership with the Nazi invaders, occupied large areas of Poland and the Baltic States, recovering at the same time much disputed territory in the Balkans and southeast Europe. Moving rapidly and daringly, the Commissars succeeded in consolidating their geopolitical position while the attention of England and France was engaged on the perils of western Europe. But the inevitable transpired in June, 1941, when Nazi Germany turned savagely on her former partner and launched the historic invasion toward Moscow and Leningrad. This reversal of fortune marked the third phase in the evolution of the Communist foreign policy, as the Nazi attack, penetrating to the gates of Moscow, Leningrad, and Stalingrad, threw Russia physically and technically, if not spiritually, into the camp of the Allies. The provocations and conspiracies of the past were forgotten by the United Nations in the light of the new dangers now common to bourgeois and proletarian States alike. The Japanese attack on Pearl Harbor with its effect of seriously diminishing the immediate striking power of the United States resulted in pragmatic acceptance, by the Allies, of Russian military co-operation and man power — with whatever reservations might be possible respecting Communist ideology.

Shrewdly timing his decision, the realistic Mr. Stalin improved this sudden international acceptability by a series of domestic accommodations designed to remove certain violent paradoxes in the conduct of a nation presumably adhering to the Atlantic Charter. He felt justified in sacrificing several minor cards in the revived game of power politics, aware that he held a precious collection of trumps in reserve for the final call. By permitting the Orthodox Church to re-establish its shattered forces and elect a Patriarch, the odium of religious persecution could be lessened and a new ally enrolled against world-wide Catholicism. By abolishing the offensive national anthem, the *Internationale,* with its insulting allusions to non-Communist States, and by substituting a new patriotic song in praise of Mother Russia, another forward step was taken on the road to conciliation and appeasement. By dissolving the centralized administration of the Third International and committing Communist activities to local parties in the several countries, a particularly obnoxious institution was curbed, though by no means sterilized, as the Party line is still uniformly and effectively maintained throughout the world without the previous open domination of the Moscow headquarters. The period which ensued was one of good will and much fraternizing which enabled hundreds of Communist officials, technicians, and members of military commissions to circulate unimpeded throughout the United States. Means and methods for clarifying the "Party line," instead of being decreased by the abolition of the Communist International, were actually increased and improved by an enlarged Communist personnel enjoying official and semiofficial status under the great alliance.

A final question in this review of the earlier tactics of World Revolution concerns the reason or reasons for the failure of that program while in the hands of the Third International. A passage from the writings of Abraham Lincoln throws much light on this aspect. Lincoln once said that in preparing a campaign speech he spent one third of his time and energy in thinking about himself and the form of his own argument but two thirds on his opponent, what he was thinking and what he might say. Lenin, though academically aware of that necessity, did not succeed in impressing the tactics of foresighted restraint on his international collaborators, and, indeed, often failed to exemplify it himself. Hence, the energy of the Third International was primarily engaged in destruction of the enemy's position; it was too little attentive to the possible resisting power of Capitalism and Democracy.

The victory over a detested autocracy in Russia had been amazingly easy and Lenin committed the psychological error of transferring the mood of conspiracy and abuse to the entire field of international controversy. His agents, for the most part, though they employed the tongues of many countries, spoke in a language and with a vocabulary alien to an outside world which was unfamiliar with the jargon of professional Marxists. Maksim Gorki very early in the Russian Revolution sensed that one blind spot in Lenin's leadership:

Lenin as a "leader" and Russian aristocrat (certain mental traits of this defunct class are not alien to him) deems himself in the right to perform over the Russian people a cruel experiment, doomed to failure in advance. Exhausted and ruined by war, the people have already paid for that experiment with thousands of lives, and will now be made to pay with tens of thousands more. . . . This inevitable tragedy does not embarrass Lenin, slave of his dogmas, nor his sycophants — his slaves. Life, in all its complexity, is unknown to Lenin. He does not know the mass of the people, he has not lived with them; only from books has he learned how one can raise this mass on its haunches, and how one can most easily infuriate its instincts. The working class is for Lenin what ore is to the metallist. Is it possible, under the existing conditions, to cast a socialistic state out of this ore? Apparently, it is not possible; yet — why not try? What does he risk, if the experiment should fail? He is working as a chemist does in his laboratory, with the difference that the chemist employs dead matter with results valuable for life, whereas Lenin works over living material and leads the revolution to perdition.[7]

The domestic revolution within Russia was achieved without a Third International. Had the resulting missionary fever been more wisely controlled, the very example of a successful proletarian revolt might have had far more serious social repercussions elsewhere, on its own merits. But the dogmatism of hordes of foreign agents scattering mystical theses about the inherent contradictions of capitalism, about the iron laws of history, dialectical materialism, the dictatorship of the proletariat, about peasantry and bourgeoisie, fell on deaf ears, particularly in England and America where most of the terms found no recognizable equivalent in the social composition of the population nor in the common vocabulary. Local reformist movements were ridiculed and the purity of the Russian revelation was made mandatory on all parties aspiring to leadership of the working classes. Deviation from the prescribed credo was heresy against Moscow. Trade unionism, growing in acceptability and power, became confused and divided, and — as happened in the United States — developed into an obstinate opponent of Russian domination. Religion was mobilized to the defense of Christianity because of the gross and blasphemous tirades on God by amateur iconoclasts who lacked the far more dangerous urbanity of Voltaire and the popular eloquence of Robert Ingersoll. Patriotism was purified by a new dignity and then mobilized to widespread counteractivity by the announcement of the Third International

---

[7] As quoted in Parkes, *op. cit.*, pp. 261–262. See Alexander Kaun: *Maxim Gorki and his Russia*, 472. Gorki died in 1936 under circumstances giving rise to an obstinate belief that Stalin permitted him to be "liquidated" by the doctors who attended him.

published in *Izvestia*, December 5, 1928: "The Communists consider it unnecessary to disguise their views and purposes. They openly declare that their aims can be accomplished only through the overthrow by force of the whole existing social order. . . . The hold of the bourgeoisie can be broken only by ruthless violence."

As the Third International and the Soviet Government were both agencies of the Russian Communist Party, one being designed to govern the Russian State, the other to reduce all other States to Communism, diplomatic intercourse and commercial relations became a tangle of paradoxical inconsistencies. Mr. Stalin himself furnished convincing evidence of this on May 26, 1929, by his instructions to a delegation of American Communists visiting Moscow. Referring to the depression then rapidly developing in the United States, he exhorted them:

I think, Comrades, that the American Communist Party is one of those few Communist parties in the world upon which history has conferred a task of a decisive character from the viewpoint of the world revolutionary movement. The force and power of American capitalism are well known to you. To many it seems now that the general crisis of world capitalism will not touch America. This, of course, is not true. Absolutely untrue, Comrades. The crisis of world capitalism is developing at an increased speed and is bound to extend also to American capitalism. Three million unemployed in America — this is the first swallow, as it were, announcing that the crisis is maturing also in America. And when the revolutionary crisis will open out in America, this will be the beginning of the end of world capitalisms. It is necessary that the American Communist Party should be able to meet this historical moment fully armed, and to take the lead in the coming class battles in America. For this, Comrades, we must make preparations, using all our efforts and all our endeavors. With this end in view the American Communist Party must be improved and Bolshevized. . . . With this end in view we must strain our efforts to forge genuinely revolutionary *cadres* and genuinely revolutionary leaders of the proletariat, who would be able to lead the many millions of the American labor classes into the revolutionary class battles. With this end in view we must eliminate all and every personal and factional consideration, placing revolutionary education of the American labor classes at the head of the corner.[8]

Fourteen years later, with Nazi armies blasting at the gates of Stalingrad, Marshal Stalin ordered the American Communist Party to sheathe its battered sword and transform itself into a cultural

---

[8] Published by the *Moscow Bolshevik*, January 15, 1930.

association for the education of the American Democracy to the blessings of Collectivism.

What Mr. Stalin abolished by a stroke of his pen in May, 1943 — after maintaining for twenty years the fiction that the Comintern was a private organization over which the Soviet government had no control — was a crude, boisterous, and provocative instrumentality which had not only failed to bring off the World Revolution but had proved an embarrassment and a stumbling block, particularly in the new circumstances to result from Russia's entrance into the United Nations. Moreover, the Third International was no longer needed. The indirect approach and the conspiratorial machinery were outmoded by the geopolitics of war. Russia's 1939 pact with Nazi Germany had enabled her to acquire immediately, in a few months, what the Communist International had not been able to achieve in twenty years. Although these territorial gains were quickly lost to the Germans, the whirligig of time and the Red Army finally restored them and much more, helped enormously by the Allied landings in Italy and the invasion of France, both of which diverted enough German divisions from the Eastern Front to enable the Soviets to smash through to Vienna and Berlin. By 1945 Soviet Russia stood within the gates of western Europe and in a wholly different guise. Where revolutionary illegality had conspicuously failed, military prowess brilliantly succeeded. Dialectical materialism thereupon became strong enough and confident enough to act officially in the name of the Soviet government without resorting to the subterfuge of a so-called private organization.

❋   ❋   ❋   ❋

This progression to the consciousness of a strong national State had been observable for some time. Even before the war, Mr. Stalin had enough of the bizarre distortion of education dominant in Soviet schools and universities during the exaltation of successful revolution. By another stroke of his pen he canceled the previous practice of belittling historic events and personalities antedating November 7, 1917. Peter the Great, Ivan the Terrible, Alexander Nevsky, General Suvorov, and numerous non-Marxian heroes regained their proper place. The works of Professor Pokrovsky, until recently the official interpretation of Marxized history, were relegated to the category of "unrealistic." Textbooks both cultural and scientific were hastily rewritten. The schools were liberated from the mob rule of zealous Comsomols and restored to teachers. Embarrassing publications, such as the *Great Soviet Encyclopedia,* were quietly withdrawn from general circulation in foreign countries. Its frequent slighting and sometimes hostile references to capitalism were too awkward for a supposedly scientific publication and were especially unwelcome in the home of Lend Lease. Military uniforms grew more picturesque; medals and ribbons appeared on stalwart proletarian chests and Mr. Stalin finally donned a well-cut marshal's uniform. When Mr. Gromyko, Soviet Ambassador at Washington, appeared at a Soviet celebration, November 8, 1944, clad in a braided diplomatic costume, with decorations on his breast and an ornamental dagger at his belt, the Renaissance of form was completed. But the deposit of faith remained unchanged.

It is not enough, then — in fact it can be extremely dangerous because misleading — to concentrate attention unduly on any one phase or development of Soviet foreign policy. Students of the Russian Revolution must regard it as a moving panorama of separate but co-ordinated forces; one must see the picture steadily and see it whole, as Matthew Arnold phrased it when describing the outstanding characteristic of Greek philosophy. You must remember, too, that Dostoevski in his *Diary of a Writer* prophesied in 1876, that all the great powers of Europe will be destroyed " . . . for the simple reason that they will be worn out and undermined by the unsatisfied democratic tendencies of an enormous portion of their lower class subjects — their proletarians and paupers. In Russia, this cannot happen . . . and therefore there will remain on the continent but one colossus — Russia. . . . The future of Europe belongs to Russia."[9]

This eschatology, though including in Dostoevski's day a mystic faith in the Russian orthodox religion, remains unaltered for the Soviet successors of the Romanov Tzars. The Marx-Lenin-Stalin

---

[9] The same conviction is found in the so-called "Last Will and Testament of Peter the Great." See Appendix I. Several additional prophecies of a remarkable character are found in the works of De Tocqueville (1835) and the Spanish author and diplomat, Donoso Cortés (1850). See Appendix II.

trinity has been substituted for the Russianized Christ of Dostoevski and dialectical materialism replaces the liturgy of the patriarchate. The combination is not unknown in Russian history. The Synod of Moscow in 1619 promised universal domination to the Tzars and a special prayer was then appointed for its accomplishment.

It is no refutation of the role of dialectical materialism in the progress of the Russian Revolution to protest that the rank and file of the proletariat cannot possibly be familiar with the niceties of such an involved intellectualism. The assumption is probably correct. But the political conclusion is false. Neither the average Communist nor the casual citizen of a democracy philosophizes over the metaphysics behind the choice he makes at the polls. The classic works of Plato and Aristotle, De Tocqueville and Lord Bryce probably count for little as an American casts his ballot for a particular candidate on election day. But both American and Soviet political thought is the end product, conscious or unconscious, of a philosophy of government originating from previous thinkers who set in motion the power of certain master ideas which then remain implicit in issues presenting themselves for decision on future election days. These principles find contemporaneous expression in the concrete act of the voter preferring one system over another, although he may never advert to their presence in his thinking. Similarly, theory, principles, and certain approved techniques to be applied in specified cases give confidence and direction to the daily work of a physician. The country doctor who vaccinates a child against contagion may never advert to the scientific theory underlying his treatment; but the philosophy of immunization and the experiments of Pasteur in Paris in 1851 are the premises giving power and direction to his practice of medicine in a small town of Ohio in 1951.

The basic role of dialectical materialism in the Soviet system was trenchantly analyzed by Pope Pius XI in his encyclical *Divini Redemptoris,* issued March 19, 1937:

The doctrine of modern Communism, which is often concealed under the most seductive trappings, is in substance based on the principles of dialectical and historical materialism previously advocated by Marx, of which the theoreticians of bolshevism claim to possess the only genuine interpretation. According to this doctrine there is in the world only one reality, matter, the blind forces of which evolve into plant, animal and man. Even human society is nothing but a phenomenon and form of matter, evolving in the same way. By a law of inexorable necessity and through a perpetual conflict of forces, matter moves towards the final synthesis of a classless society. . . .

Insisting on the dialectical aspect of their materialism, the Communists claim that the conflict which carries the world towards its final synthesis can be accelerated by man. Hence they endeavor to sharpen the antagonisms which arise between the various classes of society. Thus the class-struggle with its consequent violent hate and destruction takes on the aspects of a crusade for the progress of humanity. On the other hand, all other forces whatever, as long as they resist such systematic violence, must be annihilated as hostile to the human race.

In October, 1948, the archbishops and bishops of the Anglican and associated churches forwarded for reading to their congregations throughout the world a circular letter similar to the several encyclicals issued by the supreme pontiffs of the Catholic Church. Based on a committee report drawn up at the Lambeth Conference in London, the authorities of the Church of England and the Protestant Episcopal Church of the United States declared:

The most highly organized, consistent, powerful and destructive form of secularism is beyond doubt dialectical materialism and the type of communism in which it is embodied. This is perhaps the one live alternative to the Christian interpretation of man. Between the two there can be no compromise, and it seems to be increasingly probable that it is between these two that the world must choose.

That the dialectic is still vigorous and accepted by certain leader types is confirmed by an incident reported by Sam Welles, *Time* correspondent, who communicated it to his readers in the issue of August 1, 1949. The statement came from Shosuke Matsumoto, a twenty-four-year-old student of economics in Keio University, Tokyo: "Nothing in the world is more important than Communism. There is no truth except dialectical materialism. I wish I could go to a university in Russia where it is the only system taught. When Japan becomes Communist, we will teach nothing but Marxism here."

The world witnessed a striking adaptation of dialectical materialism in action during August, 1950, in the Security Council of the United Nations. For a whole month Mr. Malik hurled the most incredible accusations of conspiracy, warmongering, and aggression against United States policy in Korea. Utterly ridiculous to those acquainted with the facts, the indictment, however, was of a piece with Mr. Malik's basic faith that the United States has no right to exist at all; hence, all its capitalistic pomp and works are evil things. On these premises every non-Communist State is logically a warmonger and aggressor by the very fact of its not being a Communist State; its continued existence is, of itself, an act of war. What the non-Communist world is doing is to hold its position with evil stubbornness at the present crucial point of historical *antithesis* to Moscow; it is contradicting nature itself by refusing to move along in the triadic process; it is, consequently, in a state of habitual sin against humanity from which it will be purged only when it bows to the *synthesis* prepared for it by the dialectical materialism of the Politburo.

Stalin is fond of quoting Lenin's warning: "We live . . . not only in a state, but in a system of states, and the existence of the Soviet Republic side by side with the imperialist [non-Communist] states for a long time is unthinkable. In the end, either one or the other will conquer. And until that end comes, a series of the most terrible collisions between the Soviet Republic and the bourgeois states is inevitable."[10] Commenting on this Lenin doctrine, Stalin once added: "Clear, one would think."

Not only does he thus adhere to the basic Lenin postulate of inevitable war but Stalin added clarifications of his own in his *Dialectical and Historical Materialism.* From the "laws" of social development, he deduces that revolution conducted by the proletariat is a natural and logical activity. Success cannot be achieved, as the Socialists think, by gradual changes and reform but by smashing the entire existing system. Class warfare must not be checked but carried on always and uncompromisingly to its inevitable consummation. Hence, he concludes, in order not to err in policy, one must be a revolutionary, not a reformist, nor a compromiser attempting to reconcile the clash between proletariat and bourgeoisie.

Now, the term "revolutionist" has a definite and special meaning in the lexicon of Russian terminology. It is no Sam Adams or

[10] Stalin, *Problems of Leninism.*

Thomas Jefferson or Oliver Cromwell we find described there as the challenger of some existing regime. Bakunin and Nechaiev paint his portrait with precision in that revealing document: *Catechism of a Revolutionist.* He must consider himself a doomed man, with no reservations or weighing of consequences to himself; even his personality must be without name — or bear an assumed one. He has rejected all laws and all codes — except the one law, revolution. He lives in bourgeois society only to destroy it; he is disciplined, cold, and unemotional, prepared to kill all the human feelings of his breast — even that of honor, if it delays his program. By friends he means those who serve the same cause, no sentimentality allowed; when their usefulness is exhausted or found to be of inferior caliber, they must be regarded as capital to be expended for the purchase of the one thing that counts — destruction of the existing order of things. Liberals in every land are to be exploited coldly and scientifically as means to an end; they must be led to believe that the revolutionist (posing as a fellow liberal) agrees with the reforms they advocate. Then by subtle devices and planned stages, they are to be compromised by involvement with the prepared revolutionary program. They are to be carefully fished out of the mass by a hook, not by a net — and discarded when no longer useful.

To minimize the sustaining influence of theory in Soviet foreign policy is to miss entirely one of the most important components of its being. Precisely because American "realists" in high places ignored such theory, they missed the boat time and time again. Stalin himself is quite frank about the secret of Communism's successes: "Marxist-Leninist theory is the science of the development of society, science of the workers' movement, science of the proletarian revolution, science of the construction of Communist society."[11] In *Problems of Leninism* he further explains the sources of Soviet diplomacy: "The strength of Marxist-Leninist theory consists in the fact that it enables the Party to orient itself in a situation, to grasp the internal connection of surrounding events and to discern not only how and when events are developing but also how and when they must develop in the future."

---

[11] *History of the All-Union Communist Party*, p. 339.

Understand all that, he exhorts his followers, and you will understand why the Communist World Revolution is inevitable and invincible. It advances toward its goal with a rationalized feeling of scientific certainty and a sense of continuity, though not without zigzags, ebbs and flows, high crests and low waves. But the ranking Communists who determine policy are serenely confident where the trend is heading. That is the inner source of their power.

Conversely, the Achilles heel of democracies reveals itself in a paralyzing lethargy in respect to recognizing evil at its inception and controlling the beginnings of danger. We leave the initiative to conspirators and are frequently too bored or too indifferent or too dispersed in counsel to resist vigorously and articulately. To be liberal and tolerant has often meant to be debaters and procrastinators when debate and delay are exactly the attitudes desired of us by the never tiring enemies of democracy. The trial of the eleven Communist leaders before Judge Medina in 1949 is a striking example of these characteristics. The organized attempt of the indicted Communists to wreck and discredit the judicial system are matter of public record; their contempt of the court, the insults hurled at Judge Medina, the confusion, the shouting, the defiance of procedure all conspire to make that trial the most amazing but logical revelation of the virulency of Communist tactics. The patient and disciplined conduct of the presiding judge, in the face of unprecedented provocation, merited universal admiration and applause.

But one feature must not be overlooked. The final paradox of that historic trial consists in the diversity of response from Communist sympathizers and from the broad masses of the American people. The Communists on their side were organized, vocal, untiring, and aggressive. The public, for the most part, contented themselves with reading the shocking details in the daily newspapers — and then continuing their accustomed way of life. Not so the shock troops of the Revolution. Judge Medina was swamped with threatening telegrams and letters. Pickets were parading outside his courtroom. After the tragic death of Secretary of Defense Forrestal, the placards in Foley Square changed to: "Medina must fall like Forrestal." Simultaneously, he was bombarded with new letters and telegrams: "Jump now. You've got to jump eventually.

Go ahead. Get it over with. Jump, jump." A survey revealed that 99 per cent of the communications were hostile, denunciatory, and threatening. The remaining 1 per cent expressed support and encouragement. The proportion, however, was more than reversed when the jury brought in its verdict of guilty for all the defendants. Within the next six weeks approximately 60,000 letters and telegrams poured in with congratulations and expressions of gratitude for the fearless judge. An analysis revealed that one letter alone among all that number was hostile and defamatory.

It may well be that the deep silence from well-wishers during the trial was due to a sense of propriety which restrained law-abiding citizens from seeking to influence a judge on the bench during the course of a trial. If so (the present writer is dubious on that point) the disparity underscores again the heavy handicap which democracy imposes on itself in any conflict with the disciples of Marx, Lenin, and Stalin. They will attack without scruple or restraint, whereas the bourgeois world is expected to observe the rules, the conventions, and the laws of decency under conditions which could lead to loss of a just cause and even to destruction of our most precious liberties. Associate Justice Jackson of the Supreme Court of the United States doubtless had the same basic paradox in mind on May 16, 1949, when he asserted, in dissenting from a 5 to 4 decision in a case involving freedom of speech: "If this Court does not temper its doctrinaire logic with a little practical sense it will convert the Constitution's Bill of Rights into a suicide pact."

*   *   *   *

With respect to the Russian people two prime considerations must never be forgotten. The population of the Soviet Union is not the negotiator with whom Mr. Acheson or Senator Austin or Phillip Jessup or Mr. Dulles must treat. The chosen delegates permitted to venture beyond the Iron Curtain are branded and sealed with Stalin's mark. Historically, the Russian people, whether under medieval Tzar or modern Soviet, have been mute instruments of a highly centralized autocracy. The Romanovs relied on love for "Mother Russia," the Politburo on the "Party line." The second circumstance which strengthens Mr. Stalin's hand in his bid for total power is the adroit combination of Russian nationalism and Russian imperialism. Both are attractive arguments on the domestic front where dialectical materialism might be caviar to plebeian taste. Marxian Communism has been re-enforced with an organized messianic urge, a universalism unknown to the Tzars and less brash than the grossness of the shelved Third International. Stalin has hitched dialectical materialism to the Russian troika which has always been galloping across snowbound steppes toward warm water ports and the open sea. The driver and horses may change but the direction is constant. It is the dynamism resulting from these three component elements — Russian nationalism, Russian imperialism, and Marxian Communism — which characterizes the present contender for control of Europe and Asia and distinguishes him from all previous Ivans, Yermaks, Attilas, Generics, and Genghis Khans. He is enlarging the Russian National State into a universal Communist State comparable to but far more ambitious than the domination achieved by the Ottoman Empire over Eastern Christendom in the fifteenth century and by the Mongols over Russia itself in the thirteenth century. Western Europe and even the Western hemisphere are not outside the orbit of his hopes.

Whatever cannot be justified by defensive nationalism is rationalized by dialectical materialism. Both are then yoked to Russian imperialism. Taken together they constitute the present Russian troika with Mr. Stalin at the reins.

Nationalism, once so roundly condemned in Communist propaganda as a bourgeois superstition, has been legitimatized and sanctified into a flexible weapon of defense and counterattack. The momentum of victory carried the Red Army into areas of Europe where Russian nationalism, as a mechanism of defense, no longer served to justify the emerging pattern. Soviet Russia continued to rediscover its past history, and imperialism was reborn. The territorial losses suffered by the Russian Empire under the Treaty of Brest Litovsk were recovered by easy military occupation; all treaties with the Baltic States and the nonagression covenant with Poland went into that ever ready dustbin of history. Half of Poland, all of Latvia, Lithuania, Estonia, and Bessarabia were openly reincorporated into the expanding Soviet Empire. The balance of Poland, all of Roumania, Bulgaria, Hungary, Albania, and Czechoslovakia became satellites by the infiltration technique. China, always an objective of Russian imperialism, even under the Tzars, next fell within Communist control. Then came Korea. If the awakened appetite for aggresion remains unsatiated, the way is now open to advance on Hong Kong, Thailand, Iran, Burma, Malaya, Indochina, Tibet, and the ultimate grand prize of India and Pakistan. On that vast continent of Asiatics live half the population of the world.

It will not do to console ourselves with historical references to China's habit of absorbing her conquerors when the dust has settled; that will furnish excellent gymnastics for the dialectical skill of future historians generations hence. It offers no solution for present problems of statecraft and military defense. Someone in high place listened too easily to the soothing assurances that Chinese Communists were in reality only "agrarian reformers." We now know better in that instance, and we cannot wait for the centuries to ratify or disprove the appeasers. A new world is being born in Asia and old clichés sound thin and unconvincing in the tumult of widespread revolution attending the passing of colonial empires. Nor will speculation on futurities cancel out two grim facts: the once friendly harbors of the China coast are now at the disposal of an air-minded enemy who is simultaneously creating a formidable Russian navy, and the once friendly people of China have gone behind a new Iron Curtain as did Poland, Hungary, Czechoslovakia, Bulgaria, and Roumania. Equally tragic are the consequences in the field of human relationships. Friendship with the Chinese people and reciprocal confidence once constituted a cardinal principle of American foreign policy. That traditional amity is being systematically corrupted by the poisonous barrage of hatred now being poured into their ears. Synchronized with the consistent and raw falsehoods of Soviet propaganda, this organized distortion of truth has remained a constant factor in the Marxist formula of class hatred as a prelude to class warfare. There is a rich if melancholy field of scientific research awaiting the sociologist who will set himself the task of producing a documented volume on the power of the lie as a force in history.

It is cold comfort but a necessary audit at this point to recall that when Lenin began translating the complexities of Marxian metaphysics into the hard realities of life in Russia on his return from Switzerland in April, 1917, he had possibly 75,000–80,000 followers. Some records put the figure as low as 40,000. When he became dictator on November 7, his Bolsheviks had increased to 175,000 in a population then estimated at 150,000,000. Today, thirty-four years later, the power of the Kremlin reaches down and influences directly or indirectly, something like one third of the human race, possibly 800,000,000 persons. On the continent of Europe one of every two inhabitants lives under controls and policies dictated by the Political Bureau of the Russian Communist Party. With the momentum acquired by the Revolution in China, the same proportions now threaten for Asia. Who shall predict the consequences? Even the two thirds of humanity not directly subjected to the Communist empire are vitally affected by it, since the foreign and domestic policy of every government is profoundly influenced and often conditioned by what the Kremlin does.

For the sociologist and psychiatrist there arises another disturbing possibility in the field of human behavior. What will be the international consequences if the Soviet government and its satellites succeed in producing more generations whose psychological reflexes become slowly habituated to the Marxist pattern? If perpetual resistance and underground conspiracy results, as seems consonant with human nature, a large part of the world population will live in a state of perpetual siege, the repercussions of which and the turmoil cannot escape being felt everywhere. If the worst were to happen and the Russian people succumb to frustration and fatigue, habits of thought could result which could progressively degenerate into a new pattern of conduct which could give rise to a new and frightening culture of resignation to the inevitable. That is precisely what Communist thinkers and organizers of Soviet military power predict.

BOOK II

The Wasted Years

CHAPTER VI

Soviet Tactics and Soviet Geopolitics

IN 1927 a delegation of American workers visited Mr. Stalin in Moscow and exchanged views with him on the possibility of real co-operation with Communist Russia. During the interview, he frankly pictured the future zigzag of Soviet policy, adding a prophecy directed toward the United States. " . . . Thus, in the course of further development of international revolution," he predicted, "two centers will form on a world scale. . . . The struggle between these two centers for the possession of the world economy will decide the fate of capitalism and communism in the whole world."

Here we have plain talk from an expert. His general estimate of the United States is amplified by numerous passages in his other writings and addresses, in which he refers to the United States of America as "the chief country of capitalism, its stronghold." He expressed the same conviction in the interview with Governor Stassen in 1947. On other occasions, notably in conference with leading representatives of the American Communist Party on May 6, 1929, Mr. Stalin intimated that America will be a tough case for the Communist nutcracker because of the strength and power of American capitalism. Social revolution, he thought, will come to the United States only at the end of the revolutionary cycle. But that it must come is a cold, intellectual supposition always present in Communist thinking and never doubted by Mr. Stalin.

He urged his visitors to greater efficiency in hastening the revolution in the United States.

It was on February 9, 1946, however, that Mr. Stalin in a public address dropped all pretense at honest co-operation and openly proclaimed that World War II was not due to diplomatic inefficiency among negotiators, but to that old enemy, modern capitalism. He argued that wars are inevitable in the future so long as capitalism as a system continues to exist. Agreement and peaceful settlement is impossible . . . "under present capitalist conditions of the development of world economy." Coexistence of the two systems in a permanent balance of power is not possible in Mr. Stalin's logistics, though a truce is always possible — particularly when the Soviet Union is faced with a dangerous emergency. Such a temporary truce became advisable when Hitler invaded Russia in 1941. To dramatize the situation, Stalin dissolved the Third International.

The Political Bureau of the Party, those fourteen men blessed with a passion for anonymity who direct world unrest from the Kremlin, are experienced strategists and flexible tacticians. They are realists and cautious planners, though fanatic in their thought. Hence, their reaction to American foreign policy will be of a far different type from the line employed against Finland or Turkey or Norway or Iran or Korea. Such contiguous countries possess little depth in defense and can expect but little respect for their material power or capacity for resistance when the cards are down. But in the case of the United States extreme caution is indicated, in view of the demonstrated ability of this country to wage a devastating campaign once its industrial resources are mobilized and its man power summoned to technological warfare. If outright attack on America is not among the probabilities at the present time, it could take place with ruthless speed if some internal disaster, such as a paralyzing industrial crisis, overtook us. Since this hoped-for depression, long entertained in Moscow, has not yet been realized, a revision of the Kremlin's timetable is probably in progress.

Although amazing the world by the audacity of its maneuvers in eastern and central Europe, the Kremlin's assault there has been largely of the indirect and covert kind. The Politburo is letting the satellites carry the ball and harass the opposing team by constant fouls, brass knuckles in the scrimmages, and brazen defiance of rules. The offensive has been limited, moreover, to prescribed and carefully chosen areas. In Europe and Asia they are playing on their home grounds and know the hazards. But the risk of over-extension is not unknown to the planners, and the consequences of each move have been carefully calculated. Miscalculation could prove fatal. This caution seemed at one time to be operating in China, where Moscow appeared reluctant to have her Communist allies push their advantage too fast, too far, or too indiscriminately. She was not sure how far she could trust the present native leader-ship there. But the inhibition proved ineffective in the face of a tempting prize, and the red tide of conquest has rolled relent-lessly southward and eastward to the China Sea. Moreover, the new conquest of vast territory in Asia has served to offset the diplomatic defeat administered by the airlift in the West.

Although prophecy is the most hazardous form of human specula-tion, there are, nevertheless, certain salient facts in the present case which warrant consideration. First and foremost stands the fact of record that Soviet Russia, although blustering against Tito, has not launched an outright and aggressive military attack against any designated victim since the defeat of Hitler and Japan. Such a risk has not been necessary. The Politburo has achieved its purpose by means short of armed force — by not firing a shot in open war-fare, but by the indirect approach, by infiltration of trusted agents, by gunrunning to satellites as in the Chinese invasion of Korea, and by progressive domestic revolution engineered by technicians trained in the academies of revolt at Moscow and elsewhere.

Regiments of experts have been schooled for the Communist Foreign Legion in recent times and dispatched systematically to the designated fields of combat. The tactical success of these engineers of crisis was notable in Roumania, Bulgaria, Poland, Czechoslovakia, and Hungary. They are still working assiduously and boring from within, in France, Italy, Germany, Austria, Indo-china, Burma, Indonesia, and Malaya. Their influence has been distinctly felt in Japan, though waning now under the firm and vigilant administration of General MacArthur. In the United States, licensed demolition squads of native Communists were coached in a chain of training schools conducted in key cities; they furnished a classical demonstration of their technique during the trial before

Judge Medina in New York, in 1949. A more subtle form of attack by espionage was revealed in the confessions of Mr. Julian Wadleigh and the former wife of Gerhard Eisler, by Mr. Budenz, Whittaker Chambers, and Miss Bentley.

Then, too, the Kremlin has doubtless taken into account material conditions of life in Russia subsequent to the Nazi invasion. The vast areas of devastated countryside, the economic setback, the destruction of industrial equipment, and the cruel suffering inflicted on the Russian people by the Nazi invader have left the Politburo with an exhausted, war-weary people on its hands. Although the capacity for punishment and the ability to suffer incredible hardships are known qualities of the Russian people and were a source of perpetual amazement to us who worked among them during the great famine, the continuing and still unrelieved burdens of thirty-four years of constant sacrifice, privation, and tension in a land already plagued by a lowered standard of living, could bring about a total collapse of human endurance if another crushing war effort were now demanded of them. The prevalence of Draconian living conditions and the general drabness of life reveal themselves whenever the Iron Curtain is raised even by the fraction made possible through the escape of Soviet citizens whose testimony in that respect is mounting: by Mrs. Kosenkina, who flung herself from an open window in New York rather than return to the Utopia; by the Russian flyers who escaped at the first opportunity and headed for the freer atmosphere of the West; by the former Soviet citizens whose tale is told in Louis Fischer's recent book *Thirteen Who Fled;* by six disillusioned ex-Communists who confessed their errors in *The God That Failed;* by writers with first-hand experience in the symposium, *Verdict of Three Decades;* and by that mounting number of refugees who daily seek to reach the American zone of Germany and Austria. From their reports, and from such other intelligence as is available, certain probabilities may reasonably be deduced.

To repair the damage inflicted by the Nazi invasion, mobilize the necessary armament for a full-scale war, and equip the man power for such total warfare as would ensue in an atomic age is a task that must give pause even to the masters of a slave economy in a totalitarian State. Hence, it would seem more probable that the immediate effort will be one of continued preparation and organization of war potential, particularly in heavy industry, both within Russia and in the satellite countries. Few informed Communist leaders can be so unrealistic as to court open armed conflict with the power of America at this time — *unless the United States has been crippled or can be caught unaware in some devastating surprise attack.* Rather, Soviet strategy, at the present writing, points to a program of prolonging the war of nerves and thus achieving seven objectives:

1. The strengthening of domestic support — even though it be forced support — among the Russian population and in the satellite countries by an impressive show of power and determination, and by pointing to the success of Soviet foreign policy in eastern Europe and China.

2. The weaning away of any wavering European opinion from adherence to the ideals of Western democracy; meanwhile, the strengthening of subversive movements in Latin America.

3. The unifying and arming of Cominform States and the consolidation of Communist gains in China, Indochina, Manchuria, Iran, and Korea.

4. Obstruction of the Marshall Plan for the recovery of Europe; capitalizing on the lowered prestige of America in the Far East, and covert assistance to Communist China.

5. Ruination of the North Atlantic Alliance by intimidation, counterpressures, and by easily interpreted threats of reprisal. By cultivating a feeling of futility in a tired Europe and by propagandizing the spectacle of their countries again becoming the cockpit of another ruinous conflict, Moscow hopes to lead some States to decide on a policy of neutrality in the event of Soviet-American hostilities.

As for eastern Germany, the conquest of loyalty is well advanced. Those who hate Soviet Russia and hence cannot be relied on have already escaped in large numbers to the western zones — or are daily doing so. Those who remain are being subjected to an intensive form of Sovietization adapted to German environment. In addition to the Red Army of occupation, numbering 250,000 men, the *Volkspolizei*, which has already been mentioned, is estimated at over 50,000. Organized as a People's Police, these local reliables are being trained as shock troops to form the nucleus of a future German Army commanded by former German officers but controlled by the Communist authorities. On October 18, 1950, the government of West Germany charged that this force will number 200,000 by the end of 1950. Plans are also on foot in East Germany to introduce military training of all youths over 18 years of age, a draft which would provide 120,000 conscripts each year.

A similar recruitment of mercenary troops is in progress in all satellite lands; these affiliates of the Red Army will serve as the native spearhead for Moscow's military offensive whenever direct armed aggression is deemed expedient. From such information as is now available it has been estimated that these armies of mercenaries in Europe alone will number two million men by 1952. The invasion of South Korea was the first overt testing of local stamina on the Asiatic front. The fact that the attempt was, at first, frustrated there offers no guarantee that it will not be repeated elsewhere; the miscalculations and errors were corrected in the ensuing Korean campaign as they were after the initial repulse in the attack on Finland in 1939.

6. Assuming that Soviet Russia remains in the United Nations, enlargement of the Soviet bloc will be sought, by inclusion of new voices and new votes from the areas which are newly brought from time to time under Communist control. Each new delegate and his staff will constitute a new cell in a carefully operating espionage system on American soil. Domination or continuous obstruction of proceedings in the Council and the Assembly will be the Soviet pattern. If, on the contrary, the Politburo decides to withdraw from the organization (which is among the possibilities) and create a competing league of Communist States, world peace will again be subjected to the intrigues and pressures of power politics. We shall have retrogressed to 1914 — or worse.

7. By prolonging the psychological tension and requiring the United States to embark on costly rearmament at home and participation in defense of Europe, a continuing drain on our budget will result. This process could eventually weaken our financial structure and by consequence reduce our powers of resistance. While costing us dearly, the price is far less crushing in

the relatively low-standard-of-living economy prevalent in Soviet Russia. Ruination of the United States by financial bleeding to death has always figured in the hopes of Soviet planners. It is highly significant that the Kremlin has steadfastly refused to report its monetary condition to international agencies or reveal the extent of its rapidly increasing gold reserve, which is believed to be considerable. In a world monetary crisis, that reserved weapon could be dumped into the conflict in whatever manner the tacticians of World Revolution deem most harmful to the United States.

The patent improvement in the resisting power of Europe and the clear implications of General Eisenhower's appointment there have not escaped the attention of the Politburo. If no major and direct hostile move is made against the United States, it will mean that the men in the Kremlin have chosen the slow bleeding process as the more advisable tactics. Costs will mount for us as rearmament increases, as more and more men are called to nonproductive military activities, and as the internal economy becomes progressively limited in respect to goods for civilian consumption. Inflation will resume its deadly spiral ascent as purchasers enter into competition for the dwindling supply of available commodities. Price controls, rationing, black markets, and governmental "crack downs" will tend to create internal tensions. Labor leaders will oppose freezing of wages. Strikes, if not outlawed, will create new confusion and possibly violence at crucial moments; if they are outlawed under emergency legislation, the hue and cry will be raised that America is losing at home the very liberties for which she pretends to be battling abroad. If such provocative utterances are disciplined by official action, the sanctity of free speech and free press will be loudly invoked against all "muzzling." Meanwhile, the tireless propagandists of the Left will weave their own strands of psychological entanglement and seek to bind the giant to the ground, even as the little men of Lilliput swarmed over Gulliver while he slept.

How deep and how mysteriously this subversive network can penetrate became apparent in January, 1951. The official tax forms distributed in the State of New York bore a printed paragraph in Chinese exhorting the reader to support Communist policy in the

Far East. Unknown to public authorities, the subversive text had been added to the regular forms at the last minute, just before they were mailed to New Yorkers subject to the State tax.

All conjecture, however, respecting the improbability of direct armed conflict at this time between the United States of America and the Union of Soviet Socialist Republics could be wholly nullified by an unforeseen opportunity arising from some sudden shift in the balance of power. Some inviting crisis in a nearby State not too remote from Moscow or some other plausible circumstance of a favorable nature might induce the Politburo to launch its greatest gamble. But if the present rate of the stabilization and unification of Europe continues, it may well be several years before the official Soviet belief in the inevitability of war reaches the boiling point. The Politburo lost its best chance in the years of the great demobilization of the West, 1945–1950. But if an attack is contemplated for an early date, timing is extremely important. The Soviet High Command knows what winter means; hence, spring, early summer, and early autumn are times for special vigilance by intelligence and security agencies.

Decision, however, could be accelerated by desperation. The North Atlantic Alliance and the appointment of General Eisenhower to supreme command has introduced profound changes in the alignment of forces with which the Politburo has hitherto been dealing. As Hitler moved by established pattern, isolating his opponents, then conquering them one after another, so the Soviet tactics have been to move against its preordained victims one by one in a sequence determined by the vulnerability of each and the ripeness of the moment. Hitler had his Henlein in the Sudetenland as precursor of the rape of Czechoslovakia; he had his Seyss-Inquart to soften Austria for the Nazi absorption, and his Quisling to condition Norway for the Balthazar feast of occupation. That divide-and-conquer formula was disrupted by the pledged word of the United States and Canada to associate the power of both with each of ten western European States in a defensive alliance. Attack on any of them will be considered henceforth as an attack on all of them. This mobilization of power resulted in a shift of Soviet attention elsewhere, to the Near and Far East, i.e., to nonpact countries.

This wholly new form of alliance, reversing, as it does, a cardinal principle of American foreign policy which antedates the Monroe Doctrine, presents Moscow with the necessity of weighing the consequences with cold pragmatism: Shall this coalition be permitted to function and succeed? Would it not be too late if Soviet power were to hesitate for a period of years before implementing its dogma of the inevitability of war? Would not the concrete results of this solid front stimulate other States, marked for manufactured revolution, to form similar regional groups for defense under Article 51 of the Charter of the United Nations? Is it a question of now or never? What would happen if Stalin were to die?

While these momentous issues are being debated in the Kremlin, the satellite psychology of the fifth and sixth columns is moving into action with tirades of stereotyped propaganda. Warmongers; encirclement of an innocent humanitarian State; bankrupt policy; machinations of Wall Street; imperialism; aggressive coalition; preparation to crush governments of, for, and by the people, and similar accusations are being directed against a development born of historical logicality and forced on the signatories of the North Atlantic Pact by a situation not of their making but directly traceable to Soviet Russia's aggressive public policy of menace, wrecking of peace conferences, provocation, and veto. Hence came the vituperation in the Soviet and its allied press, as well as the bitter indictment of the Pact by Soviet officials, including Mr. Gromyko's stereotypes in the United Nations on April 13 and 15, 1949, and Mr. Malik's follow-up throughout August, 1950. All this is to be expected and is not, of itself, indicative of immediate danger. They always did that; the vehemence of the attack was rather a psychological index for calculating how aptly the new alliance had hit the mark. Damnation by anticipation, the creation of confusion in timid souls, and constant denunciation of any strengthening of non-Communist resistance are classic procedures in the Marxist book.

Stalin's statement in *Pravda*, on February 16, 1950, which was published here on February 17, followed the usual pattern and added little to the record. The only contribution to our enlightenment derived from the fact that the invectives came from the acknowledged head of the Soviet State, not from a subordinate. These rare "interviews" by Stalin carry weight mainly because of their origin and novelty. His denunciations of the United States, Britain, Canada, and France on February 16, were obviously intended to impress the Russian people, since the accusations of warmongering and aggression charged against the United States are so palpably false and fantastic that he could hardly expect any reaction except patient boredom on the part of free nations outside the Iron Curtain. The interview, however, may have had a purpose. His insistence on the peace policy of the Soviet Union and his assurance that war is not inevitable are familiar stereotypes. To repeat them in February, 1951, may have been motivated by a feeling of special urgency. The rearming of the West, the growing spirit of confidence observable in western Europe, and the decline of Communist strength in Italy and France cannot have failed to influence the calculations of the Politburo. A zigzag, even though verbal, may have been deemed prudent, and is good Leninism.

Stalin's strictures on the United Nations, although no different from similar tirades of Mr. Vyshinski, may, however, have had some real significance. They were publicly and officially expressed this time at the highest level and no more authoritative voice remains. Concern was felt in some quarters that Stalin may be preparing the Russian people for a proposed withdrawal of the Soviet Union from membership in the United Nations.

To dominate ruthlessly over every association which Moscow enters is traditional Kremlin policy. Having failed to prevent the United Nations from declaring Communist China an aggressor in Korea, the Politburo retreated to the propaganda sector of its highly flexible tactics and prepared for the next encounter. Although domination of the United Nations did not succeed, Russia's rule-or-ruin obsession still remains.

Those familiar with the Soviet record in international relations will recognize another factor in this unsolved equation. The Politburo, consistent with its philosophy of dialectical materialism, has little respect for the spiritual and the ideal as motives of conduct. For them it is not the power of values that counts but only the value of power. In mid-February, 1951, the skyline of the Las Vegas area of the United States was illuminated and the whole area shaken five times by the explosion of a series of atomic bombs. This testing of new weapons, the repercussion of which was felt hundreds of miles away, was undoubtedly noted and the meaning understood by the master practitioners of psychological warfare in the Kremlin.

More ominous in the present circumstances would be complete silence from Moscow, coupled with concrete measures of recognizable meaning, such as the withdrawal of leading diplomatic personnel from foreign posts, the closing of Soviet consulates, the unobtrusive but steady evacuation of their women and children from foreign capitals, and a general retreat of Russian representation abroad, including withdrawal from the United Nations, which would be reserved for the last moment. If to such storm signals should be added a heavy concentration of troops and war equipment in selected spots, or unusual movements of military forces and air power toward the frontiers of Russia and its satellites, increased stockpiling of critical raw materials, the calling home of Soviet merchant ships from the high seas, and a co-ordinated wave of Communist-led strikes in strategic centers of the non-Communist world, then, obviously, we should have specific indications of the form of things to come.

We should be particularly recreant to duty if public policy were to relax its preparations for defense of Alaska and the Arctic zone. It has been asserted by informed experts that an attack on America would most probably come across the polar seas. Russia and the United States, in the Northwest, face each other, at one point, across a bare sixty-two miles of water. Beyond, in Siberia and Kamchatka, numerous new air bases have been reported. By her presence in Manchuria, Sakhalin Island, and the Kuriles, Soviet power now encircles Japan and stands watch over the American forces under General MacArthur. These and certain other geographical considerations reveal an unfolding pattern of Soviet geopolitics which should not be overlooked. And there is a special significance in the ominous fact that the Soviet press has already referred to Alaska as "Soviet territory in the hands of an alien power."[12]

[12] On February 22, 1951, announcement was made of a decision taken by the Joint Chiefs of Staff to withdraw all combat military forces from certain

The writer of these lines is well aware of the hazard he assumes by even analyzing the logistics of Soviet Russia's present geographical position. "Warmongering" is the facile answer and the usual reply; but that is a risk inseparable from a subject in which even bare commentary makes the commentator a Guelph to the Ghibellines, a Ghibelline to the Guelphs. It will be remembered that Nazi Germany made its own the celebrated theory of the British geographer, Sir Halford Mackinder, respecting the influence of geographical environment on history. As early as 1904 and again in 1919 and finally in 1944, he warned the Western World that the pivot of history lay in that vast inner land mass of Eurasia to which he gave the picturesque title of the Heartland. Describing it as roughly coinciding with what is now Soviet territory, he declared, with extraordinary foresight, that if this natural fortress, inaccessible as it is to sea power, should ever be properly garrisoned militarily and developed economically by a virile people, it could become the center of an empire capable of ruling the world. Mackinder's brilliant hypothesis ended with the warning: "Who rules East Europe commands the Heartland; who rules the Heartland commands the world island; who rules the world island commands the world."

This thoughtful condensation of much human history and accurate observation of the influence of geography on history was conceived and formulated, to be sure, in an age when air power had not yet become a major component of military potential. Hence, the theory has been modified, but not entirely canceled out by the coming of the age of air power. Soviet Russia, consciously or unconsciously, is supplying the deficiency in terms of military aviation. I believe the unknown geopoliticians behind the Iron Curtain have adapted Mackinder's formula to the new cir-

---

exposed points in western Alaska and in the outer Aleutian Islands. These measures were taken as planned military tactics and in order the better to defend critical areas in case of war. This shift in deployment of forces was approved by a group of U. S. senators who had visited Alaska and examined military preparedness. By withdrawing from indefensible positions on the periphery and concentrating ground and air forces at more advantageous points, the Joint Chiefs of Staff considered the defense of the territory to be now improved, not weakened. It was still admitted that: "The security of every American home begins in the snows of Alaska."

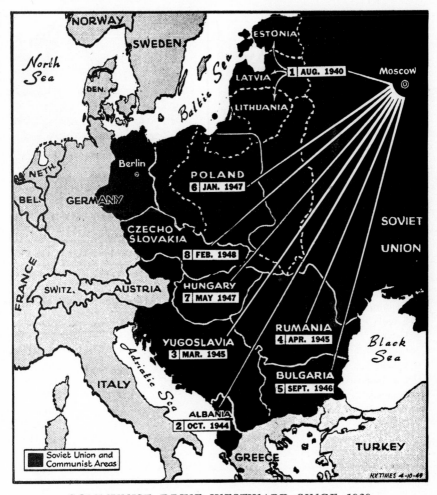

COMMUNIST DRIVE WESTWARD SINCE 1939

(1) Three Baltic nations annexed by U.S.S.R.
(2) Communist - dominated Government organized.
(3) Tito, Communist leader, is named Premier.
(4) Groza becomes Premier under Soviet pressure.

(5) "People's republic" is officially proclaimed.
(6) Communists consolidate control in elections.
(7) Cabinet change gives Communists power.
(8) Communists take over Government in coup.

COURTESY NEW YORK TIMES AND LUCAS MANDITCH

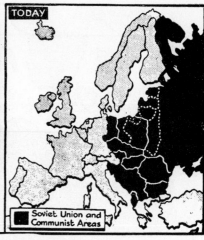

COMMUNIST GAINS, TERRITORIALLY, IN EUROPE SINCE 1939

Country	Area, in Square Miles
Estonia	18,353
Latvia	25,402
Lithuania	21,489
Poland	149,958
Czechoslovakia	54,196
Hungary	35,875
Roumania	113,887
Bulgaria	39,825
Albania	10,629
	469,614

Yugoslavia	96,010
(Communist, but not Soviet satellite)	
Communist Europe	565,624

COURTESY NEW YORK TIMES AND LUCAS MANDITCH

cumstances of the air age. They have probably changed and shifted some elements and emphasized others, so that their consolidation of land power in central and eastern Europe now leaves them free to accelerate control of marginal lands on the rim of the world island. It may well be that they are saying: "Who controls the rimlands of Europe and Asia can protect the Heartland of the World Revolution." The growth of Soviet sea power, especially of submarines, is not without meaning in such a program.

We may assume that the planners of global strategy in the Kremlin have drawn their specifications for a world State in terms of the resources at their disposal and with due consideration of the opposing forces. There are certain geographical regions of prime importance because of the number and quality of the States there clustered together. Natural location, climate, food supply, population, economic resources, industrial potential, social and political organization, and cultural development all coalesce to render such regions recognizable as reservoirs of power superior to less favored areas. Three such power centers exist in the world today — all situated north of the equator.

The first coincides broadly with the area within which the Politburo sits: it comprises European Russia, central Europe, eastern and southeastern Europe, and terminates in western Europe, including Britain. A second concentration of natural and political power, though of variable and less developed character, lies at the eastern end of the Eurasian plateau: China, Korea, Japan, Manchuria, the maritime provinces of Russia, and the teeming lands that stretch into southern and southeastern Asia. The third center arose in the transatlantic world with the principal power potential located in that area of North America which includes the eastern regions of the United States and southeastern Canada.

All three of these power centers lie in the beneficent latitudes within which the major events of world history have occurred; within that complex are found the three fountainheads of Western civilization, Rome, Athens, and Jerusalem, as well as the focal points of Oriental thought and religions. Geographers have pointed out that these regions accommodate nearly three fourths of the human race, although covering but one eighth of the land surface

of the earth. They are the favored spots of nature, richly endowed
in many instances, potentially productive in others. Effective
control of them by any one political force could guarantee
world empire.

Considering the first of these strategic areas we find that the
eastern half of it is already controlled by Soviet Russia. Outside the Iron Curtain, reaching to the English Channel, the North
Sea, and the Mediterranean, lie the critical non-Communist regions
of the West which the Marshall Plan visualizes as the last stronghold of freedom, democracy, and Christianity in Europe. The
second power center, already occupied by Soviet Russia in the
north and in process of being rapidly absorbed into the Communist orbit in the southeast, is the present major theater of
operations in the open conflict between World Communism and
the non-Communist States of the Far East.

The remaining power center in the Atlantic world is as yet
free from direct and overt assault by the Revolution. Distance
has conferred a temporary immunity; youthful vigor, resiliency,
and awakened consciousness by Americans of their inherent power
have induced considerable caution in the Kremlin. Hence the
conflict here remains in the preliminary stages of ideological warfare, diplomatic skirmishing, infiltration, manufactured confusion,
and espionage. On Mr. Stalin's showing, however, the final act
of this world drama will be played out between this formidable
power center in the West and the Oriental strongholds of World
Communism. Meanwhile the Revolution is consolidating its position
in the old world by geographic stages and by measures which
become significant when viewed in their totality and in the
relationship of each to the master pattern.

Take a map of the world and follow with your finger the
creeping progress of the Soviet empire since the disappearance
of the Nazi and the Japanese empires. Through Pechenga on the
north, acquired from Finland by force, she now has a new outlet
to the Atlantic. Drop a line from that point, through central
Europe, to Albania, her satellite on the Adriatic, noting as you
pass, Yugoslavia, slated to be repossessed when Stalin finally
decides to deal with Tito. Through Albania, on the fringe of her
power, she has access to the Adriatic and, hence, to the Mediter-

ranean. Her march toward Greece was countered by the Truman Doctrine and her hopes for Communist triumph there have been frustrated with American assistance. Had her plans succeeded in the Hellenic world, she would have been enabled to anchor her power firmly in the western end of the Mediterranean, then turn to a corresponding eastern anchor in Spain, which always remains a factor in her planning. But her hopes for gaining control of Spain, which go back even before 1935, have been frustrated thus far by the tough hidalgos. Should she finally succeed in fomenting civil war in the Iberian Peninsula, with the emergence of a satellite Communist State such as the Marxist pattern always assumes will follow a domestic revolution, Gibraltar would be the next target. Istanbul and the Dardanelles have always bulked large in the expansionist program of Russian imperialism, and this craving for that traditional objective, inherited from the Tzars, has not been neglected by the new autocrats. Unreasonable concessions have been demanded from Turkey in recent years but denied with equal determination, and the refusal has been backed up by American economic aid. But the demand will surely be renewed at a propitious moment.

Meanwhile the atmosphere of pressure will serve to maintain that psychological tension and expensive defense program along the Dardanelles which Moscow utilizes so consistently in its war of nerves. The measure of validity in Russia's historical claims for free exit through the Dardanelles is not slight. More than one European statesman has gone so far in the past as to concede publicly that Russia should have Constantinople. Both England and France so declared in 1916; but that age-old controversy between Moscow and Constantinople was limited in its application to the ancient capital of the Byzantine emperors. It now carries a wholly different significance, in view of the Communist program of World Revolution and the hope to overthrow all non-Communist governments such as Turkey. This new messianic universalism is, as we have already noted, what Soviet Russia has added to her inherited tzarist tradition. This urge to the sea and the constant process of opening up new territories and colonization of them was noted by the greatest of Russian historians, V. O. Kluchevsky, as the principal, fundamental factor in Russian history. "All other factors," he writes in Volume I of his celebrated *History of Russia,* "have been more or less inseparably connected therewith. . . . Debarred from settlement by the geographical features of their country, the eastern Slavs [in their historical evolution] were forced, for centuries, to maintain a nomad life, as well as to engage in ceaseless warfare with their neighbors. It was this particular conjunction of circumstances which caused the history of Russia to become the history of a country forever undergoing colonization, a movement continued up to, and given fresh impetus by, the emancipation of the serfs, and remaining in progress to the present day."

An entirely new factor, possessing the dynamic energy which Lenin imparted to it by dialectical materialism, has now been superimposed on Kluchevsky's summation of Russian national history. The evangel of World Revolution and the specific instruments to achieve it, whether in the form of the Third International or the Cominform, are commonly ignored by those who seek to justify Soviet conduct. They keep referring to certain old grievances, such as Russia's land-locked isolation, her legitimate striving to acquire warm-water ports, the ignoring of her existence at Versailles, the refusal to accord diplomatic recognition during so many years, and her exclusion from the powers which met at Munich — although the latter should now be cause for gratitude and not a stigma. Soviet Russia was predestined to bellicosity from the very moment Lenin turned the successful domestic revolution of 1917 into an organized Marxist revolution on a world scale. And each decade as it passes will add to her man power. Her population trend and fertility rate indicate an increase by 1970 which should bring her population to something over 250,000,000, whereas the rest of all Europe combined will probably not exceed 400,000,000. And if we consider the population of newly acquired territories, the Soviet total should be 270,000,000 by 1970. This is not to include non-Russian satellite countries of Europe, and China, in both of which fertility is high. Since population is one of the important components of power, these new acquisitions will progressively encourage the Politburo to more frequent use of its favorite weapon — aggression by proxy.

Return now to the northern perimeter of Eurasia and continue along Soviet Russia's Arctic coasts with a geopolitical eye. She is dominant there, and has no contestant in those icy solitudes. She already claims approximately 50 per cent of all offshore territory lying within the Arctic Circle, including such potential landing fields as Novaya Zemlya, Wrangel Island, Franz Joseph Land, and the new Siberian group. Rounding the eastern shoulder of Siberia as it projects into the Bering Strait you will note that she possesses not only Kamchatka, Sakhalin, the Kurile and Komandorskie Islands, but exercises control over North Korea and still controls the important harbors of Port Arthur and Dairen, both of them strategic ports of China. The encirclement of East Asia, by control of its rimlands, is nearly complete. These developments underscore a cardinal point in the program of World Revolution: Communist strategists have always maintained that the way China goes furnishes the key to all problems on the international front. The General Headquarters for the forthcoming struggle for Asia is believed to be located in Thailand, where Soviet personnel in Bangkok is reported to be enormously in excess of any legitimate diplomatic need. From the Pacific, then, to the Iron Curtain on the west, she will be in a position to mount an outer ring of offensive and defensive installations around her Heartland, particularly in marginal regions adapted to land-based air power.

If her efforts to secure a base in Tripolitania, the western half of Libya, had not been refused in the United Nations, she would have gained a coveted foothold in the Mediterranean basin. That great inland sea, if ever dominated by Soviet influence, would prove of inestimable strategic value in sealing the outer rim of protective areas, providing at the same time a sea route to western Europe and the Atlantic world. That is why Tito's rebellion particularly enrages the Moscow geopoliticians.

The invasion of Tibet in early November, 1950, by Communist troops from China reveals two constant factors in Soviet strategy. The geographical position of that hitherto inaccessible region makes it a strategic, though difficult passageway for a military advance on India, provided suitable airfields can be located somewhere among its towering mountains. Reports are already current that locations for the first potential air bases have been surveyed by Russian agents on a flat plain in western Tibet between Lake Rakas and Lake Manasarowar. This would bring Soviet striking power dangerously near the heart of India. New Delhi, the capital, lies approximately 300 miles to the southwest, an easy two-way run for Soviet bombers through negotiable passes of the Himalayas.

To meet the requirements of political strategy, the planners of the aggression invoked their usual pretext. They welcomed the existence of a rival Dalai Lama, another claimant to the position of ruler and high priest, who was living in exile in China. By supporting the claims of a second living Buddha of Mercy against the actual incumbent, the Communist Politburo of China staged another "liberation." They activated the familiar pattern of a civil war to be instigated by Communists and utilized by the Soviet Union for hidden intervention. The device is an old one and was employed in Greece, China, and Korea. It was tried in Finland, where a Communist regime was first installed under Kuusinen as prelude to the invasion of 1939. The erection of a puppet State usually follows and the Iron Curtain falls. Then, to preclude assistance from outside powers, the Communist legalists invoke international law as forbidding foreign intervention in a purely civil war. This concept was introduced into the Soviet argument against the United Nations' resolution to come to the assistance of South Korea. It makes both the United Nations and the United States of America not only iniquitous warmongers, but actual aggressors by unilateral, legal definition. Since, according to Mr. Vyshinski and all Communist jurists, the Soviet concept of law is the only valid interpretation of legality in any situation, the invasion of Tibet, like that of South Korea, became an act of moral heroism and dialectical purity.

There may well be other considerations arising from the historical development of Tibetan autonomy. China, to be sure, has never officially acknowledged the separation of that remote province from her sovereignty, although for a long time Tibet has acted independently. The significant fact for humanity is the steady advance of the Communist World Revolution into another area of Asia and the establishment of new outposts in what has been called "the roof of the world." This geographical pattern would seem to extend itself to other significant spots much nearer the

Western World, where forward bases would be indispensable for logistical preparation of the eventuality prophesied so unequivocally by Mr. Stalin: " . . . *a series of the most terrible collisions between the Soviet Republic and the bourgeois states is inevitable.*"

Two other Soviet maneuvers acquire special geopolitical meaning when related to this persuasion of inevitability, and when integrated with the concrete position already taken by Soviet strategists and diplomats. In December of 1946, Ecuador was requested to grant "fishing rights" to the Soviet Union in .the waters adjacent to the Galapagos Islands, a highly strategic area off the west coast of South America approximately 1000 miles from the Panama Canal. The distance could easily be covered in five hours by hostile war planes launched from the deck of a properly camouflaged "fishing" bark. One bomb would be enough to cripple the locks and sever one of the vital defense lines of the two Americas. Then, in January, 1947, Norway was presented with a Soviet demand for bases on Spitsbergen, the ice-covered group of Arctic islands, 3500 miles from New York, Chicago, and the industrial heart of the United States. Modern bombers, with a 5000-mile one-way cruising range from Spitsbergen, could reach not only industrial centers represented by Detroit and Pittsburgh, but penetrate deep into continental America.

Should the Communist empire ever advance as far as the English Channel on one side of the world and eventually dominate the full coast line of China and its pendants on the other, the position of the United States would indeed be perilous. Consult your map of the world again — a Mercator projection will do if no other is available — and note the geographical position of the United States. But be sure to take a map which does not put the two Americas off on the fringe of the land mass of the earth but midway between Europe and Asia. That is our true position in the composition of world movements and world forces — an insular power encircled east and west by the two major old-world continents. Soviet Russia, if finally dominant in both of them, would then be ready for the kill.

It is as important to analyze what Soviet Russia has refused to do as it is to understand the things she is trying to do. She has exercised the right to veto, in the United Nations, over forty-five times and claimed veto by absence in the session on Korea. She refused to accept the forty-year treaty offered her by the United States under the terms of which we would be obligated to come to her instant defense in case of attack by an axis aggressor. "There never was a greater example of friendship and good will," said Senator Vandenberg on October 19, 1946, when explaining the offer of a defensive pact. She has repeatedly rejected similar friendly advances in the field of human relations and cultural exchanges. The State Department, through Francis H. Russell, Director of its Office of Public Affairs, declared on April 20, 1949, that thirty-four proposals had been made by this country over a period of three years to arrange for the exchange of students, orchestras, and similar good-will visits to and from the Soviet Union. In every instance, he reported, Communist authorities in Moscow either returned no reply or refused to accept the invitation. They have likewise refused to participate in the International Bank, the World Health Program, the International Trade Organization, and numerous other constructive forms of international co-operation, including UNESCO. Even the proposal to create a modest United Nations police force of 800 armed men to protect the personnel and property of United Nations' missions in foreign lands was attacked and denounced by Soviet delegates in the General Assembly.

Moscow has consistently blocked every honest attempt to arrive at a peace treaty for Germany and Austria. She has refused to participate in common efforts to stabilize the European economy and has prohibited her satellites from sharing in the Marshall Plan. She has manifested inflexible opposition to all proposals for effective control of the atomic bomb, despite the willingness of the United States to sacrifice the overpowering advantage which is temporarily ours by possession of a stockpile of these ghastly weapons. Because of that particular denial of co-operation, and refusal to submit to the same inspection in the field of atomic energy which all other nations have agreed to accept, the result is now no control at all.

Commenting on this aspect of the tragic *impasse*, the *Washington Post* made an impressive prediction on August 13, 1947: "No control at all would be a virtual death warrant for civilization.

International control, without Russia, will necessitate the retention and improvement of atomic weapons as a safeguard against an attack when that country comes into possession of atomic power. The possibility of a world-destroying war cannot, therefore, be ruled out, but it can be minimized." It is precisely to the minimizing of that possibility that men of good will are obligated by a conviction of responsibility as well as by the innate instinct of self-preservation. The road to that goal and the prevention of a general shooting war will be facilitated by a combination of countermeasures in the several fields which are examined in Chapter IX of this volume.

CHAPTER VII

Five Years of Cold War

Marshal Stalin's greatest Five-Year Plan began in the spring of 1945 with the launching of planned psychological warfare against the United States. That the grand alliance of the Roosevelt-Hopkins era was definitely at an end became apparent when Soviet forces first met Allied troops at the Elbe, although warning signals had already more than once appeared on other sectors of Soviet-American relations. But with the collapse of Hitler's military machine and with the joint occupation of Nazi territory the honeymoon of cordiality and the toasts drunk in vodka soon gave way to an official policy of calculated estrangement, the details of which have filled the press of the world. The number and the quality of the provocative incidents engineered from the Kremlin make it possible to draw up a trial balance of our present position after five years of constant skirmishing.

Among the losses and failures must be entered the profound and widespread incredulity current in the United States respecting the continuing role and the unchanged tenets of Soviet Russia's revolutionary philosophy. Until the average American's dislike of anything savoring of philosophic discipline be exorcised from his mind, his reaction to the realities will continue to be expressed in terms such as fantastic, incredible, amazing. Quick and expert in evaluating the points of form and operation in a new model automobile, or balancing the batting averages of favorite ball players and forecasting the make-up of an All-American football team, he is still slow to understand the most important thing for him in the world today — the onward sweep of the Third Russian Revolution. He is face to face, though he appears to know it not, with the most fundamental single political event since the fall of the Roman Empire. It goes that deep and recalls what Napoleon said of his times: ". . . there will be no real peace in history until the whole generation contemporary with the French Revolution is extinct to the very last man."

In the early stages of the cold war there was a curious and disturbing blend of apparent fatalism coupled with a kind of tone deafness in the reaction of the average American to the probability of an open war with Soviet Russia. There has been, to be sure, a sudden awakening to the reality of the danger during the past year, due to the shock of events in China and Korea, and the emerging specter of the hydrogen bomb. The anticipated horrors of a new war, crowding so close on the heels of a devastating conflict barely terminated, stunned the imagination into bewilderment and a sense of frustration. Into this ferment of the private mind was injected a series of public pronouncements tending to confound the confusion. Secretary Acheson's ambiguous comment on the conviction of Alger Hiss left many sympathetic readers in doubt whether his refusal to turn his back on a friend in trouble meant condonation of guilt or compassion for all sinners. Secretary of the Air, Mr. Symington, had solemnly warned us even before the invasion of Korea that the striking power of the Soviet military establishment was superior to our own; but the then Secretary of Defense, Mr. Johnson, kept assuring the nation that we could lick them out of hand. To cap it all, an English scientist closely connected with atomic production both in England and the United States was arrested by London police for having transmitted critical information to Soviet authorities and was condemned to fourteen years of imprisonment. It was later discovered that he was assisted by numerous collaborating spies in the United States, all of them American citizens. A group of American physicists, also experts on atomic knowledge, issued a joint appeal that the United States should never use the hydrogen bomb unless it has first been employed against us.

Senator McMahon made a deeply moving appeal to the Senate that fifty billion dollars be assigned to a project calculated to induce Soviet Russia not to proceed further in an armament race that must lead us all to self-engineered destruction. To suggestions for one final conference with Mr. Stalin, the State Department replied that further direct negotiations are superfluous in view of the offers of concrete co-operation still considered open by the American government. The President was then quoted by Mr. Krock of the *New York Times* as stating he can no longer put trust or credence in any promise made by Moscow. Mr. Churchill on the contrary announced during the electoral campaign in England that he favored the idea of one more attempt at agreement through another top-level conference with Mr. Stalin. Mr. Clayton, former Undersecretary of State, proposed to a congressional committee an immediate federation of North Atlantic powers. The suggestion was opposed by his successors in the State Department. While Mr. Clayton was making his recommendations to the Senate, Soviet Russia and Communist China signed a thirty-year alliance patently directed against non-Communist States. The Communist Premier of China, Chou En-lai, at the signing of the pact in Moscow made direct reference to "American imperialism" and "disgraceful attempts" to prevent friendship and alliance with Soviet Russia.

Meanwhile Soviet Russia, showing no confusion of mind or divided counsel, continued unabated her accelerated program of warlike preparation. The insincerity of the "security" pretense was unmasked as far back as the conference of foreign ministers at Paris in the summer of 1946. Not only was the Kremlin offered the security of membership in the United Nations but a direct forty-year treaty with the United States which guaranteed instant assistance in case an axis aggressor should ever threaten Soviet Russia again. It was refused.[1] She already has the atomic bomb, partly in consequence of the secret information and the specimens of uranium (U 233 and U 235) which Soviet diplomatic agents had filched in Canada some five years ago, and partly from the

---

[1] Senator Vandenberg, in a radio interview, after his return from Paris, October 19, 1946.

information supplied by spies in America. She will, it has been predicted, have the hydrogen horror in due time. She welcomed the consternation of her Western opponents because such confusion and indecision are precious weapons in her arsenal of psychological warfare. The decline of the West was progressing smoothly and by appointed stages; she planned it that way.

The tenseness of a near-battle psychology had thus been cultivated for five years; it had been conducted and stimulated by all the media of modern communications: press, radio, lecture platform, television, by the sounding board of United Nations' facilities, by veto exercised more than forty times, by agreements cavalierly repudiated, by denunciations from the Kremlin, and by diplomatic insults from satellite governments. Wherever a nerve was exposed it was manhandled by experts in the art of provocation. The complete documentation of that amazing period is not yet available and may never be laid before an incredulous public. But sufficient testimony is at hand — and in increasing volume: in the memoirs of Generals Dean, Eisenhower, Clay, and Howley; in the accounts by ex-Secretary of State Byrnes and Admiral Leahy; in the monumental annals of Mr. Churchill; in the memoirs of General Bedell Smith covering his three years as American ambassador in Moscow; and in the testimony of similar authentic witnesses. The violent fluctuations in Soviet attitude deliberately created by the Kremlin and enlarged by official harassment at the hands of Communist China, Bulgaria, Hungary, and Roumania, if plotted as a fever chart, would probably constitute a record in the history of crisis diplomacy.

One element in the pattern appears and reappears with a consistency which makes it extremely significant and offers an additional clue to Soviet psychology. The internal situation in each of the conquered areas was always carefully estimated before resort to direct action. Stalin has never attempted to absorb a designated country into the Communist empire without the assurance of effective assistance from a native Communist Party controlled by reliable Moscow-trained leaders. Lenin warned against premature military action in his analysis of the abortive attempt at a Communist revolution in Finland in 1918; it perished, he pointed out, because of the lack of an adequate, organized

Communist Party. The Fourth Congress of the Communist International went on record in the same vein with respect to the failure of Communists to seize power in Italy after World War I: ". . . the objective premises for revolution were present, only a Communist Party was missing." Stalin repeated the diagnosis in his *Problems of Leninism:* the attempted revolution in France, 1871 [the Paris Commune], suffered from a fatal division of leadership between two parties, "neither of which can be called a Communist Party." Once the Party edges its way into the political arena, particularly into the Cabinet of a coalition government, the pattern enters on its final stages. Like a cat crouching in a corner, the Politburo observes the progress from obstruction to confusion, from confusion to crisis after crisis, until the great collapse occurs. Then it pounces on its bewildered victim. Since such an infiltration into the government of the United States has not been effective, though attempted, the attack was concentrated on foreign sectors of American interest, such as Germany, Korea, and Austria. Tactics in Austria have taken the form of procrastination, until the Kremlin completes its organization of a reliable Communist Party. The technique is revealed in a laconic press announcement: *London, July 10, 1950 (U.P.). The Western Powers conferred today with Russia for the 256th time on the Austrian Peace Treaty but reached tentative agreement on only one point — to suspend the talks again.*

This organized war of nerves first reached a peak of potential danger during the blockade of Berlin, 1948–1949; at one stage of the airlift General Clay felt that the worst could happen at any minute. But the Politburo was not yet ready for the supreme gamble. The impossible had been achieved in fact, and Berlin was saved from starvation by the superhuman accomplishment of flying in food, supplies, and coal, sometimes 10,000 tons or more in a single day. On April 16, 1949, 12,849 tons were landed at the three airfields, one plane arriving every 63 seconds, making a total of 1383 flights in 24 hours. Moscow calmly capitulated before the power thus demonstrated, after putting the United States to an unnecessary expense of 32 million dollars a month for nearly a year. New pin pricks and a kind of minor blockade of Berlin began again in the winter of 1949–1950, followed by the great adventure in Korea.

❊   ❊   ❊   ❊

The composite record of the cold war on its several fronts adds up to something extremely important because extremely revealing. A new weapon of attrition has been invented by the Marxist organizers of World Revolution. It has been fashioned from long experience with conspiracy in the police State that Imperial Russia was and Soviet Russia became. We detect in the Communist technique certain characteristics also found in Hitler's attempt at total power. But there are many differences, gaps, and deceptive resemblances.

The Führer of the Third Reich inherited no organized theory of social revolution from his Teutonic predecessors. He had no ready handbook of appropriate strategy beyond the philosophy of power, the function of naked force, and worship of blood, race, and soil popularized by a long succession of Pan-Germanists from Fichte and Hegel to Rosenberg and Streicher. In all their premises to total power, it was the iron in the will of Prussia, the argument of superior force and massed might, that was to carry the day. There was little subtlety, small finesse, and slight regard in their book for a cat-and-mouse diplomacy. From them to Hitler, with Clausewitz supplying the military counsel, the line runs straight.

Although experienced diplomats and candid statesmen early realized what Hitler was about and were able to forecast the ultimate tragedy from events following the Nazi seizure of the German State in the mid-thirties, the intervening years were not undiluted crisis; peace of mind was not kept hanging on a thread all the time. Circumstances were not ripe and the Nazi re-armament program was not ready until September 1, 1939. Such deferment of direct assault did not mean that the seeds of conflict had not matured in the soil of Hitler's mind. Despite the several respites conceded, out of prudence, to a tired Europe, he never deviated from the broad pattern of his projected conquests nor foreswore the ultimate consummation of his resolve. That much we know with certainty from the captured documents at Nuremberg. We know, moreover, that he advanced his date for beginning hostilities from 1943–1945 to 1939 because he discovered how demoralized, unprepared, and disarmed his opponents had become. "We have nothing to lose; we can only gain . . . our enemies have men who are below average; no personalities; no men of action. . . . Our enemies are little worms. . . . I saw them in Munich."[2]

When we turn to Hitler's successor on the continent of Europe we find him profiting from a set of circumstances peculiar to the Eastern Slavs, rooted in Russian history and very favorable to a dictator. The technique of sustained crisis and calculated panic with which Mr. Stalin has corrupted international relations since 1945 was particularly adapted to the human material on which he must rely for support. At home he manipulates a population already molded to patient submissiveness by centuries of autocratic rule. Few nations have suffered more from their own rulers and few peoples have accepted suffering with such melancholy mysticism. The mood is expressed in their household word *podvig* — expiation for sin, which runs through Russian psychology and literature like an extra letter in the alphabet. It is a frequent theme in Dostoevski, Gogol, Nakrassov, and in the leading Russian writers already cited in a previous chapter.

In *Under Western Eyes* Joseph Conrad tells, as only Conrad can, how a chain became symbolic of Russia. He narrates the history of Peter Ivanovich, the gloomy Russian exile whose story was known not only along the *Boulevard des Philosophes* of Geneva but in every capital of Europe. Escaping from a fortress where he had been imprisoned by "administrative order," he could not rid himself of the iron fetters that had been affixed to his limbs by the tzarist jailers. Winding the loose end around his waist he learned to creep furtively from village to village in the endless forests of the Okhotsk province. He acquired genius in the art of moving about without betraying his fetters except by a faint clinking of metal. He felt that no man on earth could be trusted with the temptation of the unfastened chain. It seemed impossible that some fellow Russian could resist the

2 U. S. Document 798 P.S.

urge to fasten the loose end to a staple in a barn door and then rush away to find a policeman. The presence of the hidden fetters and the muffled rattling of them is felt throughout all Conrad's chapters.

Mr. Stalin knows the unbelievable capacity of his people for sustained trial short of rebellion. The boiling point in the blood stream of a Russian muzhik is high. He has been rendered docile to command by weight of traditions reaching far back in his genealogy. The political temperament of his forebears was profoundly affected by centuries of autocratic rule: by two hundred and fifty years of Tatar domination, by four Ivans, by twenty-nine years of domestic anarchy intervening between the death of Ivan IV and the coming of the first Romanov, by the peremptory reforms of Peter the Great — and by the repressive measures of the early nineteenth century followed by the constant frustration of the Duma under the last of the Romanov line. Then followed the bloodletting of 1914–1918, the iron discipline of Lenin's militant Communism, the devastation of civil war, the demoralization of two famines, the rigors of Mr. Stalin's five-year plans, and the inhuman brutalities of the Nazi invasion.

Calculating shrewdly on the qualities of a people capable of heroic resistance to foreign invasion, twice proved, he knows, however, that they have been broken so often on the wheel of adverse fortune that their resignation to hardship relieves him of undue domestic anxiety during the prosecution of his present daring international adventures. Should the giant which is the Russian people begin to stir uneasily in their bondage, he will be the first to recognize the portent — and he will act accordingly. Should dissidents become too annoying he has large areas at his disposal in Siberia, and large precedent for their colonization by "unstable elements in need of social rehabilitation." President Truman has stated that the number of prisoners in Mr. Stalin's concentration camps may reach 16 million. Complete control of press, radio, speech, public assembly, food rations, and housing furnishes Stalin an unparalleled field for the imposition of official ideas ranging from genetics, music, and economics to geopolitics, submarine architecture, and linguistics. His foreign policy in particular is publicized as a logical vindication of Russian right against Western wrong, of Soviet peace plans against Western warmongers, of Communist nobility against bourgeois hypocrisy.

* * * *

In its external strategy and tactics the GHQ of World Communism capitalized successfully also on one of the psychological qualities of the American mind. Your average American will readily grasp an issue arising from things in the concrete or from events discernible to one or more of his five senses: the imprisonment and dishonoring of an American consul in China, the cost of the airlift, the economic impact of the Marshall Plan on social stability in Italy, the shooting down of an unarmed American airplane over the Baltic, or the warfare in Korea. The hurried, unphilosophic reader of daily headlines — and his name is legion — is impatient of theory. He wants cold facts and he is more at home among them than he would be during the tough process of analyzing their causes. By and large he walks briskly away from the abstract. To be sure, he will take up some great moral or charitable issue which seizes his imagination, and he will crusade for it with a measure of intensity and generosity which amazes his more sophisticated European contemporary. But the issue must be concrete in form and immediate in menace before he gets angry to the point of seizing a musket and taking battle station, if needs be in far-off Korea.

The American Revolution had precisely such a dramatic appeal because of a parliamentary injustice concretely connected with taxation without representation on the part of the colonists. The burden and the consequences of King George III's imbecility were computable in shillings and pence; the tyranny was then dissected by the metaphysicians, extended widely in the public domain, and finally dramatized by Jefferson in the ringing phrases of the Declaration of Independence so that the conflict was eventually elevated to defense of inalienable human rights. The metaphysics came later than the material provocation. The original grievance, in point of fact, might have been compromised away on practical terms, with no thought of the colonists seceding from the British empire. Benjamin Franklin made that clear to the Parliament at Westminster during his testimony there in 1765. It is one of the ironies of history that the celebrated Olive Branch Petition, pledging the colonies to remain loyal subjects of the British Crown, if only certain administrative abuses were corrected, was drafted and dispatched to London after blood had been shed at Concord, Lexington, and Bunker Hill.

The controversy which finally plunged this nation into fratricidal conflict in 1861 had revolved for fifty years on a politico-economic issue. The territorial extension of chattel slavery as new states entered the Union raised the practical issue of states' rights and involved the legal prerogative of any one state or group of states to withdraw from the Union. The moral issue of slavery (already solved by Russia in the emancipation of the serfs by Alexander II in 1861) lay among the roots of schism, to be sure, and had to be met some day, as it was by Mr. Lincoln's proclamation of 1863. But it was the concrete fact of the secession of eleven southern states, followed by the bombardment of Fort Sumter in April, 1861, which made civil war inevitable. Mr. James Truslow Adams had much history and considerable documentary evidence on his side when he wrote in the *Epic of America:* "There is, of course, no doubt that slavery was in everyone's mind and that it made the best concentration point for all the vague and emotional substratum of the sectionalism which had now become deadly. The mere abstract morality of slavery, however, would not alone have been adequate to plunge the nation into war."

Similarly, it was the specific violation of American freedom on the high seas which carried us back to Europe in 1917 and committed us irrevocably to the fortunes of the Old World, although we did not fully appreciate the permanency of the commitment at that time. The decision to become a belligerent was taken, as a matter of historical fact, on the basis of legal rights. It was a pragmatic decision, although Mr. Wilson's language was keyed to high idealism. The ethical, the moral, and the social implications were chiefly emphasized after political decision had been taken on the grounds of wounded sovereignty. It took Von Tirpitz' unrestricted submarine program to stir us up to final action. The problem of human solidarity and international responsibility became formal in the hot debates of the postwar period but, again, no moral or legal obligation was assumed respecting collective maintenance of world peace; we declined to enter the League of Nations and American policy reverted to isolationism. It required the stunning shock of Pearl Harbor, a concrete humiliating fact in the material order, to organize the soul of America into indignant mobilization. The philosophic, ethical, and moral aspects of Nazi racism, of Japanese imperialism, and the Soviet aggression of 1939–1940 against Latvia, Lithuania, Estonia, Finland, and Poland had proved insufficient. We needed the blow to the body which so nearly reached our heart on December 7, 1941. We shuddered, recovered, mobilized, and conquered, then demobilized, only to be shocked into new indignation by the spectacle of American troops dying in Korea.

Mr. Churchill's pithy epigram about Soviet policy being a riddle wrapped in a mystery inside an enigma can do considerable damage, if taken too seriously and outside the context of the Marxist dogmas which control the course of the Russian Revolution. Many who are fascinated by Mr. Churchill's undeniable gift of language and brilliancy of style do not pursue his thought in that particular speech of October 1, 1939, to its better and more reasoned conclusion. As a result, that picturesque phrase occurring early in the text served as a poultice to solace the bruised feelings of many a frustrated diplomat at the close of some futile round of exhausting negotiations. The Churchillian figure of speech comes easily to the lips as some Soviet negotiator suddenly reverses an encouraging show of co-operation and abruptly stalks out of the conference, laying another veto on the hopes of a tired Western world. The riddle-mystery-enigma label is not a correct description to pin on his retreating back or hang on his approaching breast as he returns with some unexpected concession. It is not a correct assessment of any Soviet move in the game for such high stakes now being played across the board of Europe and Asia. Neither does it discriminate between incidental phases of Soviet tactics and the unchanged permanent pivot on which Kremlin diplomacy swings.

The plain truth of the matter is that Soviet policy is the most logical and consistent political phenomenon that emerged from World War I or prevailed after World War II. That is why the Russian Revolution has advanced to the points of longitude and latitude where it now stands on the map of Europe and Asia. The vacillations, the empiricism, the half measures, the weakness and compromise were all on the other side of the table — at least, until recently. They have not characterized the counsels of the Politburo. Communism advanced simply and basically because it maintains a monolithic policy deriving from a deposit of faith with many dogmas, a system of special ethics with no inhibitions, and a set of fixed geopolitical objectives. The Revolution never demobilized.

Communists do not have opinions or impressions or sentiments. They have convictions which, whether they be noble or ignoble, true or false, constitute a navigator's chart for procedure in debate at the United Nations and serve as a lamp of guidance for Molotov, Vyshinski, Gromyko, and Malik whenever they are maneuvered into the narrows of a critical situation. Soviet diplomats are not negotiators seeking an adjustment of international differences. They are professional revolutionists for whom the art of revolution has no fixed rules, only fixed objectives. They know what was meant when Saint-Just warned his colleagues of 1789 that he who stops halfway in a revolution digs his own grave. They are scientific Marxists, not Jeffersonian Democrats. They know their Machiavelli, and the logicality of the emergent philosophy is baffling only to those unacquainted with the special nature and content of their resolve. No government in history has been so frank and circumstantial in spelling out and publicizing its basic policy and its ultimate intentions. Candor leaves but one conclusion: the tragedy of unpreparedness lay not in our stars but in ourselves.

What Christianity and Democracy are dealing with is the Third Russian Revolution in the flesh, not with isolated events on disparate sectors of the international scene. It is the same Revolution in a diplomatic conference at Washington, Berlin, or Vienna as it is under the guise of a Chinese invasion of Korea. Its genius lies as much in the use of a dynamic philosophy of conflict as in the weakness and compromise so long manifest in its mounting roster of victims. The still evolving World Revolution has created that most dangerous of all intellectual siege guns — a false absolute adapted to the temper of the times. It has not been afraid of theory or dogma or metaphysics, provided the Revolution controlled the metaphysician's mind and his printing press.

Permanent in Soviet policy, and pervading it from top to bottom of its substance, is the absolute conviction that the Revolution of November 7, 1917, was not an historical incident, however striking, but a shift in the foundations of civilization, the end of one major epoch in the annals of the race and the beginning of a new world order. Like Cato's incessant warning against Carthage, this truth needs to be reiterated over and over again. The French Revolution had something of that universalism, but not the systematic and coherently progressive body of dogmas that the Communist has at his disposal. His is no mere declaration of the rights of man but a resolve to re-create the whole man to the image and likeness of Lenin and Stalin. Democracy is not his only target. He recognizes another formidable opponent still standing squarely across his path. Christianity wrought a profound transformation in the culture of the ancient world and led Western man from paganism to monotheism and the ethics of Christian culture. Hence, it was persecuted by the Caesars for over three hundred years. The faith which created Christendom and held it together when the last Roman consul had retreated to the seat of his threatened empire on the Tiber is not expressed in dogma alone. It is not only a religion; it is an accepted outlook on life that permeates the whole man. It is a cast of thought that colors a man's way of living and influences his legal, his social, and his domestic relations as well as his ritual of worship. He has been elevated to the sonship of God not for Sundays only but for weekdays as well.

Communism and Christianity part company at a very early point of thought. It has sometimes been claimed that the early Christian communities practiced collectivism and, since they were nearer to the Founder in time, place, and inspiration, it would follow that their customs reflected the true image of Christian idealism.[3] Those who cite the Jerusalem community and the

---

[3] "The Communist regime in Czechoslovakia has set up a working committee to search the Bible and religious texts for extracts suitable for Communist propaganda. Its purpose is to reinforce the Red Government in its struggle against the Roman Catholic Church. A major objective will be to

common way of life described in the Acts of the Apostles ignore
the totality of circumstances. The texts which commonly give
rise to the false conclusion describe a voluntary pooling of
material resources in what today might be called a community
chest. The motive was Christian charity involving not only belief
in God but love of God in His creatures. Obviously, such a
motivation is anathema to the Communism of Marx, Lenin, and
Stalin, with its compulsion, atheism, direct action, class warfare,
and dictatorship of a minority party. Moreover, there is no indication that Christ Himself ever condemned private property as
an economic institution; on the contrary, there is abundant evidence that He accepted it, condemned only the abuses, and, in
the case of the rich young man, warned His followers how hard
it would be for him to enter the Kingdom of heaven. The
Redeemer did not declare it impossible but emphasized the
impediment which riches are wont to interpose on the narrow
road to the Kingdom. The fact that Matthew was a practicing
banker did not prevent him from accepting the call and becoming
the first Evangelist.

Private property as a natural right not only was not denied by the
Jerusalem community but was affirmed by St. Peter, the Prince
of the Apostles. The relevant texts in the Acts describe how the
destitute were provided for by the generosity of those who sold
their farms, homes, and similar capital "so that each might have
what share of it he needed."[4] But Ananias secretly kept back
some of the purchase money from the sale of his property and
handed the balance to St. Peter as if it were the full amount.
Sad, but indignant, Peter reproached the racketeer: "Unsold, the
property was thine; after the sale, the money was at thy disposal;
what has put it into thy heart so to act? It is God, not man, thou
hast defrauded." Ananias, continues the Scripture, straightway fell
down and died on the spot. The punishment was meted out to
that chiseler, not because of his retention of all or part of the

---

persuade the highly religious Czech peasants that the regime's land collectivization projects have a sort of Divine sanction" (*Newsweek*, November 18,
1950).

[4] Chapter 2, 44–47, Chapter 4, 32–37, Chapter 5, 1–12.

price received, since he was free to retain his entire estate or sell it, turn in all the receipts or part of them. It was the lie that brought judgment on his head, as it did on Sapphira, his wife, who shared the conspiracy and repeated the falsehood.

The special way of life practiced for an unspecified time at Jerusalem was unique of its kind. In no other apostolic community is such a type of voluntary collectivism recorded by the Scriptures. On the contrary, various epistles of St. Paul, who was a contemporary of Peter, reflect the practice and the legitimacy of conventional property holding. Thus he instructs the Corinthians in the opening lines of the Sixteenth Chapter of his first Epistle to them, how each should economize and save so that a fund might be created to send to needy fellow Christians in Jerusalem. The same system of organized community budgeting had already been set up among the Galatians. In his second letter to Corinth, St. Paul invokes the example of a charity program to the needy set by the churches of Macedonia which, despite their poverty, showed exceptional generosity toward other communities in need of help. He counsels moderation in the collections to be made for the distressed areas: ". . . there is no intention that others be relieved at the price of your distress. No, a balance is to be struck, and what you can spare now is to make up for what they want; so that what they can spare may, in its turn, make up for your want; and, thus, the balance will be redressed." In Chapter 9, he succinctly defines the nature of their contributions for the relief of Jerusalem: "Only it is to be a free offering, not a grudging tribute."

From these exhortations to Christian charity and generosity it is apparent that no Communism could have existed in communities to which such appeals were directed. Generosity is the virtue of those who possess and willingly share their abundance with others. From the evidence at our disposal, we may conclude that the emergency at Jerusalem was not a permanent economic condition and the drastic measures adopted there can by no means be considered as obligatory or derived as dogma from Christ. Otherwise, they would have been common among all Christian communities of the apostolic age.

The teachings of Christ, St. Paul's interpretation of them, and the subsequent development of the Christian ethos follow a very definite scale of values in respect to fundamentals and accidentals. As the first Christian sociologist, Christ directed the major emphasis of His teaching to the individual soul, because He knew it to be the source and fountainhead of the collective conscience of mankind. He then progressed to the next component element of civil society, the family, and made but limited references to the political and economic features of the State. By far the greater proportion of His revelation is concentrated on the first two elements and in the order indicated; the smallest portion deals with the techniques of social organization and the material conditions in which men live. These latter are neither excluded nor minimized, but they do not constitute the prime obligation of the Christian Church, except when the externals of political and economic institutions impede the spiritual welfare, endanger the inner life of the soul, or challenge the supernatural mission of Christianity.

Even the Old Law which Moses promulgated, and which Christ did not disdain to obey in many respects, wrote its ten commandments in the singular number: *Thou shalt* and *Thou shalt not*. The obligations and the penalties are personal; judgment for sin will be passed on Matthew and Luke, on Mark and John, or Martha and Mary and Magdalen, not on families as such, nor on cities nor democracies nor autocracies, but on individual members of families, on separate citizens, on single democrats, republicans, and autocrats. Naked and alone each of us came into this world; solitary and stripped of worldly trappings we shall leave it; stark and alone we shall stand responsible before the judgment seat. Man's sojourn in socially organized communities, though important and natural, is only an interlude between two eternities. It is not his ultimate destiny.

Even on the rare occasions when the Founder of Christianity promulgated dogmas of a political character, He directed them to individuals: "Render therefore unto Caesar the things that are Caesar's and to God the things that are God's." That simple but majestic commandment established the distribution of power and constitutes the master key to Christ's political preachment. The limitation of secular authority was equally laconic and in the singular, addressed to Pilate: "Thou wouldst have no power over me if it were not given thee from on high."

If the kingdom your Christ came to found is not of this world, the sophist argues, Christianity should not concern itself with political problems domestic or international. The fallacy is an easy evasion for those who have not learned the discipline of defining terms. If by politics one means the heated partisanship and polemics of election campaigns, the curbstone vulgarities of party conflicts, the smoke-drenched caucus rooms of national conventions which so often degenerate into three-ringed circuses, obviously the Christian Church as such has no mandate to descend into that arena. But if by politics is meant the art of government and the science of regulating the mutual relations and the social conduct of men living in organized societies anywhere, then the Christian Church is not only in politics but she cannot stay out of politics any more than human beings can live outside the atmosphere which envelops the earth. To breathe oxygen is an inescapable condition of our bodily existence; to refuse to do so brings death. By reason of her surroundings, both human and institutional, the Christian Church faces many a challenge to the vitality of the mission confided to her. Some of these are direct; others are indirect, but not less relevant in the long run.

Contradictions arise from abuses in such overlapping fields as government, economics, education, and social welfare, for it is in the midst of such human adjuncts that the Church must live. They meet and sometimes jostle her at many a crossroad of life. Her children, who are citizens as well as members of a religious faith, may be penalized by invasion of their most sacred rights of conscience, as happened in the Oregon Schools Case of 1925 in which the Supreme Court of the United States eventually upheld the parental rights of Protestants and Catholics alike against the claims of the state legislature to monopolize education. Slums breed unhealthy moral conditions, as well as unhealthy bodies; gross industrial exploitation, social injustice, callous abuse of financial power, and similar excesses constitute such palpable menaces to the Christian sense of moral responsibility as to warrant positive intervention on the part of the Church. So long as the soul of man may be inclined to good or evil by the quality and pressures of environment, just so long is the Church obligated to pronounce judgment on the spiritual consequences of legislation, on political platforms, economic programs, and civic administrations. To do less would be default in the essentials of her stated mission.

In the performance of her primary obligation to the supernatural order she will not neglect the temporal and the visible needs of human nature, the daily welfare and the material necessities of the lowly, the widow, the suffering, the outcast, and the orphan. Since, in the Christian heritage, the body of man has been elevated to new dignity by the indwelling of a ransomed soul, Christianity the world over has not been wanting in works of compassion, collective charity, and social service. The Christian Church was active and eloquent in that domain long before the State became conscious of social responsibility. She respects the body, because it bears the signature of divinity. But she will not adore it. She knows that it was the eternal Logos which became flesh, not *vice versa*. To compromise on that primary issue is to surrender utterly. Henri Ghéon, in his book *The Curé D'Ars,* puts his finger on the alternative: "If truth is inescapable, what use is it to anybody to try to whittle it down?" Any Church which devitalizes the supernatural substance of religion pure and undefiled by overmuch and disproportionate solicitude for the transient and corruptible part of man's nature will have lost the reason for its existence. It will progressively degenerate into a disguised social welfare agency and might better merge with some solid humanitarian foundation before it ends by becoming a losing competitor with the Red Cross, Hollywood, and Broadway.

Marxian Communism has set itself to reverse the effects of the Incarnation and drive men back to an impersonal paganism more material and more despiritualized than any heathen religion of antiquity, because of the cold rationalism of its processes. Its most significant victory has been its success in emphasizing the abuses close to hand and to eye: economic inequalities, social discriminations, and low standards of living among the teeming masses of common men throughout the world. The main objective — control of the total soul and the complete body of mankind — is kept under cover until its full conquest is achieved. The incidental fact is made to serve as the visible argument. "Facts," wrote Macaulay, "are the mere dross of history. It is from the abstract truth which interpenetrates them and lies latent among them, like gold in the ore, that the mass derives its value."

Because of this setting up of perishable flesh to be the eternal Logos and the fascination of manufactured gadgets to be the be-all and the end-all of intellectual capacity, Soviet philosophy creates a secret loneliness of heart which seeks incessantly to fill the void created in man's nature by the elimination of the concept of God. The vacuum must be filled somehow and by something. Man cannot repeal the law of his being. The Soviet Government — every government — is made up of men. There is no more lonely man than the Godless man even when he is absorbed outwardly with his wine, his women, his song, and his luxuries. He may stifle conscience but he cannot wholly kill his awareness of it. There is something forever lacking in his mind, something haunting his intellect; to satisfy the ever constant urge to find the absolute he increases the tempo of his fling at life and enlarges the inquiry. Science will engage one type of tempera- ment; art, literature, gold, music, and endless speculation will pass the hours for others. If a libertine, he will seek felicity in the flesh and still come back unsatisfied; if a Darwinian, he will find repose in man as a mere "social vertebrate." Fatigued and frus- trated he not infrequently reaches a point in his quest for happi- ness where no thrill remains to be explored except the final gamble of suicide. What he was forever seeking, but always afraid to find, was God. What pursued and drove him ever onward, though he never turned to look, was that Hound of Heaven whose immanence is the subject of Francis Thompson's absorbing poem of that name:

> I fled him down the nights and down the days,
> I fled him down the arches of the years,
> I fled him down the labyrinthine ways of my own mind. . . .

So, too, a purely materialistic civilization with no vision beyond the horizon of industrial productivity, pleasurable things, utilitarian objects, and earth-bound motion must become a lonely introvert. It has nothing better than itself to satisfy the yearnings of its rational nature and reply to the nostalgia. It is inevitable, with a kind of dreadful logicality, for such a dwarfed culture to turn to power on a grandiose scale for satiation of that innate appetite for perfectibility and to slake its unsatisfied thirst for a lost paradise which distinguishes man from the beast in the field. General Eisenhower, in his *Crusade in Europe,* relates an incident which illustrates the practical consequences of a materialism that ignores the origin and the destiny of human personality. In company with a Soviet officer he was watching a picked group of American soldiers, trained technicians, carefully and methodically locating hidden land mines in an area soon to be passed over by a great mass of troops. The Soviet general expressed surprise and disagreement: the way he would do it was to send a large body of men across the field, the weight of whose bodies would explode the mines. The area would then be safe for the tanks, artillery, and supplies. The dignity of the human person and the value of the individual were ciphers in his accounting.

By another of its macabre inventions, the Politburo has enlisted Soviet science to a modernized form of diabolism. The spectacle of convinced Communists, tried and true Party stalwarts, suddenly changing their very personality, eagerly and eloquently confessing treason and welcoming punishment, first appeared in the purge trials of Trotskyites in 1937. The avenging spirit and often the very language of the public prosecutor, Mr. Vyshinski, took possession of the defendants. In the satellite countries the technique was extended to non-Communist prisoners as well and was apparently improved, as the paradox of self-accusation became more frequent there. Bulgaria had its Evangelical pastors confessing improbable iniquity. More recently Alexander Shipkov, whose courageous account of the torture to which he had been subjected to extort a false confession in Sofia was published by the State Department on March 4, 1950. The Communist government of Bulgaria promptly retaliated on March 6 by publishing a counterconfession from Shipkov who had been rearrested in the meantime and put on trial for espionage. In it the harassed victim is made to retract his former statement and assure the world that the conduct of the Security Militia had been "Very good. . . . A humane attitude. No torture." Following the conventional pattern he described his statement given while at liberty as "false and calumnious." Another recent example is that of the American citizen Robert Vogeler and the Englishman Edgar Sanders admitting guilt and begging clemency in Hungary. But the most compelling instance is that of Cardinal Mindszenty whose entire previous character of firm, unshakable opposition to Hitlerism and Communism alike was suddenly transformed into something unrecognizable as emanating from the same individual.

The bold, uncompromising figure of a saintly prelate whose personal status as a Prince of the Church and the tenets of whose faith required martyrdom, if necessary, became, in thirty days, a broken, self-accusing penitent who threw himself on the mercy of a usurping power whose pretensions he had combated up to the hour the doors of the Andrassy prison closed on him on the night of December 25–26, 1948. It has been ascertained that one of Moscow's specialists in the art of extorting confessions, a certain Dr. Kaftanov, accompanied the prisoner to the "processing room." What went into that secret chamber was not the figure produced for public trial a month later.

The corporeal structure of the man was the same; but the soul was blurred and shriveled. Even the eyes, which are the windows of the soul, were not the same. Whether this terrorizing of the inner spirit and the patent transformation of the Cardinal's publicly known personality without destroying the union of soul with body was accompanied by prolonged physical torture, by psychological terrorism, or induced by drugs such as actedron and scopomorphine or by hypnotic control after a tampering with the brain, may continue to be debated by students of the subconscious ego, by psychiatrists and toxicologists. What confronts humanity is the end result of some hidden process capable of effectively killing the completely developed personality of a mature man and substituting another mind subservient and responsive to the will of the conqueror — all achieved with the apparent consent of the victim and without his being conscious that his freedom of will and integrity of intellect have been damaged. The skill to effect such a sublimation of one personality and rebirth of another, even if exercised by practitioners obedient to the natural law and conscious of their moral responsibilities, would be frightening enough. That fearsome power now reposes in the hands of unscrupulous totalitarians and amoral pragmatists sworn to world revolution and the extinction of religion. The political and ethical possibilities foreshadowed in the courtroom at Budapest give as much pause to civilized men as do the social consequences of atomic fission in the physical constitution of matter.

The pioneer delvers into the secrets of the atom, whether enclosed in uranium or hydrogen, are now recoiling in dismay before the capacity for evil they there discovered. Soviet science is plunging deeper and deeper into the unexplored depths of man's innermost personal nature. They have unlimited clinical material for their satanic alchemy. Their motive is not scientific research for the benefit of humanity, but for the political profit of the Soviet State. That objective has been specified by public decree. We may rest certain, they will not retreat before the sanctities of life and conscience, nor spare them either, if the rapine smells sweet in the nostrils of the new barbarians. This tampering with flesh, blood, and nerves, ending in the domination of the mind to a prescribed party pattern, may well turn out to be a more sinister triumph of the Revolution than all its territorial and political conquests.

CHAPTER VIII

The Wheel Comes Round Full Circle

ON WHITSUNTIDE, May 28, 1950, whatever ghosts still haunt the ruins of Berlin beheld a spectacle which gave new meaning to the old French proverb, *Plus ça change, plus c'est la même chose.*[1] The mobilization of German youth in the Eastern zone, the regimented columns of 500,000 semiuniformed zealots massed to make a Soviet holiday, their marching in military formations, their acclaim of Stalin and Communism, the banners and the 10,000 militarized police participants were all paraded with techniques and psychological overtones identical with the monster demonstrations that prepared the German people for World War II. The appeal to the eye, the communicated feeling of massed power, the stirring up of emotions to stylized chanting of defiance against the Western Allies needed but an occasional substitution of other faces and other slogans to make onlookers imagine that the *Hitler Jugend* was on the march again or that a new rally of a resurrected Nazi Party was taking place in Nuremberg.

Not far away, at the same moment, in the Spandau prison, Hitler's organizer of youth, Baldur von Schirach, was making expiation for his crime of having achieved a similar regimentation of eight million German youth as prelude to Hitler's attempt at a World Revolution. One wonders if Von Schirach could have heard the echoes of the Whitsuntide march of 1950 and recognized

---

[1] The more that changes, the more it comes to the same thing.

the portent. Or perhaps he repeated to himself the confession he had made from the witness stand at the Nuremberg trials on May 24, 1946:

It is my guilt, which I bear before youth and the German Nation, that I have formed the younger generation of this people for a man who for many long, long years I believed in as a Leader, as Head of the State, whose authority I considered could not be questioned. . . . It is my guilt that I educated youth for a man who was a murderer a million times over. . . . But German youth is innocent . . . today they wander bewildered among the ruins of their fatherland . . . they knew nothing of these crimes . . . they saw in him an ideal and went to death for him. . . . I believed in this man, that is all.

The memory of man is amazingly short for comparatively recent events, let us say in respect to the period during which Germany's rearmament program was achieved after the defeat of 1918. But the sequence of events should not be forgotten by those who would draw profit from a comparison between what was then accomplished by stealth and what Moscow is now achieving in the occupied zones under her control. The secret rearmament of Germany after World War I led directly and inevitably to World War II. The public rearmament of the Eastern zone of Germany today is following a pattern which it would be folly to ignore. The rearming of the Soviet zone of Korea has already had a bloody aftermath.

From the earliest years of the Soviet regime, the Politburo has considered Germany as the key to World Revolution in western Europe, as it has deemed China the basis for Communist control of Asia. These two premises, like a constant among variables, run through the revolutionary literature of the Party and recur consistently in the programs of the Communist International. The role and position of Germany as second to Russia itself in a chain of future Communist States appears as early as Brest Litovsk (1918) when Trotsky, over the head of the German Army there facing him, openly appealed to the population of that country to join the new proletarian regime in Moscow by taking the road of domestic insurrection and class warfare. His propaganda and printed material, directed to Germany even from within the German lines where the negotiations took place, so angered the German High Staff that

Lenin was obliged to withdraw the firebrand and have Chicherin sign the treaty on March 3, 1918.

German social democracy was always the model and the hope of Lenin. In the Seventh Congress of Soviets he described the Russian effort as "raw" and needing the mature political experience of Social Democrats in Germany, as well as the general technological skill of the German worker, whom he described as "intelligent . . . educated . . . because he is used to living in an advanced culture." In February, 1918, the Petrograd Soviet elected Karl Liebknecht an honorary member in tribute to German leftism. Lenin's writings were first translated into German. Jaffe and Bukharin, two old Bolsheviks, were later installed in the Russian embassy in Berlin, under cover of terms provided in the Treaty of Brest Litovsk. Among the most active of leftist Germans of the period was Wilhelm Pieck, still, in 1950, a Moscow-trained Communist leader in the Eastern zone. When internal convulsions threatened the Communist cause in Germany in 1920, Lenin showed his concern by composing what was virtually a foreign policy for German revolutionists. In July, 1923, Karl Radek, active in developing Communism in Germany, issued his program for the future of Germany in a special edition of the *Rote Fahne*.

The most significant influence of Moscow, however, was felt in the secret process of rearming Germany, by which the *Reichswehr* circumvented the Treaty of Versailles under the Weimar Republic. Defeated in the field but never entirely conquered, the militarists of the General Staff looked eastward for solace to the rising power of Soviet Russia. As early as 1921 Radek made his proposal to the intransigent generals: arsenals could be built on Russian territory and armament built up for the day of reckoning with the Western powers which had triumphed over Germany in 1918. In 1922 the Rapallo Treaty established political relationship; ambassadors were exchanged and commercial ties strengthened.

The author of this volume had considerable to do with the first German ambassador in Soviet Russia, Count Brockdorff-Rantzau. An unreconstructed Junker, tall, hair *en brosse,* monocled, and bitter, it was he who refused to sign the Treaty of Versailles, though delegated to do so and a substitute had to be named by Berlin. During the tense days of religious persecution in 1923, the

German Foreign Office had sought, out of courtesy to the Vatican, to exert a restraining influence on the Kremlin. But their Chief of Mission in Moscow turned the occasion into an opportunity for political bargaining. In answer to my pleas for assistance in averting the death sentence from the Petrograd clergy, the Count suggested that my delicate mission might be facilitated if I, for my part, would do him a favor. The French had recently occupied the Rhineland. France was a Catholic country. Could not the Pope bring pressure on the *Quai d'Orsay* to effect a withdrawal of French troops? I could only answer that my powers did not extend to such matters, but that his observation would be transmitted without comment to the Cardinal Secretary of State. Nothing happened — beyond the killing of Monsignor Budkiewicz, the death sentence against Archbishop Cieplak, and long terms of imprisonment for the others.

On another occasion, during a sudden crisis that looked dangerous I was engaged in making emergency provisions for transferring certain members of the papal mission to places of greater safety. The Count invited me to his embassy to discuss the current uneasiness in Moscow and to inquire about the disposition of our personnel. I replied that those of Italian nationality had been offered lodging by the Italian Commercial Agent, Signor Amadori, others would be received by the Poles or by Mukhtar-Bey, the Turkish diplomatic representative. "And yourself?" he queried. "I have been offered hospitality by Sir Robert Hodgson, the British representative." The Prussian in him bristled — *"Alors donc,"* he murmured, twisting the stem of his wine glass, *"Vous allez transporter votre lit virginal aux Anglais."* This catty remark was intended to let me know he was aware that I was a Catholic priest though clothed in lay costume. The mood was outwardly playful, hence I felt free to reply in the same vein. I ventured to suggest that there would be no net loss in that field, as certain well-known members of the diplomatic corps would probably continue to make compensation by their private activities and roving eye. No offense was taken, so far as I could judge. He lifted his glass, clicked it against mine, and said: *"Touché, mon père."* He followed the code of his regiment — except that he did not splinter his glass on the stones of the fireplace.

But to return to His Excellency's government and its secret rearmament program on Russian soil.

Traveling constantly throughout Russia after the German-Soviet understanding at Rapallo, we could not escape noticing the presence, in growing numbers, of German engineers, consultants, businessmen, and military experts. The concrete results of their collaboration appeared during the next three years. By 1928 it was estimated that 800 special German agents had been dispatched to Soviet Russia for work with the Red Army. Factories arose under Junker engineering and direction, such as those at Samara and Saratov; an airfield blossomed in the Tambov area; German officers conducted training courses in chemical warfare and aviation; the Hugo Stolzenburg firm constructed a plant for the manufacture of Phosgene and Lost, two types of poison gas. The Stinnes group and Krupp were prominent in the program. It later developed that the trade agreement between Moscow and Berlin was utilized to ship separate parts of knocked-down military equipment to Germany, labeled as commercial supplies. Hand grenades were delivered to the *Reichswehr* via Baltic ports such as Stettin, a transaction which was discovered, however, by longshoremen at the time of unloading and revealed to the Social Democrats who systematically collected the evidence and exploded the news in the *Reichstag* on December 17, 1926. The conspiracy was published in the Social Democratic *Vorwärts* and the *Berliner Tageblatt*, as well as in the series of articles in the *Manchester Guardian* during December, 1926. But the power of the *Reichswehr* and the interest of the German government combined to stifle opposition and defeat the demand for a parliamentary investigation.

Meanwhile, within Germany itself, the process of preparation for war was organized with characteristic German efficiency. The Inter-Allied Military Control Commission was often circumvented by ingenious devices; double walls in warehouses, subterranean storehouses, entrances blocked with brickwork, and subterfuges such as renting private storage space under the name of a legitimate business enterprise. Even lighters were loaded to capacity and then anchored offshore in charge of a trusted agent or a soldier in civilian clothes. In the first disarmament period, after the demobilization of the defeated army, large numbers of rifles of the

Free Corps had been greased, packed in cases, and buried at remote border spots in Upper Silesia.

The training of future troops in excess of the 100,000 permitted under the Treaty of Versailles was accomplished by indirect maneuvers. "Automobile clubs" increased; "glider corps" were formed; student organizations flourished; war veterans' associations preserved contact among the rank and file, while the Prussian Officers' Corps maintained an intact leadership. As Hitler approached his final triumph, the SS contingents and Brown Shirts became, to all intents and purposes, a private army for the liquidation of Communists and Jews, while the Hitler Youth furnished reserves, and the Labor Service provided training in the field. For the intellectuals an appropriate indoctrination was supplied from their own ranks. Karl Haushofer, the father of German geopolitics, encouraged the eventual and open alliance of Germany with Russia in his voluminous writings; he wrote the preface to the joint work of Lt. Colonel von Niedermayer and Juri Semjonov, on the geopolitical potentialities of Soviet Russia (1934). All in all, the hidden purposes, the extent and technical execution of the German-Soviet collaboration must be regarded as "one of the best kept secrets of modern history."[2]

The emergence of Hitler and his seizure of power in the midthirties effected a distinct transformation in the hitherto hidden process. It was no longer necessary to conceal the facts. What is more important was the change of form, of tempo and association. Rearmament now became an exclusively Nazi weapon, divorced from the ties and the hopes which Moscow had cultivated toward Germany since the days of Rapallo. It became, in effect, a public menace and a direct challenge to the Russian Revolution, a menace

---

[2] Cited from the conclusions reached in the exhaustive study by Ruth Fischer, *Stalin and German Communism* (Harvard University Press, 1948). No writer in modern times has more intimate and authoritative documentation on the relationship between German Communism and Soviet Russia. The present author is much indebted to her account, particularly Chapter 24, which supplements my observations of 1922–1923 inside Russia, coincides with much of the evidence contained in the captured documents examined by me at Nuremberg in 1945–1946, and rounds out data obtained during a sojourn in Japan during the winter of 1947–1948 when Tojo and other Japanese leaders were on trial before the International Military Tribunal for the Far East.

clearly discernible in the violent language of Hitler's *Mein Kampf*
and made concrete in the civil war waged by the new praetorian
guard, the paramilitary units such as the SS troops and the
Brown Shirts mobilized by Hitler for his private warfare against
Communists and Jews. The traditional ascendancy of the Prussian
military caste declined; the *Wehrmacht* finally capitulated to the
elite represented by Göring, Hess, Himmler, and Von Ribbentrop.
Step by step, Hitler absorbed all organizations into the orbit of
the National Socialist revolution until the Nazi Party became the
German State.

Then Moscow took alarm, recognizing a formidable competitor,
and new directives were drawn up for the Seventh Congress of the
Communist International which was hastily convened in the summer
of 1935. Fascism became the public enemy in the Party line
imposed on World Communism, the Trojan Horse was groomed for
service, and Stalin liquidated Marshal Tukachevsky as well as all
other agents and colleagues who represented the previous policy
of co-operation with German militarists. It was another violent
zigzag in Communist tactics always responsive to sudden emergencies. The orthodoxy of one phase became heresy and treason over-
night in the rapid shifting of policy characteristic of the Politburo.
It is this ever present danger of being charged with "deviationism"
which hangs like a sword of Damocles over the head of every
Soviet official, not excluding Mr. Molotov or Mr. Vyshinski or
Mr. Malik. Greater than they met sudden death from it.

The braggadocio of Hitler and the cold opportunism of Stalin
met on common ground in August, 1939, and another zigzag took
place on both sides. The inviting vision of joint domination of
Europe possessed both dictators, stirred their imagination, and
found voice in the Nazi-Soviet pact in which they buried their
hatchets after pledging mutual consent to a carving up of Eurasia
between themselves. The pact revived certain historic tendencies
latent in the thinking of many German publicists. A condominium
in some form or other had often been advocated in previous years
by Haushofer who followed Bismarck's canny diplomacy and
cautious benevolence respecting the role of Russia in preserving
a balance of power favorable to Germany and irksome to France.
Neither a geopolitician nor a Pan-Germanist, the Iron Chancellor

sought not so much German expansion as German security. A strong, unified Germany, dominated by Prussia and not menaced by Russia, was his basic policy. To that end he revived the Three Emperors' League (Germany, Austria-Hungary, and Russia) in 1881, effected a secret "reinsurance" treaty with the Tzar in 1887, and, in general, skillfully isolated France, appeased England, and impressively increased Germany's strategic position on the Continent from 1871 to his retirement from public office in 1890. In the succeeding years, the balance was reversed under the bellicose Wilhelm II, as Russia and France gravitated more and more toward solidarity of understanding in a dual alliance which was later enlarged into the Triple Entente — England, France, and Russia — with Japan in sympathetic though unstable co-operation. To compensate for the shift, Germany and Austria wooed Italy into the shaky Triple Alliance and waited for the next turn of the wheel in power politics.

Resolved to profit by the debacle of 1918, Haushofer devoted much of his genius and physical energy to restoring Russia to the Germanic camp and enlisting Japan as an Eastern ally. *"Never again,"* he wrote after the German-Soviet alliance of August, 1939, *"shall Germany and Russia endanger the geopolitical foundations of their adjustable spaces by ideological conflicts."*[3]

It was the allocation of spoils as proposed by Soviet Russia that frightened Hitler — or enraged him. The Politburo had described its aspirations of empire as stretching far beyond Soviet borders in the direction of the Indian Ocean and southward of Batum and Baku in the general direction of the Persian Gulf. It was this evidence of a rival geopolitics that convinced Hitler, as early as December 18, 1940, that Soviet Russia would have to be crushed even before the conclusion of the war against England. This momentous decision, embodied in the *Operation Barbarossa*, was revealed at Nuremberg and described by Hitler in his letter to Mussolini, June 21, 1941, as designed "to put an end to the hypocritical performance in the Kremlin."

The Nazi invasion of Russia will doubtless be accounted by future historians as Hitler's most fatal error; by the same token,

---

[3] *Zeitschrift für Geopolitik,* 1939, p. 773.

it must be regarded as a providential miscalculation in favor of the hard-pressed Allied cause not yet reinforced by the entrance of the United States into the war. If the Soviet-German pact had held and been developed to its logical consummation, the map of Europe might today be all red and brown from the Baltic to the Mediterranean and from Vladivostok to the English Channel, with the last remnant of British power established as a guest in Ottawa.

The defeat of Von Paulus before Stalingrad and the surrender of the Sixth German Army, followed by other contingents, transferred to Soviet control some 300,000 seasoned German troops whose subsequent treatment as special prisoners of war made them an important pawn in the contest for Germany. The Free German Committee, composed of German officers in Moscow, served as a propaganda agency under Soviet auspices. Disbanded officially in August, 1945, this group's subsequent activities have been nebulous; Von Paulus appeared for a brief sojourn at Nuremberg, but how many German soldiers continue as an organized secret army on Russian soil cannot be ascertained. It would be a highly profitable enterprise, however, to attempt to find out how many of them are enrolled for future military use in the German Police, the *Volkspolizei*.

In addition to its political and ideological conquests in eastern Germany, Soviet policy is busy with a program of military preparedness in her other satellite provinces of Europe. Wholly master of the government of Czechoslovakia, Hungary, Poland, Roumania, and Bulgaria, the Kremlin is systematically building up reserves of trained man power in these subject areas. Already in control of the police — a prime requisite in every seizure of power — their next step is now in process of execution. Satellite armies under "reliable" leadership are being organized which, in effect, will serve as reserve corps of the Red Army. All Cominform countries are included in this system of border levies. It has been estimated, as we have already noted in a previous chapter, that the total strength of these well-armed, well-trained, and Soviet-led mercenaries will be approaching 2,000,000 by the year 1951–1952. It must not be forgotten that one of the most productive centers of military armament in Europe is the Skoda works in Pilsen, Czechoslovakia. It is operating full blast and the products, for the most part, are moving eastward or to Cominform allies. And it will be remembered that one of Europe's most important sources of uranium was found in the Joachimsthal region not far from Karlsbad; a northern spur of the deposit extends into Soviet-occupied Saxony.

In January, 1947, the slowly maturing fruits of the Marshall Plan convinced Moscow that a countereconomic move was imperative. The Council for Mutual Assistance, the so-called Molotov Plan, was the answer. By virtue of the bilateral trade agreements between Soviet Russia and its satellites, economic relations with the West are rigorously controlled with a view to increased production of war materials, a prescribed percentage of which must be exported to the Soviet Union, which had already supplied much of the raw materials at a price always favorable to Moscow. Thus Hungary is obliged to export 60–70 per cent of her finished industrial products to the Soviet Union or to a market approved by Moscow. In the latter case, the Soviet Union manipulates the transaction in a manner to insure a sort of broker's fee. This limitation of market diminishes the possibility of commerce with the West, a handicap which can fatally impair Hungary's ability to achieve economic stability. By assigning similar quotas to Poland and Czechoslovakia, Moscow feeds her own appetite for industrial products and heavy equipment suitable for war industries, while at the same time keeping her exploited satellites chained to the Kremlin's program and crippling the export trade of western Europe.

This exploitation of satellites internationally has its domestics counterpart in Soviet Russia's forced labor system applicable to citizens within the Union. It has been estimated that 10,000,000 economic serfs, at a minimum, are detained in her labor camps and other State enterprises. Many competent authorities place the number much higher. The laws permitting this new form of serfdom were published within Russia by the State Political Publishing House in 1941 and revealed to the outside world by the British delegate to the United Nations Economic and Social Council at Geneva on July 22, 1949.

This code, with its 147 subsections, provides in detailed language for the recruiting of forced labor for the needs of the Communist empire. Wide latitude is accorded to the government to round up persons considered to be "class hostile elements" or "unstable

elements" for the purpose of "re-education . . . to socially useful
ends." One of the most sinister and revealing phrases to be found
in these statutes is the provision that suspected persons may be
deprived of liberty by that most characteristic device of tyranny —
"by decree of an administrative organ," which means, of course, by
the arbitrary, star-chamber sentence of some governmental bureaucracy. It is as if the National Democratic Committee in this country
had the power, through a Party agency located in the Interior
Department, to arrest and deport for re-education in Alcatraz or in
the uninhabited wastes of Alaska all Republicans deemed to be
unreliable or socially unstable.

The code states textually that the armed guards who control the
economic slaves may be recruited, as they commonly are, from
convicted criminals, a procedure which guarantees ruthlessness and
callous administration. This practice had been widely adopted by
the Nazis in their concentration camps. To stimulate zeal among the
supervisors, the Soviet code further provides that 5 per cent of
the net proceeds from the sale of products shall be deposited in
a "bonus fund for officials of corrective labor institutions."

❊ ❊ ❊ ❊

Lenin's conviction of the prime importance of Germany in the
logistics of a Communist World Revolution is thus revealed as
persisting unchanged in the Soviet policy so rapidly maturing in
the Russian zone of occupation. By the time these lines are in
print, East Germany may already have been incorporated into the
Communist empire as another compliant satellite State under a
bogus treaty unilaterally imposed. The fictitious sovereignty thus
created could then claim place and delegates in the United Nations,
together with the unpredictable number that could also be demanded for a Sovietized China whose sprawling bulk, historic splits,
and geographic divisions offer specious pretexts for the setting up of
several pocket States in the service of the Kremlin.

Throughout this panorama of conspiracy and organized violence
runs a constant technique based on a systematic distortion of
values in the field of semantics. With the boldness which relies on
attack as the best defense, the followers of Lenin have turned the
meaning of words upside down and attached special definitions to

traditional terms. In order to confuse adversaries and mobilize support among the unwary, they have excelled in the double talk which Lenin describes in his treatise on Imperialism.[4] He there discusses the use of "Aesopian language" — the form of speech used by the Greek writer of fables, Aesop, who made animals talk in a manner to convey criticism of human foibles and spread sarcastic innuendoes without formally offending the reader. Although in that passage Lenin pretended to a distaste for double talk, he openly advocates all and any deceit in *The Infantile Delusion of Leftism* where he counsels his followers: "We must be prepared to employ trickery, deception, lawlessness, withholding truth and concealing truth."

The Soviet adaptation of the Aesopian method takes the form of evasion of known truths, emphasis on half-truths, covering up illegal programs under color of legal privileges, hammering incessantly on ideas favorable to the Communist program, and inserting guidance and signposts recognizable to Communist eyes. A special vocabulary was created in which, by dint of repetition, the accepted meaning of familiar terms was smothered under the new semantics of the Communist ideology. Truth became synonymous with Marxism; falsehood meant any statement not in accord with dialectical materialism; democracy became the form of State organization now prevalent in the U.S.S.R. and satellite lands; justice — whatever advances the cause of the Revolution; injustice — whatever impedes the progress of Communism; morality — everything Stalin does or Lenin recommended; freedom — the ability to submit to the inevitability of Communist truth unilaterally defined; peace — the tranquillity following the conquest of a country by the Red Army; war — any attempt at self-defense by a nation unappreciative of Soviet aggression; warmonger — any person or government adhering to the sovereignty and natural rights of a non-Sovietized society; fascist — every non-Communist; reactionary — one who pushes against the latest decree of the Politburo; logic — the dialectic working up to an aggression by proxy after infiltration by instructed agents; history — a manner of thought first appearing in 1848 in the *Communist Manifesto;* beauty — an anthology of the

---

[4] Little Lenin Library, Vol. 15, p. 7.

writings of Marx, Lenin, Stalin; art — any approved representation of life in Soviet Russia; ugliness — bourgeois culture; up — down; right — left; white — the absence of red.

In the field of police control and public administration, Aesopian methodology endeavors to hide certain grim realities and ignore them when it is impossible to conceal them. From the outset of the Revolution, the propagandists adopted a uniform terminology respecting the evils of the Tzarist autocracy, which were serious enough and hastened the end of the Russian empire. But they were mildness and softness in comparison with the penal measures soon to be adopted by its Soviet successor. Since Lenin, Stalin, and many old Bolsheviks had done time in Siberia, the propaganda value of the exile system under the Romanovs was utilized to the hilt. Little was said or indicated of certain very important, but embarrassing facts. It is possible, however, to make an estimate of the number of exiles sent to Siberia from 1823 up to the fall of the Romanov dynasty. The records of the Tzarist Bureau of Exile Administration, erected on the initiative of a well-known reformer of earlier times, Count Speransky, shows a total of 772,929 exiles sent there up to 1887.

This date is selected because of the careful investigations made in that field by George Kennan, the American journalist who first explored Siberian prison life and published his monumental work, *Siberia and the Exile System*, in 1891. Supplementing Kennan's report by a computation based on comparison and analogy, we may add another 400,000 to account for the years before the establishment of the Tzarist Bureau and the unrecorded years after 1887. One may assume with fair accuracy that, in the space of a hundred years, the Tzars banished something like 1,250,000 Russians to Siberia, a figure which probably errs on the side of exaggeration. But the liberators of the proletariat uprooted some 3,000,000 Russian peasants during the first two years of the First Five-Year Plan and transported them to penal service somewhere. The additional millions confined in Siberia and in concentration camps at the present moment may only be estimated in figures already cited, i.e., probably much in excess of 10,000,000, not counting the victims in satellite regions.

If we wish to pursue one of those tzarist political exiles to his place of confinement and examine with objectivity the nature of his punishment, we meet another semantic triumph of Soviet propaganda. It will probably be conceded that Lenin himself will be an informed and authentic witness in his own case. He was exiled to Shushenskoye in 1897 and spent three years under conditions which are typical of administrative exile under the Romanovs. Let us consult his memoirs and review his sufferings. They are recounted with considerable detail in his *Letters* published by the official Lenin Institute, and printed by *Gosizdat,* Moscow, in 1931, 1932, and 1933.[5]

While awaiting his departure to Siberia, he writes to a friend from the House of Preliminary Detention, Petersburg, January 2, 1896, a long letter setting forth a program for the exile period. There was ample time and permission for literary work in prison, hence he decided to embark on the writing of a book; he encloses a list of supplies for his friend to obtain for him; he is even able to allot a sum of money for their purchase; some of the desired reference works were obtainable in the prison library, however, and he crosses them off.

Another letter from the Petersburg prison, dated January 24, 1896, acknowledges the receipt of a quantity of conveniences from his friend — tea in abundance, a suit of clothes, a waistcoat, and a shawl. He is permitted to order mineral water from a chemist, and it is delivered on the same day. He sleeps about nine hours a day "and dreams about the various chapters in my next book." He adds a postscript asking for a special kind of pencil with the lead inserted in a holder. It appears that the rules required the old-fashioned kind to be sharpened by the prison warden and he "takes his time over it."

The remaining letters from the preliminary detention prison at Petersburg are in the same vein: thanks for the various supplies, but no more underclothes should be sent . . . he has such a complete supply that there is no more storage room . . . he is having dentistry work done . . . needs a new German dictionary . . . has a traveling rug . . . but needs pillowcases and towels.

By March 14, 1897, he is on his way to Siberia and writes to his

---

[5] A selected group of these letters appeared in an English version *Letters of Lenin* (New York: Harcourt, Brace and Co., 1937).

mother that he is proceeding partly by slow train and partly by horseback. He foresees that he will need a sheepskin coat, felt boots, and perhaps a fur hat . . . he is sleeping splendidly . . . he feels much better than he did in Moscow.

At Krasnoyarsk, on March 22, he visits the famous Udin library but notes that it is located two versts from the town which affords opportunity for a brisk walk.[6] He hopes to use the collection as a source of reference in his task of writing the projected book. . . . He is enjoying the pleasant town. . . . He has heard rumors that his eventual residence will not be Krasnoyarsk. . . . His case of books can be sent to him at the new address. . . . He makes arrangements for the use of the money he will receive for a recent article . . . send it in three installments, about 50 rubles a month. . . . He will subscribe to some periodicals which may not be available at his new address, Shushenskoye, a small community of about 1500 inhabitants.

His letter of May 30, 1897, from the permanent address, exhibits some querulousness about the nonarrival of his books. . . . But the hunting is good, though difficult without a dog . . . he rode out twelve versts and shot duck and snipe. . . . He is sorry he did not have a mackintosh cape. . . . Could one be sent to him . . . he is thinking of buying a revolver.

From this date to the termination of his sentence, his letters recount the bucolic life of a middle-class country gentleman . . . he swims in the Yenisei, hunts frequently, writes books and articles, has a stream of current literature coming and going, visits friends in other towns over week ends, acknowledges receipt of his government allowance, discusses the possibility of having a good sporting dog sent from Moscow . . . looks forward to the arrival of Krupskaya, the lady who is coming out soon to marry him . . . have her bring some gentleman's kid gloves . . . also send a seal and sealing wax for letters, together with a penwiper and small scissors.

On the 7th of May his fiancée arrives and preparations for the wedding begin . . . the invitations are being prepared . . . his book, *The Development of Capitalism in Russia,* is published and

---

[6] This collection was purchased by American funds in 1907 and is now in the Library of Congress, Washington.

he experiences the author's thrill of holding the first volume in his hand . . . it looks so good that he recommends the price should be raised . . . students should have a 25 per cent discount but not more. . . .

In February, 1900, Lenin's exile terminated and he returned to European Russia. On April 20, 1900, he addressed a petition to the Director of Police of Pskov respecting certain permissions he needed to travel to Ufa. He signs it: *Hereditary Nobleman, Vladimir Ulianov, Pskov.* In August he is in Germany, writing from Nuremberg, later from Munich, Paris, London, Geneva, Zurich, Bern, Naples, Copenhagen, Krakow, Zorenberg (Sweden), and other strategic centers frequented by Russian émigrés. The signature is no longer *Vladimir Ulianov* but *Nicholas Lenin.*

These recollections of a prominent political prisoner under the Tzars may with profit be contrasted with the ruthless treatment of similar dissidents under the Lenin and Stalin regime. The Aesopian language appears at the outset. Opponents of the Soviets are condemned to labor camps "for rehabilitation" . . . "for social education" and "correction of unsocial conduct." Once behind the domestic Iron Curtain they undergo the brutal process of extermination and exploitation first revealed to the world in 1934 by Vladimir Chernavin, a former professor in the Agronomic Institute of Leningrad. Arrested for "political unreliability," he was confined in one of the most notorious concentration camps on Solovetsky Island in the White Sea. Escaping in August, 1932, he published his moving account in a volume entitled *I Speak for the Silent* (New York: Hale, Cushman and Flint, 1935). It reveals where the Nazis got their model for Dachau, Auschwitz, and Buchenwald.

Prisoners were deliberately worked to the limit of human endurance, exploited to the last ounce of energy during 14 to 16 hours of the day. Frozen and hungry, they frequently were unable to do the heavy tasks of sawing wood or constructing roads; as punishment they were "put out in the cold." This meant that the helpless victim was stripped naked, made to mount the stump of a tree and slowly freeze to death — or die later of gangrene. Suicide was frequent. Desperate men often shammed an accident by letting their ax cut off a finger or even a whole hand at the wrist. But the penalty was of a piece with the barbarian code of the wardens.

After the conventional beating, the "self-cutters" were obliged to stand before their assembled companions on parade and hold up the severed fingers or entire hand and proclaim: "I am a shirker." If the victim still survived, he was sent to an "invalid gang," a battalion of sick, aged, crippled, and tuberculous prisoners, where a lingering death awaited him.

The policy of inhuman extermination described by Chernavin was modified in later years, as the loss of man power was felt in the economic structure of the country. Concentration camps were reorganized and are now commonly conducted with an eye to business efficiency and with more refined cruelty. Hardened criminals, who constitute perhaps 10 per cent of the population of the camps, are put over the slave laborers and productivity is stepped up by rigor, bribery, and use of food as a weapon. The enormous increase of prisoners in recent years, augmented by thousands of war prisoners and displaced persons from zones occupied by Soviet troops, furnish one of the main sources of labor for the heavy industries serving the present war economy and armament program. It is a special function of the Secret Police to provide a steady flow of new "workers" from the still silent masses of the U.S.S.R.

The relentless memory of the Soviet government pursued its victims even into western Europe after the cessation of World War II hostilities. Those of us who observed Soviet activities in occupied Germany at that time will not soon forget the groups of Soviet officers and officials who combed the American zone to repatriate the "non-returners," i.e., the hundreds of thousands of Russian refugees who were unwilling to return to their native land out of a well-grounded fear of the fate awaiting them there. Because of a mistaken policy, American military authorities were obligated to round them up and hand them over to the waiting Russian slave-drivers and probable executioners. Fortunately, the repulsive practice was halted when the tragedy became unbearable to humane administrators.

CHAPTER IX

Counterattack

FREEDOM, of itself, is an undisciplined concept and a self-serving impulse. By nature and definition it is impatient of restraint. If no controls of private or public conduct be acknowledged beyond the reach of those possessing the power to tamper with them, the path of freedom can become the road to suicide. "All power tends to corrupt," was Lord Acton's terse summation, "absolute power corrupts absolutely." The rarest fruit of freedom is the spectacle of power voluntarily setting limits to its own power and curbing man's innate appetite for more and more domination of other men and new things.

Therein lies the profound significance of the present conflict between Soviet Russia and the American concept of freedom limited by responsibility to moral law. There lies the difference which lifts the cold war in Europe and the hot war in Korea to the level of a contest of ideas and beliefs, which is a form of antagonism far more decisive for the future of humanity than a clash of arms over a strip of territory, a disputed frontier, or a right of way to the sea. Because the tug of war with Soviet Russia since 1945 had not involved explosives on a grand scale, the conflict has been called a cold one. Such a description becomes illusory when one meditates on the issues involved; it is, moreover, a disturbing indication of the miscalculation to which the modern mind so frequently tends whenever the visible things of the market place are measured and weighed against the unseen things of the spirit.

The admixture of truth and falsehood in Soviet State policy constitutes a growing challenge to the alertness and vitality of the truths upheld in the Christian credo and in the dogmas of democracy. Orestes A. Brownson, that long-neglected figure in nineteenth-century American thought, has an arresting and wise passage in one of his works. It deals with the attitude one should adopt respecting balance of mind in winnowing truth from error in an opponent's claims. We shall never rightly comprehend any system, he argues, until we understand how much truth it embraces. We shall never rightly comprehend it by merely detecting its errors and fallacious conclusions. The main burden of refutation consists in discovering, distinguishing, and accepting the measure of truth which incomplete thinkers misapprehend, misinterpret, and misapply.

Acknowledgment of whatever is legitimate in the claims of Communism must have place in the case now before us, accompanied by reconstruction of the social order in ways and steps conformable to enlightened conscience. The patent iniquities will usually carry their own refutation. The errors and exaggerations of Communism, while meriting vigorous opposition, may even be considered as beneficent occasions. They challenge stagnation where it exists and purify vision that may have become jaundiced by easy living. The Communist persecution of religion may well serve as a purgation of incidental human weaknesses in the Church and Lenin's dictatorship by one class can serve to enhance the value of a chastened democracy made conscious of its social obligations.

In their aggressive mobilization of motives and resources for combat, the Communist crusaders have far outdistanced those who have most to lose whenever Marxist tactics succeed in a given country. The heralds of revolt are never timid propagandists; they assume a confidence of manner and act as if their beliefs are worth any and every sacrifice. On November 23, 1946, one of Soviet Russia's most prominent novelists, Constantine Simonov, analyzed the monopoly claimed by Marxist truth in the publication *Literary Gazette,* an organ for correct orientation of Soviet writers:

In literature and on the stage we must show the Soviet person — the builder of the future — in such a light that the audience and the whole world will see the moral and spiritual superiority of people who have been reared in a socialist society.

Our diplomats speak from the world tribune with such brilliance and so convincingly not only because they are great statesmen and orators, but also and mainly because, in spite of the lies and libel spread about them, they alone speak the truth about humanity, a truth supported by our entire people which makes our representatives superior to all others in the world tribune.

The subordination of cultural forms to the political objectives of the Communist State now includes music as well as linguistics. Dimitri Shostakovich once held an honored place in the world of music and expressed in many symphonies the universal appeal of the most stirring of all the fine arts. But the Agitation and Propaganda Committee of the Central Committee of the Communist Party haled the famous composer before the tribunal of Marxian dialectics in 1946 and accused him of cowardice in abandoning "warm ideological conviction." Shostakovich's Ninth Symphony, it was charged, showed no awareness of modern social problems; it toys with musical harmonies when it should be expressing Marxism and converting the world to the Soviet cause. In his abject surrender, Shostakovich promised to harmonize his compositions "with social and state interests . . . the voice of our Soviet Epoch."

In 1950, a Soviet scientist, a woman biologist named O. B. Lepeshinskaya, was awarded the Stalin prize for adding another "discovery" to Marxist science. She established to the satisfaction of Soviet criteria, that the living cells of plants and animals are formed from nonliving elements. The inanimate particles became cells "under the right conditions," which, however, were neither specified nor clarified. But the political and propagandistic value of the alleged scientific discovery was high. Hence the prize. According to the genetics now popular in Marxist circles, environment (if the right kind) is much more potent than heredity. The Party line requires Soviet scientists to believe that Marxism is capable of transforming Nature itself into new forms. The Moscow news bureau added the inevitable commentary: "Soviet science is approaching the solution of the great problem . . . of the transformation of nonliving matter into living. . . . " Obviously, the origin of life will be "discovered" some time in the future, to be followed by Soviet creation of life with no primeval taint of capitalism in it. The elimination of the Creator will then be not only a political tenet, but a biological certitude. It will no longer be necessary nor good form to have recourse to the crudities of earlier days. On June 19, 1929, the Association of the Godless contributed to the government a new airplane which was named *The Atheist*. Its special function was described in the deed of gift — "to make war on heaven." The pilot dramatized his mission by cruising over Moscow on the lookout for God.

Now, the romancing and propagandizing, though patent and often ridiculous, is not to be minimized as a component of Communist power. The world membership of the Party was recently declared in the Moscow Press to be approximately 25,000,000. An unreflecting reader might be inclined to discount the strength of such a small fraction of the 2,300,000,000 human beings in the world. Nothing would be more dangerous or more unrealistic. Each of these registered Communists is a chosen man; he has been selected after careful examination and rigorous testing. He becomes, not a passive, individual adherent of the Party line, but an agent trained to be an active leader, the dynamo of a cell, the organizer of more malleable minds, and a local powerhouse of energy and direction for hundreds, perhaps thousands, who come within his specific circle of influence. How such fractional minorities of a population manage to exercise a radiating control over millions of non-Communists has been developed in a previous chapter. In his discussion of events in France in 1789, Lord Acton, the learned professor of history at Cambridge, put his finger on a similar phenomenon: "The appalling thing in the French Revolution is not the tumult but the design. Through all the fire and smoke we perceive the evidence of calculating organization."

The Soviet creed must be met and answered by chapter and verse of an integrated philosophy of life. But faith in democracy is not enough; there is work to be done. And the order of the tasks is determined by the character and timing of the assault.

At the present moment, the predominant, though not the exclusive menace, is the military posture, i.e., the rearmament pro-

gram, Moscow's support of Communist China, and the general
logistics of the Soviet Union's geographical expansion. It is small
consolation to have demonstrated the truth, the beauty, and the
justice of the four freedoms if we find ourselves suddenly confronted with a gigantic war machine on the march by land and
sea and air. "How many divisions has he?" was Stalin's pragmatic
answer to a reference made by President Roosevelt to the position
of the Pope on certain aspects of the world crisis. The Communist
conspirators have profited mightily from the tendency to inertia
bred of long enjoyment of freedom among men who inherit liberty
without having to bleed for it. The freedoms of democracy and
the spiritual patrimony of Christianity were all purchased at heavy
price. They have not been set up as a perpetual trust to be
administered painlessly with automatic revenue for heirs-at-law.
They must be rewon and merited by each succeeding generation.
They will not be safeguarded by alleluias unaccompanied by
vigilant defense.

First and foremost among the practicalities, the military power
of the United States must continue to be so apparent and so alert
that any aggressor will think more than twice before provoking
another devastating conflict with America. That argument of power
is quickly grasped by the one government which has based its
social philosophy on the function of force and violence in ac-
complishing the overthrow of non-Communist society. For Soviet
Russia, the value of power far outweighs the power of values.
An opponent with no adequate power behind his just claims can
only beg for, not require, respect and reciprocity from an armed
dictatorship with a Marxian conscience. Appeals to the divine
law, to international law, to Christian charity and the discipline
of the moral law left the Hegelians of Berlin untouched. They are
leaving the Hegelians of Moscow cold and unresponsive. What
brings them to respectful attention quickest is a formidable air
force in being, with adequate bases. Air power is no stronger
than the bases which serve it.

Concomitantly with military force must go a renaissance of
spiritual power in the souls of men through recognition of the
strength religion supplies to the stability of the mind. The value
of human personality, the image of divinity which man carries in

his soul, the consciousness of heritage as sons of God, the resulting obedience to the instincts of brotherhood — all coalesce to constitute a bedrock of motivation for the good life and for fulfilling the responsibilities devolving on the good citizen. That is why every totalitarian Caesar across the centuries has attacked religion on his road to conquest. He cannot bear the challenge of divided allegiance and acknowledgment of a higher law than his; by the logic of his position he must annihilate the contradiction. That is why Archbishop Stepinac is a prisoner of Tito; that is why Cardinal Mindszenty has been subjected to scientific barbarism, the Protestant pastors persecuted in Hungary and Roumania, the Archbishop of Prague threatened with similar oppression, and hundreds of missionaries martyrized in Communist China. Such uniformity of violence can only stem from the depths of a great resolve to Communize the world — or else destroy it. By fiat of Marxism the fierce energy of its collective will has set up a material divinity in the form of economic and scientific productivity to fill the vacuum created by banishment of the concept of Deity. One may speculate, possibly with apprehension, on the consequences to society if Communism retained its political, social, and economic totalitarianism but ever abandoned its atheism. Jacques Maritain raised that paradox when he expressed fear of the day when the dictator of Soviet Russia might order his people to adore God above the electron.

It is disheartening after thirty-four years of public experience with Marxian Communism as it evolved from a cabal to a world power, to hear people of intelligence and good will maintaining that the core of the conflict is economic. Normal trade conditions, they assert, industrial stabilization, and material prosperity will solve the problem, or at least tend to lessen the aggressive psychology of Soviet Russia. That such desirable achievements in the material order can strengthen resistance to the Communist program for world domination is obvious and, hence, to be cultivated at every turn. That they can cure or eliminate the basic antagonisms of a moral and spiritual character inherent to the Soviet fanaticism can be seriously maintained only by those who have never penetrated to the roots of the official Soviet philosophy of life. That philosophy cannot change so long as Soviet means

Marxian Communism. It might conceivably be temporarily discarded or modified in certain aspects if found to be unsatisfactory or not workable either within Russia or at the international level. To that extent stabilization of Europe may be contributory; but so long as class hatred, class warfare, and militant atheism characterize the Soviet mind, economics alone are not the key to world peace. The ax must be laid to the roots of the evil; it will not do to stop on the surface of things. It is not enough to point to the absence of pure Communism in Soviet Russia and call the system State Capitalism.

Peace begins in the mind and the heart. As men think and feel so will they act, individually and collectively. It is the sum total of the habits resulting from deliberate thoughts, accepted ideals, and customary conduct which creates the character both of individual citizens and of a nation. Economic stability is only a part of that frail and elusive thing called peace; what we must aim at is the whole man, for he does not live by bread alone. The *homo oeconomicus* is a myth derived from a warped and narrow conception of what constitutes the full dignity of manhood or nationhood. Man is an integrated unit and his soul cannot be departmentalized, like the shops and factories. What a fearful engine of iniquity would confront civilization if the United States, with its giant capacity in material productivity, in technological skill and military power, should suddenly be stricken with the insanity of total and militant atheism fostered by a ruthless federal government dedicated to world conquest.

The issue lies between *two moral opposites* and will not be resolved by physical power alone. Hence, to combat Soviet Russia with her own weapon will not suffice, for that leaves the roots of the evil unconquered no matter in what direction the fortunes of battle may eventually incline. Even a technical knockout or a decision on points would not mean that the West had vindicated the primacy of those inner, spiritual values which World Communism has challenged everywhere. Awareness of what is at stake and how deep the lunge at the vitals of human freedom goes is the first condition of a satisfying victory.

Half measures may bring a military stalemate — or even something that might look better to the outward eye — but not permanent liberation from the overhanging menace now haunting the soul of humanity. Worse still, uneasy compromise, or dreary appeasement, or hollow bargaining would only whet the appetite of a temporarily restrained absolutism. There would be no solid substance to the truce. External peace at any price is indeed an appealing argument in normal circumstances. But if the vital issue of the present hour remains unwon, the yearning for peace can become a seductive fallacy that could end in surrender of the supreme principle of moral survival. Though the horrors of war are ghastly, they are not the worst alternatives now confronting Western Civilization.

Mr. Arnold Toynbee, in his monumental work *A Study of History,* discusses the disintegration of twenty civilizations from the Minoan and Sumerian to the Mongol empire in China and the Tokugama Shogunate in Japan. He then puts the question: Can Western Christendom, before it is too late, regenerate itself through spiritual rebirth after having shamefully succumbed to the special temptation of neopaganism, "the intoxication of a showy victory over physical nature?" It had applied the spoils, he continues, to laying up treasures for itself without being rich toward God. It had tried to stand alone but failed. To the question of Nicodemus: Can a man enter the second time into his mother's womb and be born again? Mr. Toynbee replies in the words of Nicodemus' instructor: "Verily, I say unto thee, except a man be born of water and of the spirit he cannot enter into the Kingdom of God."

In the field of American jurisprudence one subversive tendency needs constant attention. Confined at present to a limited group of thinkers in the domain of law, it could, nevertheless, become an element of infection if not countered step by step. The legal philosophy of the late Associate Justice Oliver Wendell Holmes has acquired an undeserved respectability because of the high position of its advocate on the Supreme Court of the United States. Yet, if it were ever to become a widely accepted pattern of judicial thinking or a precedent to influence the evolution of American jurisprudence, the logical results would be disastrous both to the concept of natural right developed by Jefferson and to the traditional respect for human personality on which the liberties of the Bill of Rights repose. If wholly accepted and made

operative by an entrenched government it could lead straight to
the abhorrent totalitarianism that wrecked Germany and makes
Soviet Russia synonymous with despotism.

From certain judicial pronouncements, as well as from his
occasional addresses, published works, and from the long correspondence he conducted with Sir Frederick Pollock of England,
it is possible to draw up a series of conclusions respecting Justice
Holmes's beliefs and dogmas.

He holds, in effect, that there is no intrinsic difference between
right and wrong, good and evil. These terms, he maintains, and
the legal system that interprets them are mere historical expressions
of social habits at a given time; they correspond to the fluctuating
ideas and customs of successive generations who may find them
convenient or inconvenient for maintaining order in the market
place, but they have no roots deeper than the consent of the
majority that enacted the covering laws. Hence law is to be
squeezed dry of any moral content; truth is what the majority
thinks; law is what the majority wills; justice is what the crowd
wants; man has no natural rights antecedent to grants legally
defined and recognized by the State; humanity has no inherent
spiritual value other than as a functioning organism of unknown
destiny; man's place in the cosmos is similar to a ganglion in the
nervous system, a comparison of which Mr. Holmes is very fond.
He asserted that he saw "no reason for attributing to man a
significance different in kind from that which belongs to a baboon
or a grain of sand." In another place he writes: "And I bid myself
accept the common lot; an adequate vitality would say daily:
'God — what a good sleep I've had!' 'My eye, that was dinner!'
'Now for a rattling walk' — in short, realize life as an end in itself.
Functioning is all there is — only our keenest pleasure is in what
we might call the higher sort. I wonder if cosmically an idea is
any more important than the bowels." Force is admitted to be
the ultimate determinant of right; hence, in Mr. Holmes's philosophy, war is an admirable activity which, though horrible, carries
a "divine" message. "The students at Heidelberg with their sword-
slashed faces inspire me with supreme respect."

All this, of course, is very old wine in a modern, cut-glass
decanter scintillating with Mr. Holmes's sophisticated diction,

wide learning, and Rabelaisian imagery. At bottom and as a set of principles it is a distillation from many sources. It has something of the subjectivism of Kant, the Hedonism of Epicurus, the pragmatism of Henry James, the positivism of Comte and Austin, the instrumentalism of John Dewey, the skepticism of Descartes, the religious agnosticism of Robert Ingersoll, the callousness of Treitschke, and the animal quality of the Nazi jurisprudence that created the gas chambers and ovens for human sacrifice at Dachau and Auschwitz. Like all synthetic philosophies it snips and culls from many masters, although achieving a certain consistency — the consistent negation of anything like an absolute value. While publicly dogmatizing on the relativity of all values — except power — it publicly accepts the exception as a private absolute. Jacob Burckhardt, the noted Swiss historian, once characterized the escapist attitude later adopted by Justice Holmes as shallow and unsatisfactory. "To begin with," he declared, "not all things are necessary, not by a long way, but much is accident and personal guilt; and second, the worst verdict — namely, the approval of the *fait accompli* of success — is easily substituted for what was intended to be a suspended judgment." The moral relativism which continually avoids an absolute judgment was, for Burckhardt, a perpetual "staring into chaos."[1]

Neither time nor the scope of the present chapter permits a metaphysical rebuttal of Mr. Holmes's contradiction of Thomas Jefferson nor his flat negation of the principles on which the American system of government was founded and on which it continues to exist in a shattered world. Our direct concern is with the consequences in the practical field of social control should his philosophy become a dominating influence in American life. Happily, it should be said in passing, Mr. Holmes's official decisions and opinions as a judge were often better and sounder than his declared principles and his advertised conviction that empiricism is the only stable element in the evolution of law.

Our comments will be illustrated in the first instance by important facts revealed in the trial of the main Nazi leaders at Nuremberg, 1945–1946. Göring, Hess, Von Ribbentrop, Streicher, Rosenberg, and the other key figures of the Hitler regime made

[1] *Force and Freedom* (New York: Pantheon Books, Inc., 1943), p. 71.

one point crystal clear and in a manner that remains one of the most valuable lessons of that trial. The Nazi State with its totalitarian apparatus was erected and made to function on principles identical with the fundamental tenets of the Holmes philosophy of law. Day after day those trapped sadists poured out their justifications of tyranny and bestiality by citing the formal legitimacy of the legal enactments under which they operated: what the State decreed by positive statute became justice; what the Party thought became truth; what the dominant government willed was law, to the exclusion of all or any other human rights. The legal competency to slaughter six million Jews, shanghai and transport to Germany five million foreign workers as slave laborers for the Nazi war economy, assail the sovereignty of ten independent States and reduce half of Europe to a shambles followed smoothly from the existence of decrees duly enacted and accompanied by power to enforce them. They had the might and hence they had the right, because they banished the moral law to the museums of superstition where Justice Holmes believed it should be kept. Listening to that year-long revelation of the logical consequences of positivism in law and raw Kantian subjectivism in philosophy, no thoughtful man could fail to recognize how dehumanized the human animal can become when he follows to the bitter end Mr. Holmes's functional concept of law limited only by power of enforcement. Man did become no more important than a baboon and the corpses did become as grains of sand in the Warsaw ghetto and the gas chambers of Dachau and Auschwitz. And Göring had many a fine dinner during the saturnalia, Hitler had many a good sleep, and Rosenberg many a rattling stroll along the Philosophers' Walk at Heidelberg.

The application of similar principles has served Soviet Russia extremely well and made it the leviathan that has crushed the common instincts of humanity beneath its weight of power and filled satellite countries with phantom memories of a vanished freedom. Mr. Holmes's conception of law as a transient manifestation of social will, no moral basis allowed, is analogous to the doctrine of economic materialism already mentioned in a previous chapter. It will be remembered that one of the basic tenets taught by Marx in his *Critique of Political Economy* was the dogma that it is not consciousness or the mental processes of men that determine the social conditions of man's existence, but, on the contrary, it is the fluctuations of social environment that determine his inner life and ethical judgments. Change a word here and there and you have Mr. Holmes on law. Lenin's teaching on the nonexistence of objective morality has likewise been cited: it is exclusively a rule of conduct created by the will of the governing group as an instrument of class control and interpreted in a manner to insure the dictatorship of the proletariat. It creates its own absolute and then declares it a universal norm to which all nations must submit. In the name of a majority, whose voice is still muted, Soviet jurisprudence justifies the worst excesses of the Revolution, rationalizes the present enslavement of cowed peoples behind the Iron Curtain, and validates Moscow's organized attempts to overthrow every non-Communist State weak enough to prove vulnerable. In following Justice Holmes's philosophy of functionalism as measuring the validity of law and in putting force as the origin of rights, Lenin and his successors are strictly logical and ethical unto themselves.

It will not do to protest that the humane and liberal Justice would be horrified at the callousness of Soviet Russia as well as at the bestiality of the Nazi sadists and would probably resist both to the best of his ability. Undoubtedly so. His humaneness and native instincts would probably move him to do vigorous battle against all flagrant abuses of despotic power in the concrete. He might at times even use the language of moral law in deference to convention and circumstances. But such opposition, as we gather from several passages of his works, would be based on feelings and sentiments responsive to a case at hand; it would not flow from principles or conviction that the dignity of man must be respected. His concern would not be with inherent justice or injustice, but only with bad manners in the aggressor. It would rather be the reaction of a behaviorist resisting a player who disregarded the rules of the game. ". . . I don't see there was anything to be said [about Germany, in World War I] except: we don't like it and we shall kill you if we can." He further explains himself: "Our morality seems to me only a check on the ultimate domination of force, just as our politeness is a check on the impulse of every pig to put his feet in the trough." From such a cynical libel on the decencies of human relationships to the purely functional concept of law was an easy descent. Degradation of justice to the level of an umpire in a dogfight over a bone, with the contestants held, not to respect of rights and equities, but only to observe Marquess of Queensberry rules, is frail foundation for the erection of a rational and viable system of domestic law or international peace. It is the very definition of moral nihilism, a degeneration one step short of the ethics of the jungle. It is another melancholy example of an incomplete thinker slaying reason in the name of thought and giving point to the remark of another New Englander, James Russell Lowell: "The idol is the measure of the worshipper."

* * * *

The two primary reinforcements of security for America, the one military, the other of the spirit, will be accelerated and enhanced by a strengthening of our physical well-being as individuals and by stabilizing our domestic economy. Except for saints, it is profoundly difficult for a man to maintain a clear mind and a tranquil soul if beset and harried by the daily worries of an impoverished existence. An empty stomach has no ears, only a mouth. Hence, a robust citizenry providing sound bodies for the habitation of the soul of democracy involves continuous guardianship and development of national health; it means the minimizing of social injustices; the combating of racial and religious inequalities should they exist anywhere; co-operation, not antagonism, between capital and labor; and provision for exorcising those two specters which haunt the common man — insufficiency of income in the present, insecurity in future years when his earning capacity has vanished. Every successful effort to meet these obligations of social justice means one more nail driven into the coffin of Communism, for then the cunning lies of Moscow-trained or Moscow-duped propagandists will fall on deaf ears in America, because alien, mendacious, and superfluous.

The government of the United States is now engaged in recovering some of the ground lost in recent years and warring openly with Communism in Korea. Pitiless publicity by radio, press, and platform must accompany the activities here advocated. No opportunity should be neglected to expound the peace policy of the United States, particularly in radio broadcasts to foreign lands and to Iron Curtain listeners not by half-hour broadcasts but around the clock. Refutation of Soviet propaganda; accurate accounts of the defensive nature of the North Atlantic Pact; documented comparison between a slave economy and rational, free enterprise; catalogues of the liberties enjoyed in Western democracies under a Bill of Rights; the status of labor unions in Soviet Russia and here; comparative wage scales; the steps being taken to eliminate social and political inequalities compared with the huge numbers of political prisoners in Soviet concentration camps and in the prisons of satellite lands; the police control of Soviet citizens which requires an internal passport to move from one locality to another; the frequent purges; the recounting of that particularly barbarous oppression by the Soviet government in the annexed Baltic States of Latvia, Lithuania, and Estonia, where so many thousands of peaceful persons have been ruthlessly transported from their homeland to distant uninhabited wastes; the reasons for a high standard of living in the United States — all such affirmative rebuttal will go far to put the present world debate on a solid foundation of fact. In a word, while the conflict remains a cold war, no sector of the ideological front should be left undefended. And above all, Soviet "peace propaganda" should be unmasked and shown to be what it really is — Aesopian language contrived to induce non-Communist States to disarm themselves and make ready their neck for the sacrificial knife.

No relaxation of cordial relations should be permitted with respect to the Latin-American peoples. The solidarity of the Western Hemisphere is one of the basic conditions for the defense of the Atlantic world. The continuing freedom of the Atlantic world is the bedrock of confidence for freedom in the entire world. Weakness or disunion in the Western Hemisphere will mean weakening the cause of liberty everywhere.

The division of labor and of function which becomes necessary in our enterprise of conducting a world-wide mobilization for peace requires an active and planned diplomatic campaign.

Representation and formal negotiation by the foreign service branch of government, if integrated with American economic and financial agencies engaged in the international field, will achieve that unity of defense measures which alone can match the oneness of control vested in the Politburo. The menace of total war must be countered by total mobilization for world peace. The hotter we make the logistics of the cold war, the colder will become the probabilities of a shooting war.

The diplomatic service of the United States constitutes the primary eyes and ears of national security; its permanent character and career personnel, as contrasted with emergency agencies, guarantee not only a continuous stream of authenticated information to the State Department from all quarters of the globe, but provide a direct channel for the steady application of matured national policy at every level. In addition to matching wits with Soviet diplomacy, American diplomatic action will further strengthen a constructive peace program by daily contact with foreign opinion on every sector of international relations. A diplomatic victory has been often won at a dinner table, in a casual conversation with a Minister of Foreign Affairs or with his wife or with the head of the National Banking System. Obviously, diplomatic preparation for the planned objectives of a peace offensive presupposes a fixed American policy, which has not been in striking evidence in past years. Too late and too little, with a sporadic rushing to some point of the line where a breakthrough had already occurred, kept us in a purely defensive psychology. The bare containment of Soviet Russia within the confines of her present holdings gave place to the more positive attitude represented by the Marshall Plan, the North Atlantic Alliance, and the Point Four Program.

The validity and success of the new psychology was strikingly demonstrated in the Italian elections of April, 1948, during which American policy was advertised and openly advocated in terms of the realities of the Italian situation. It was there, at long last, that we dared to take the initiative; the issue lay not so much between Togliatti and De Gasperi as between Soviet Russia and the United States. Had Italy gone Communist on that fateful 18th of April, 1948, France, in all probability, would have been next. The mobilization of every resource of publicity, from the placards on public buildings of Rome and in the provinces to the avalanche of letters to relatives in Italy from Americans of Italian descent, was visibly reinforced by the tireless and repeated appearance of the American ambassador, Mr. Dunn, at every port, to welcome relief supplies and Marshall Plan commodities arriving in American ships. In addition to the courageous attitude of Pius XII, particularly in that eloquent address on spiritual values before 400,000 people on Easter Sunday, the concrete assurances of solidarity from official America contributed much toward convincing the Italian electorate that they would no longer be betting on a losing horse if they arrayed themselves on the side of the United States against World Communism. The valiant decision of Norway to take her stand with the western States of Europe in a North Atlantic Alliance, despite her 122 miles of frontier contiguous with Soviet territory, was another fruit of an enlightened and positive diplomatic policy. The same may be said of the results achieved at the London meeting of foreign ministers — Mr. Acheson, Mr. Bevin, and Mr. Schuman — in May, 1950, and more recently in September, 1950, at New York.

It is far from being sterile speculation to reconstruct the possible evolution of events had the firmer and more informed posture of 1950 been adopted sooner in negotiations with Soviet Russia. Franklin Delano Roosevelt entered on the momentous wartime conferences at Yalta and Tehran with heavy odds against him, not only because of the pressing nature of the problems on the table, but because of certain qualities inherent in his character, and in his psychological make-up.

The diplomatic history of that crowded period and of subsequent years emphasizes again the wisdom of the observations made by that seasoned negotiator, Mr. Harold Nicholson, in his thoughtful little book on *Diplomacy*. If diplomacy is the art of the possible, it is not less a process of negotiation involving mutuality, reciprocal obligations, and the recording of agreements in carefully worded documents. Whenever it stops short of precision and relies on loosely worded guarantees, secret promises, or unilateral agreements, the way is open for fatal misunderstanding, deliberate misinterpretations, and slippery evasions of the given word. The personal conference method, unless supplemented by precise protocols and clear-cut obligations on a reciprocal basis, opens the way for dangerous improvisations and the play of volatile personal characteristics. Charm is no substitute for the long spoon one needs when dining with disciples of Machiavelli and Karl Marx.

Mr. Roosevelt's title to a ranking place in the roster of American presidents will rest more securely on remembrance of other services to his people in great domestic crises and international emergencies than on his highly personalized conduct of Soviet-American relations, whether in peace or in war. The elements compounded in his nature created violent antagonisms, such as those revealed in Mr. Flynn's indictment, *The Roosevelt Myth,* and Professor Beard's Prosecuting Attorney's brief, *President Roosevelt and the Coming of the War.* Against the almost total blackness of these summations stands the enthusiastic admiration and devotion of the school which has elevated the Roosevelt personality to the dimensions of a cult similar to the quasi-idolatry indulged in by some hero worshipers of Justice Holmes. The judgment of history will seek to establish balance between such extremes.

Even the closest and best-informed intimates of Franklin Delano Roosevelt have not minimized the defects of character in their President which, because of the time and the circumstances of their elevation to international significance, had a distinct and probably permanent influence on the destiny of millions upon millions of human beings. Thus Mr. Morgenthau records in his diary, portions of which have been made public, that the President often came to vital decisions on "hunches" and trivialities. Professor Arthur M. Schlesinger, Jr., though by and large defending Mr. Roosevelt's Russian policy, concedes that "Yalta represented the downfall of Rooseveltian pragmatism." He correctly concludes that the President miscalculated his Soviet opponents.[2] Mr. Adolph Berle, an important official in the inner Roosevelt circle during a long period, also concedes that the Yalta Conference "was a failure with tragic consequences."[3] But he is not so close to the facts when he inclines to John Gunther's version that Mr. Roosevelt,

[2] Roosevelt and His Detractors," *Harper's Magazine,* June, 1950.
[3] *New York Times,* Book Review, June 4, 1950.

on military advice, underestimated the strength of the American position and so was outtraded. A full-length portrait including Mr. Roosevelt's earlier and total attitude in dealing with Soviet negotiators requires some additional lines of character: it was not only underestimation of the logistics of the situation at that moment but his recurring overestimate of his own powers of persuasion as a good horse trader that betrayed the President into the fateful appeasement of Stalin.

Mr. Robert Sherwood in his exhaustive and documented study, *Roosevelt and Hopkins,* comments on the "complex mind" and "heavily forested interior" of his chief. He likewise reports the Roosevelt habit of dodging immediate issues "by maneuvering the conversation into the realms of irrelevancy." Mr. Sherwood frankly paints into his portrait the obstinacy of Mr. Roosevelt's belief in his personal capacity to surmount obstacles "which would have held other men earth-bound." He is frank to recognize the deterioration in the President's physical condition at Tehran, as well as the evil consequences of the secret agreements with Stalin at Yalta regarding the increased number of votes Soviet Russia would have in the forthcoming United Nations. Mr. Sherwood, certainly not a Roosevelt hater but one of the President's most trusted advisers, describes this concession as "one of the worst all-round botches of the war." Another secret pledge to Stalin — that Soviet demands in the Far East would be unquestionably fulfilled after the defeat of Japan — is qualified by Mr. Sherwood as "the most assailable point in the entire Yalta record."

After Tehran, Mr. Sherwood points out, President Roosevelt was confident that the Soviets would prove tractable and co-operative; he felt sure that Stalin was "getatable."[4] Similarly, the secret commitment to Stalin regarding Soviet claims in China were based on Mr. Roosevelt's belief in his own powers of persuasion. "I believe," writes Mr. Sherwood, "that he was hopeful that when the time came to notify the Chinese, he would be able to straighten the whole thing out with Chiang Kai-shek, but the hope, of course, was not realized."

No man served President Roosevelt more faithfully and in more diversified capacities than former Secretary of State, James F.

---

[4] *Op. cit.,* pp. 798–799.

Byrnes. Describing the course of events in his memoirs, *Speaking Frankly*, he considers Yalta as the high-water mark in the tide of Soviet-American relations. "But President Roosevelt," he writes, "had barely returned to American soil when the tide began to ebb." Mr. Byrnes further indicates in his text that foreboding and disillusionment weighed heavily on the President in his final hours. This is confirmed by a cablegram to Churchill from Roosevelt shortly before the fatal seizure at Warm Springs. We shall never know how much the realization of the renewed hostility of Soviet Russia may have saddened his soul and contributed psychologically to the final tragedy of sudden death.

We now have additional testimony of the unreality which so often appeared in the thinking of a man otherwise gifted with unusual political foresight. In September, 1939, President Roosevelt was visited by the then Chinese ambassador, Hu Shih. Disturbed and worried by the outbreak of a new war in Europe and the continuance of hostilities between China and Japan, the President explained to the Ambassador that he believed he had found a solution for effecting peace in the Far East. As Manchuria was the main obstacle, he believed he had found a workable formula which would settle the case. As mediator he would invite both belligerents to accept an agreement similar to the plan recently worked out between the United States and Great Britain to last for 50 years respecting Anglo-American interests and joint control of two disputed islands in the Pacific, Canton and Enderbury. Such an arrangement, he thought, could be applied for the joint benefit and security of China and Japan in Manchuria.

Not familiar with the dimensions of those two coral islands south of the Equator, the scholarly Ambassador did some quick research. He found that Canton Island was 9 miles long, 500 yards wide at maximum, with a population of 40 persons. Enderbury was 3 miles long by 1 mile wide with 4 persons living on it. He could have added that the entire Phoenix group of islands, of which Canton and Enderbury form a part, have a combined area of some 16 square miles. "Manchuria, of course," he writes,[5]

---

[5] "China in Stalin's Grand Strategy," by Hu Shih, *Foreign Affairs*, October, 1950, pp. 38–40.

"has a population of 33,000,000 and an area of about 413,000 square miles."

Hu Shih ends his account with an expression of undiminished respect for the generous idealism of a great humanitarian. But he cannot escape the conviction that this favorite Canton-Enderbury precedent played a definite role in Mr. Roosevelt's handling of the Chinese problem at Yalta. He further states that history will not forgive Stalin for deliberately deceiving and blackmailing the President.

Analysis of the human elements in this record confirms what Aristotle meant by his observation that great men come to disaster through some weakness of psychological structure, by some defect which, at the same time, appears to them to be a factor of great strength. Men, like trees, fall on their leaning side. With no intimation here of failure in other policies, and with no blanket endorsement of the bitter criticism leveled at the late President by undiscriminating critics, one cannot escape the relevancy of Aristotle's dictum in respect to Mr. Roosevelt's Russian policy, which is the sole and exclusive object of the present inquiry.

His capacity for leadership and daring initiative proved a welcome asset for the country when we were confronted with the crisis of the great depression of the thirties and the challenge of December 7, 1941. But overconfidence was an unjustified and dangerous attitude when transferred to the international arena where he was to encounter a wholly different breed of men. His opponents there were no longer a minority of Republicans in Congress who, though dissidents, were still Americans with the tradition of democracy, the responsibilities of freedom, and the discipline of Christian principles bred into the marrow of their thought. He was no longer dueling with the National Association of Manufacturers or with chivalrous individual opponents such as Al Smith and Wendell Willkie. The President's opening remarks at the Tehran conference, in which he welcomed the Russians as "new members of the family circle," did much credit to his amiability and love of domesticity, but were small tribute to his comprehension of Communist psychology, if he really meant what he said. The historian, however, must take the record as he finds it and learn what is there to be learned.

It has been argued that it was no time for cautious diplomacy or conventional bargaining. President Roosevelt and his advisers may have had good reason to fear that Soviet Russia was an unstable ally and might have gone over to the Nazis as she had done once before. Such a catastrophe would have thrown her immense weight into the balance against the United States at a moment when such a new alignment of power might well have changed the whole course of the war. Hence, it was the moment for quick, unqualified strengthening of a new ally against Germany and Japan. So be it. The argument is tenable and commands a measure of respect. Candor, however, and the gravity of the consequences, require objective exploration of the circumstances.

Yalta, it is admitted by Mr. Roosevelt's friends and supporters, was a calculated gamble that failed. In extenuation it must be remembered that the precedents there set of conceding the maximum to Soviet Russia had the approval and recommendation of the President's military advisers. But it was a gamble, others insist, that should not have omitted certain prudent reservations and more cautious playing of high cards. The basic power position of the United States, the flow of Lend-Lease supplies, and the still unimpaired resources of America for disposal in the postwar period warranted clearer, firmer, and enforceable guarantees of reciprocity from Soviet Russia respecting her obligations in the reconstruction of Europe. The assumption that the bully had become a welfare worker was an amazingly naïve conclusion for men who had demonstrated such exceptional skill in the human relationships and hazards of domestic politics since 1932 and achieved the unprecedented record of persuading an intelligent electorate to retain Franklin Delano Roosevelt as President of the United States for four terms.[6] They hurdled the most formidable obstacle in American political history, only to see their President come a cropper before an obscure revolutionary from Georgia whom Trotsky once described as the outstanding mediocrity of the Russian Communist Party. The nature of Stalin's probable

---

[6] No longer possible in consequence of the constitutional prohibition recently accepted by the required majority of states.

maneuvers in the hour of allied victory were inherent in the historical premises and should have been forever in the consciousness of responsible negotiators.

The misplaced confidence of Mr. Roosevelt did not begin at Yalta nor was it the result of the new optimism which flourished during the strange but necessary alliance with Moscow from 1942 to 1945. It was not due to the prevailing climate of enthusiasm for Soviet Russia as an ally against Hitler. It was not due to the pressure of events nor the concurrence of Mr. Churchill. Its case history goes farther back than that. It is spread on the record as a political and moral miscalculation as old as the policy of appeasement and credulity that began with the recognition of Soviet Russia in 1933.

However valid and persuasive Mr. Roosevelt's pragmatism toward Soviet Russia may have seemed during the uncertain and tense crises of war when quick decision was imperative and bold risks had to be taken, it still remains a lamentable improvisation to have committed so much destiny for so long to a negotiator so little acquainted with the special complexities of Russian history, Russian mentality, and Soviet dialectics as was Mr. Harry Hopkins. Again, a distinction must be made. The total record of Mr. Hopkins and the controversies arising from his special role among the President's intimates and counselors are not under examination at this point. We are concerned with a limited and specified area of his activities, the Russian phase.

The deficiencies in psychological preparation for such a supreme role are revealed in the official Hopkins report of his last special mission to Moscow in May, 1945, after the death of President Roosevelt. The text covers nearly sixteen pages of Mr. Sherwood's book and runs to something over 8000 words. This record of the intimate conversations with Stalin at a moment when the pattern of the future was being formed are indeed revealing. Mr. Hopkins' analysis of the rapid deterioration in Soviet-American relations since the collapse of National Socialism is accurate enough but not his understanding of the underlying causes. He seemed to have no appreciation of the ultimate objectives of Moscow: hence he complains to Stalin that friends of the Soviet Union were experiencing "a sense of bewilderment . . . could not understand why. . . ." Nothing in the text indicates that Mr. Hopkins realized the complete change that had taken place in the contemporary Soviet tactics, now that the elimination of Hitler had cleared the way for Soviet Russia's return to the permanent aggressive strategy inherent in the nature of the Russian Revolution. And Stalin, unperceived by Mr. Hopkins, discarded the temporary role of Russian patriot and reverted to the belligerent universalism of Marxian Communism. Nothing basic was changed, only a cloak was dropped.

The progressive stages in the Hopkins-Stalin conversations constitute a classic example of the manner in which Soviet dialectics can confuse basic issues and hide the Marxist objective by weaving a complicated web of minor issues around the central problem. We had new specimens of the ancient formula from Mr. Malik in the Security Council of the United Nations during August, 1950. Despite his energy and zeal for a specific argument then as in negotiations of earlier years, Mr. Hopkins was put on the defense from the start. He was forced to discuss the admission of the Argentine to the United Nations, defend the personnel of the new Reparations Commission, explain the attitude of the United States toward the Polish question, the curtailment of Lend Lease, the surrender of the German fleet, etc., etc. All these were alleged by Mr. Stalin as proof of American default. Mr. Hopkins gave a satisfactory answer to the great bulk of organized objections and Mr. Stalin admitted in most cases that the explanations were true and understandable. Nevertheless, Soviet policy continued to run counter to what Mr. Hopkins concluded was a meeting of minds, a sequence not unknown to experienced negotiators with the chameleon of the Steppes.

In his report to the State Department and to President Truman, Mr. Hopkins — himself a sick and dying man — accepted at face value Mr. Stalin's assurances that nothing would be done to weaken the leadership or unified policy of Chiang Kai-shek in China, that Soviet Russia had no territorial claims against China, that he agreed with America's "Open Door" Policy in China, etc., etc. Mr. Hopkins ends this section of his report with the comment: "We were very encouraged by the conference on the Far East."

With respect to Poland, Mr. Hopkins made damaging concessions, particularly in the light of President Roosevelt's late discovery: "The Russians do not use words for the same purpose that we do." Mr. Hopkins agreed that Poland should have a government "friendly" to the Soviet Union; apparently he was in blissful ignorance as to what that word "friendly" means to the anaconda appetite of the Politburo. He likewise declared to Stalin that "the question of Poland *per se* was not so important as the fact that it had become a symbol of our ability to work out problems with the Soviet Union." Subsequent events showed how tragically Mr. Hopkins was deceived on both counts. Poland was the first major casualty in an important series of enslaved peoples, which is an important fact *per se*. The symbolism of Poland as an index of success or failure in reciprocal understanding with Soviet Russia was laconically described in that unprecedented rebuke administered by President Truman to the first Sovietized Polish ambassador, on February 4, 1947. Recalling the pledge to guarantee free elections, Mr. Truman asserted: "It is cause of deep concern to me and to the American people that the Polish Provisional Government has failed to fulfill that pledge."

All this, to be sure, is water over the dam. So is all history, recent or remote. The value of hindsight consists in its contribution to foresight applied to new situations, particularly to the American position in 1951. History in its finest form is something more meaningful than a bare narrative of human events accurately assembled and verified under canons of scientific research. Thucydides, the father of interpretative history, has a celebrated passage on that quality of historical writing: ". . . but whoever shall wish to have a clear view both of the events which have happened and those which will some day, in all human probability, happen again in the same or similar way — for these to adjudge my history useful will be enough for me. And indeed it has been composed, not as a prize-essay to be heard for the moment, but as a possession for all time."[7]

The norm may well be applied to the facts of record in Soviet-American relations. Although the historical mind as such is not required to prophesy or philosophize from cause to effect, the facts

---

[7] Thucydides, *History of the Peloponnesian War*, Chapter 22.

of history may do both — unless they are read out of curiosity or for entertainment in leisure hours. A thoughtful man, looking into the depths of the vast mirror which historians hold up for contemplation of the past, will see what mankind has done, which means what he as man of the same clay is capable of doing under similar circumstances. He will profit by the procession of avoidable errors and unnecessary tragedies, leaving denunciation and partisanship to the pamphleteers. But a mirror is intended for seeing men. It is useless to a blind man.

CHAPTER X

The United Nations and the Revolution

FOR over six months before the outbreak of hostilities in Korea, the chair of Soviet Russia in the Security Council of the United Nations had been vacant. That symbol of veto by nonparticipation in the work of the organization clarified, as little else has done up to that date, the basic paradox of a promoter of World Revolution sitting permanently with power of obstruction on the board of directors of an institution dedicated to world peace through mutual understanding and enforcement of international law. The great attempt to conciliate great opposites and make the inflammable oil of class warfare blend harmoniously with the waters of reconciliation reached its most revealing stage during the crisis precipitated by the invasion of South Korea in June, 1950, by one of the affiliates of World Revolution. The return of Mr. Malik on August 1, followed by his month-long filibuster, served at least one extremely useful purpose. It brought into the open the latent contradiction between Soviet Russia's public pretensions to be considered an advocate of peace, and her patent conspiracy to organize and support aggressive conflict whenever and wherever the cause of World Communism can be advanced. Television of Mr. Malik's efforts to sabotage the work of the Security Council brought the hard facts into American homes with a force not previously experienced.

By reason of its postwar strategy Soviet Russia has come in

closer geographic contact with the West than ever before, far closer than imperial Russia penetrated, or desired to come. The new provinces of the Communist empire have acquired a double importance: first, geopolitically, as buffer states, and, second, as inviting areas for propagating the evangel of Marxism. The urge to spread Communism outward from each satellite State stems from a messianic consciousness characteristic of political religiosity in its youthful stage. The older counterpart of Christianity, Mohammedanism, passed through the same exaltation during the age of its missionary advance by fire and sword into the heart of the Christian West; but, now, much older than Marxian Communism and less virile, Islam has learned how to coexist with non-Muslim peoples in adult tranquillity. Of the other historic religions of the East, Confucianism has not been a crusading faith but rather a code of morals, philosophic behavior, and good manners. Buddhism is a contemplative faith, a search for the Nirvana of personal repose and liberation from conflict. Shintoism was as much an expression of Japanese nationalism as it was a religion, its main tenets being: obey the emperor, follow the inspiration of your heart, and venerate ancestors and heroes. Shorn of its political character by the defeat of Japan, it now occupies a reduced position in Japanese civic life. Hinduism, with its multiplicity of sects, is a distinctly national growth of India and shows no aggressive tendency to propagate its beliefs on a world-wide scale. Judaism, until lately and since the destruction of the Temple, has been in exile and on the defensive. Communism alone retains the vehemence of its adolescence.

Though entering into the United Nations' organization, Moscow never renounced its exclusiveness and sense of overpowering destiny. The very universalism which the Council and the Assembly embodied in their members was a latent challenge to the particularism of the Soviet creed and the universalism of its revolutionary dogmas. Hence, its every maneuver and veto was parry or thrust in a duel which, at bottom, is as much theological and philosophic as political and economic. The Kremlin's god is not the God of Christianity or Mohammedanism or Hinduism or Judaism or Confucianism, but a scientific deity created by Marx, Engels, and Lenin. Hence the Soviet mind, now committed to Mr. Stalin's trusteeship, always considered itself as a segment of the elect quartered among the heathens of Lake Success, a beleaguered outpost of the Revolution that must stay always on the alert against the Philistines. This inner persuasion of special assignment to a dangerous mission manifested itself in the private life of Soviet delegates and their families whose isolation and secluded home life in New York created social barriers against contact with the nonelect. The same atmosphere of suspicion and defensive aloofness enveloped Soviet delegations in occupied Germany and Japan. Even when fraternizing with us (on rare occasions), they gave the impression of uneasy men living in enemy territory, but armed to the teeth and waiting for some prearranged signal from their Muscovite Mecca. There was always a member of the Soviet Secret Police circulating among the guests and keeping a vigilant eye on his sheep, lest they become too cordial or comradely with the bourgeois Americans. It was not uncommon for us to see this guardian of Marxist tribalism tap even some high-ranking Soviet general on the shoulder at any moment and whisper that it was time to leave.

The dilemma which the Politburo faced in consequence of President Truman's historic decision to come to the assistance of the stricken Republic of Korea was solved — to their own satisfaction — in the usual way. The Kremlin refused the invitation, promptly dispatched from Washington, to use Soviet influence and the Soviet position in North Korea to force the invaders to withdraw to their proper place north of the 38th parallel. The Communist-controlled and Moscow-trained North Koreans ignored the United Nations' order to cease firing and observe the common agreement of humanity respecting a pacific solution of international conflicts, a charter and a pact to which Soviet Russia was a signatory. The action of the United Nations' Council against the evident breach of peace was likewise repudiated by the Kremlin as being null, void, and illegal since Soviet Russia was absent from the session at which the vote was taken. Then, as the only alternative, though a logical one in the Marxist premises, the government-controlled press and radio of Russia deluged the land and the airways with fantastic distortions of truth. The people of Russia, bereft of all sources of independent news and helpless prisoners of the Politburo, were made to believe that the invasion had been launched by South Korea under the auspices of American warmongers and that the military measures taken by North Koreans constituted, in reality, a heroic counterattack in defense of peace and outraged liberty.

Mr. Malik, on his return to the United Nations, used his position as presiding officer of the Security Council to repeat the stereotypes. Mr. Vyshinski continued the set pattern as soon as the Assembly convened in September. General Wu, on arriving at the United Nations to represent Communist China repeated the formula down to identical phrases and abusive epithets. It was noted that the Chinese delegation was met at the airport by the Soviet representatives in the United Nations. The first words spoken by General Wu on American soil were read from a prepared text handed to him by Mr. Malik as soon as the Chinese had stepped from the airplane.

How complete this mastery of public opinion has become inside Russia may be realized by recalling the domination over schools, public gatherings, the press, literature, art, science, radio, film industry, theater, and Orthodox Church by the Communist dictatorship. Broadcasts from the United Nations and programs of "The Voice of America" encounter two barriers. It has been estimated that in 1947 only 18 per cent of all radios in Russia were in the form of private sets, with no available data on the proportion of short-wave instruments capable of receiving foreign broadcasts, even if such programs could survive the powerful "jamming" technique of governmental stations. The Soviet information, on the contrary, is blasted into every community by "wired speakers" which are said to be set up in public places in numbers exceeding six million. Hence no uncensored communication can reach the great masses of common folk.[1]

With Soviet logicality and in conformity with the Marxist

---

[1] These and similar controls are well set forth in *Public Opinion in Soviet Russia* by Alex Inkeles (Harvard University Press, 1950). The distortion of truth systematically broadcast to the Russian people and the hatred of the United States officially inculcated by Soviet policy are also described in the documented report of a seasoned observer who resided in Moscow from 1942–1947: *The Soviet Image of the United States*, by Frederick Barghoorn (New York: Harcourt, Brace & Co., 1950).

monopoly of truth, Mr. Gromyko, Deputy Foreign Minister of the U.S.S.R., transmitted to the Security Council of the United Nations on July 4 an abusive indictment of the United States which demanded the immediate withdrawal of American armed forces from Korea. The cue was followed by the *Literary Gazette*, one of the many mouthpieces used by the Politburo, which described the Security Council as a body of "bloody fools" and ridiculed the entire United Nations as lap dogs led on a leash by Mr. Truman. The General Secretary, Mr. Lie, who shortly before had visited Moscow on a peace mission, was denounced with scurrility as a coward and a stooge of Wall Street who had fallen to the level of "an abettor of American aggression."

The immediate mobilization of public opinion throughout the world, the endorsement of the positive policy of the United States by 52 of the 59 members of the United Nations and the promise of military support by several powers, sent a new wave of optimism through the corridors at Lake Success where gloom and pessimism as to the future of the organization had lately prevailed. On July 14 Trygve Lie, on behalf of the United Nations, appealed to the 52 supporting governments to provide combat troops, particularly ground forces. Korea had become the supreme test and if the United Nations survived the challenge there would be less danger of the frustration and disintegration which ruined its predecessor on the shores of the lake at Geneva.

Mr. Churchill's moving phrase about England's finest hour seemed to have found its fellow in the vocabulary of the times. Mr. Truman's prompt decision may well go into history as marking America's day of greatness. One must not only be right respecting alternatives; he must be right at the right moment. One can be wholly right but at the wrong moment which, in the unpredictable flux of human relationships, could turn out to be as dangerous as being wrong at the right moment. The stunning reverses suffered by United Nations' forces under the massive onslaught of the Chinese invasion of Korea precipitated wide debate as to the wisdom of Mr. Truman's original decision. Although a great battle was lost, a crucial campaign was won. The mental fog and indecision so long obscuring the minds of too many Americans was at long last dissipated. But indecision of policy again seemed to paralyze the Security Council. The order to the Chinese Communist government to cease firing and withdraw beyond the 38th parallel was ignored; the defiance provoked divided counsel and procrastination in the United Nations, wholly at variance with the prompt measures taken in June, 1950, against the aggression of North Korea.

It is too early, at the present writing, to predict the ultimate resolution of the crisis. But it is not too early — on the contrary, it is high time — to examine with frankness and realism the prospects of world peace under the present constitution of the United Nations. And such an examination of conscience would not be complete without considering the defects and weaknesses of the previous League of Nations, as the present organization is a lineal descendant of the old and embodied much of its philosophy, internal structure, and public procedure.

If collective security is ever to be realized in a world shrunken and consolidated by modern inventions, by instantaneous communication and swift transportation, the new police power must be clothed with real sanctions quickly available, not left to become the pawn of international rivalries and not subject to the whim of any one member of the Council. These deficiencies were among the fatal defects of the first organization. It is historically incorrect, and unjust as well, to lay responsibility for the failure of the League of Nations so heavily on the conscience of the United States. Nonparticipation by this country was not due to a partisan conspiracy hatched by Henry Cabot Lodge but to the inherent dishonesty of the League's structure. It was not a league of co-operating States but a holding company organized by five great powers to maintain a definite *status quo* and balance of power favorable to the senior partners. When an agency of equitable representation and practical democracy had been devised, it was felt that it would merit the popular approval denied its ineffective predecessor. The frightful ordeal of World War II and the bitter experience acquired across the past five years supplied the education and psychological preparation so conspicuously absent from the previous experiment. Both these elements are indispensable to bring men to the acceptance of that sacrifice and reciprocal confidence which are the invisible cement required in constructing any workable international agreement.

The League of 1919, even if it had been more perfect structurally, was premature. It sought to by-pass too many historical and psychological realities. Public opinion throughout the world was not prepared, either by understanding or moral fraternity, to scrap abruptly the habits of sovereignty and nationalism which had been so widely cultivated since the Congress of Westphalia in 1648, systematized by Bodin in 1576, and reaffirmed by the Congress of Vienna in 1815. There were also undercurrents of thinly disguised hatred in the instrument of 1919. Bad psychology attended its birth. While admirable in expressed ideals and daring in their vision of a humanity emancipated from the ancient fears and shibboleths of war, its advocates were unrealistic in their estimate of the time element; they were impatient at the slow, laborious processes of education required to convince the world of a new and daring revolutionary idea.

Twenty years would not have been too many for adequate preparation. Political wisdom comes by experience; it is a birth, not an instantaneous creation, and is accompanied by the pangs attending all birth. Men are born in another's pain and die in their own. Ideas run the same gamut. It is an amateur and futile pedagogy which berates men for not straightway accepting untried assurances. No competent educator, and surely no compassionate student of human nature, will wax wrathful and sarcastic at a humanity whose intellect and emotions have been submitted to the outrages of categoric imperatives and scientific arrogance for so many generations. No. He will roll up his sleeves and continue his pedagogy, having incurred the primeval curse of learning the hard way. It has taken Christianity nearly two thousand years to evangelize approximately one third of the human race — and the issue at stake was far more important than the League of Nations.

To what extent did the United Nations profit by the experience of the past and avoid the pitfalls revealed by the record of the old League? A dispassionate comparison chapter by chapter and verse by verse would show a mixed balance of success and failure at Geneva, the successes mainly achieved in relatively minor issues involving smaller States and collateral welfare activities, the

failures arising from inability or unwillingness to deal courageously
with the challenge presented by great powers intent on aggression.
The League foundered on the rocks created by the rise of Fascism
under Mussolini, by Japan in Manchuria, by the aggressiveness
of Hitler's National Socialism, and the problems created by the
Spanish Civil War. The atmosphere of frustration was further
clouded by the lack of any military sanction available for the
enforcement of decisions — if, indeed the League had ever
screwed its courage up to the sticking point. The flag of the
United Nations flying side by side with the colors of the United
States in Korea marked a decisive step in the evolution of collective security.

Since it is Soviet Russia's relationship to the non-Communist
world which is engaging our attention in the present chapter,
her short membership in the League must be recalled, though
summarily. At the outset Moscow denounced the Geneva organization as a den of thieves, an assembly of brigands, and a bourgeois
iniquity similar to National Socialism. But as it was with the
Nazis, so was it with the League. Conscious of the growing
menace of Japan in Manchuria, the commissars turned complete
somersault and joined the League of Nations in 1934 only to
become such a thorn in its flesh that Russia's membership was
canceled and her delegates expelled in 1939. The wanton invasion
of Finland was an obvious breach of international peace. Hence
the reasons for the expulsion were not trivial nor ephemeral nor
purely administrative. They were inherent to her revolutionary
character as a force hostile to the very purpose for which the
League was founded.

The Assembly had already been warned of the inevitable by
Dr. Joseph Motta, Chief of the Swiss delegation, on the very
day of Soviet Russia's admission, September 18, 1934. Voting
against the adventure, the spokesman for Switzerland declared:
"From the point of view of sound international relations and the
indispensable principles of life that govern those relations, the
essential and outstanding feature of Russian Communism is its
invincible, inevitable, irrepressible tendency to secure universal
domination. Sovietism of its very nature scatters its seeds to the
four heavens. Of set purpose it aims to bring about world Revolu-

tion." Replying to the argument that Russia's presence in the League and closer contact with the West would have a beneficial effect by tending to facilitate a gradual evolution in Soviet psychology and policy which would help to eliminate the danger of future wars, the farsighted Dr. Motta replied: "We are unable to put one scintilla of faith in such a view. . . . The Swiss have no confidence in the unnatural union of fire and water." But the voice of prophetic realism was lost in the chorus of opportunism and appeasement. The League welcomed the Russian delegation, soon came to know them, then expelled them — and itself expired soon after.

The next appearance of the Revolution in a resurrected society of nations in 1945 was accompanied by a generous wiping out of the previous record and a spirited show of enlarged expectations. Not only was the Soviet Union welcomed with high optimism and without reservation at San Francisco, but a grant of special privilege was made in the form of three votes whereas every other member nation was limited to one. The sequel is contemporaneous history. By midsummer of 1950 — in five years — the Revolution had so multiplied its veto in the Council and maneuvered its satellites in the Assembly that the United Nations was reduced to a state of paralysis and coma from which it was rescued only by the prompt action of President Truman in pledging the influence and resources of the United States to the defense of the Republic of Korea against the Soviet-supported Communist invasion from the North. It was compensation full and overflowing for the absence of the United States from the first League. This dramatic assertion of a resolve to meet the obligations of membership in the present United Nations and the carefully executed procedure of working in accordance with its charter furnished a welcome demonstration of loyalty to the concept of collective security and vindicated the rule of law over the unilateral dictates of aggressive power. It cleared a murky atmosphere. But while it postponed, it by no means solved the underlying paradox created by the continuing presence of a revolutionary force dedicated to class warfare in the Security Council and Assembly of a peace organization. The record of five turbulent years of cold war culminating in hot warfare clearly demonstrates how futile were the hopes of those who believed in the gradual evolution of World Communism into a partner who could be trusted. Dr. Motta's prophecy was justified and his foresight proved to be entirely accurate.

The course of events since 1945 reveals how obstinately and consistently the Kremlin adheres to Lenin's doctrine of embracing parliamentary institutions in order to dominate them, or, domination failing, to destroy them. This Machiavellian policy is developed in Lenin's celebrated treatise: *Left Wing Communism, An Infantile Disorder*. German Communists had raised the question: Should we participate in bourgeois parliaments? Their reply was negative, on the grounds that such institutions were "historically and politically obsolete." Lenin rebuked them with withering sarcasm for their error and for their absurd pretentiousness in mistaking their subjective desires for objective reality. Parliaments, Congresses, Chambers of Deputies, Senates, popular elections, and the whole political apparatus of the bourgeois world *exist;* hence, he concludes, ". . . you must work inside them . . . otherwise you run the risk of becoming mere babblers. . . . The conclusion which follows from this is absolutely incontrovertible: it has been proved that participation in a bourgeois-democratic parliament even a few weeks before the victory of a Soviet republic and even after that victory, not only does no harm to the revolutionary proletariat, but actually makes it easier for it to *prove* to the backward masses why such parliaments deserve to be dispersed; it *facilitates* success in dispersing them, and *facilitates* the process whereby bourgeois parliamentarism becomes 'politically obsolete.' To refuse to take this experience into account and at the same time to claim affiliation to the Communist *International*, which must work out its tactics *internationally* (not narrow or one-sided national tactics, but international tactics), is to commit the greatest blunder and actually to retreat from internationalism in deeds while accepting it in words." The italics are all Lenin's.

In view of this declared intent and in the face of facts developing over the years in consonance with such established principles culminating in the Korean War, he who still clings to the hope of converting World Communism to harmonious co-operation with the United Nations is a hopeless sciolist and, if a statesman, he is a reckless and dangerous leader. He will end in the frustration which engulfed Mr. Beneš and Mr. Masaryk and made Czechoslovakia a house of bondage.

Whatever final consequence emerges from the war in Korea, one conclusion seems inescapable. If successful there, the Russian Revolution would have gone far toward destroying the United Nations. That would usher in an unpredictable period of interstatal anarchy for an exhausted humanity newly disillusioned. It would mean a return to the ice age of international relations and the triumph of totalitarianism. It would mean another long step on the road to the vision of the world in flames which Zinoviev, then head of the Third International, pictured to the visiting Asiatics at the Congress of the Peoples of the East held at Baku in September, 1920:

> The real revolution will blaze up when the 800,000,000 people who live in Asia unite with us . . . when we see the hundreds of millions of people in revolt. Now we must kindle a holy war. . . .

If checked after Korea, the Revolution will assuredly strike again, directly or indirectly, on some other sector of its extended battle front and at a moment of its own choosing. It can never consent to become a nonpracticing World Revolution. At best, its managers may accept a prorogated truce — until a safe opportunity to strike presents itself.

Its tactics, however, are calculated to keep the heart and the central military force of the Revolution uncommitted to direct conflict. The risks and the wearing-down process are left to others. By stimulating class warfare on the periphery of the bourgeois world, now here, now there, now in Burma, now in Malaya, now in Iran, now in Indochina or Greece or Turkey or Italy, it will force the United States to be forever committed to the piecemeal defense of democracy on an expanding global front without conceivably ever meeting the real enemy face to face except in the form of bootlegged Russian tanks, Soviet-made planes, and disguised Soviet personnel. This exhausting process of attrition can continue without the stronghold of the conspiracy ever experiencing direct assault, while the cost in men, money, and supplies will become a permanent and heavy charge on our national economy.

Moscow, on the other hand, can husband its unspent forces against the hoped-for day of complete exhaustion on the part of the United States, which will be expected to bear the lion's share of global defense. Should the lion falter or sustain a crippling wound, the Politburo will recognize the moment and send its horde across the moat already provided by its expendable satellites for the final encounter with the West. Japan will be a prime target. The Philippines, bound to the United States by many ties, will be in mortal danger; and it is not outside the possibilities that Soviet Russia will one day claim Alaska as rightful Russian land and attempt to repossess it, declaring the sale of that territory by the tzarist government in 1867 to have been a null-and-void betrayal of Russian interest by the Romanov dynasty.

The rule-or-ruin psychology was again manifested in late October, 1950, on the occasion of the debates in the United Nations on the reappointment of Mr. Trygve Lie as Secretary-General. Despite the obstinate attempts of the Soviet bloc to repudiate Mr. Lie, because of his performance of duty during the crisis over Korea, the Assembly voted to re-appoint. Whereupon Mr. Vyshinski announced that the Soviet delegation would have nothing to do with the Secretary-General and would ignore the decision of the majority. On November 1, an attempt was made by two gunmen to assassinate the President of the United States in Blair House. Two men were killed and several wounded. Telegrams of sympathy and congratulations on his escape reached Mr. Truman from virtually all major foreign powers — except from the Kremlin.

Mr. Henry L. Stimson, long an advocate of conciliation with Moscow, finally, though reluctantly, came to the only tenable conclusion open either to intelligence or charity. There can be no lasting settlement, he wrote in 1947, until the men in the Kremlin "either change their minds or lose their jobs." At the present moment there is no sign of either miracle. And should one be announced, the players in this prolonged game of global geopolitics must keep a sharp eye on the prestidigitator as he shuffles the elusive pea back and forth among the walnut shells. He is an old hand at it. And there always lurks in the offing another explosive possibility. Good faith and reciprocated confidence are, we repeat, the cement which makes the diverse human elements cohere within the structure of international relations. Because of the habitual lying and twisted propaganda of Soviet negotiators, it can easily come to pass that no man will believe them even in some great emergency when they may be forced into the necessity of wanting to tell the truth.

The United Nations, like every predecessor of its kind in history, from the Amphyctionic League to the North Atlantic Pact, represent the age-long yearning of mankind to forge an instrument capable of reshaping international anarchy into international order and stable peace. Wars and new wars bulk through the annals of the race as mankind's deadliest invention for self-torture. The conscience of a tired humanity demanded at long last that the scourge be ended. The presence of Soviet Russia among the consulting physicians and her use of the prerogatives accorded her in the veto power, in her triple vote, and in the unlimited franchise of denunciation and obstruction have resulted in corrupting the present constitution of the organization into another invention for continued self-torture.

CHAPTER XI

Atom Bombs and the Christian Conscience

THE place of A-bombs and H-bombs in this complex clash of power between East and West is, like the ghost of Banquo, the uninvited guest at every international conference. Ready to scrap the advantage conferred by those ghastly weapons if all other nations would agree to effective controls, the government of the United States has been blocked by the constant veto of Soviet Russia. Thus she gains time while the sands run out, until she has a stockpile of atomic bombs. Hence, regretfully but categorically, President Truman announced on April 16, 1949, that he would authorize use of atomic bombs again, should the dreaded necessity arise and if the welfare of the United States and the democracies of the world are at stake. "I hope and pray," he added, "that will never be necessary."

The frightful effects of that dreadful weapon are known by personal observation to the present writer, as he spent some ten days in the ruins of Hiroshima in 1947 and interviewed many of the victims who survived the tragedy. The ethical problem of employing such a lethal weapon, which by the very nature and intensity of the explosion will exterminate thousands upon thousands of civilians and innocent bystanders not directly employed in military activities, is not easy to resolve. Discussion of that moral aspect is made intricate and inconclusive, moreover, by the new fact of total warfare.

The concept of total war was advocated in Germany even before Hitler launched one in fact. The premise that all previous theories of war were erroneous was published by General Ludendorff in his work *Der Totale Krieg* (Total War) in which he developed the new strategic conceptions. They were extracted from his book and published in *Winged Warfare* by General H. H. Arnold and Colonel Ira C. Eaker.[1]

1. You must wage war with the entire man power and material resources of the people. War must become a mode of national existence.

2. It is absolutely essential to introduce universal service, and twelve workers are needed at home for every soldier in the field.

3. The war program must engulf the entire people wiping out all civilian activities which are unnecessary. Private business obviously would not be tolerated except under the most stringent government regulation.

4. No internal politics would be allowed to continue within the State.

5. One of the most essential instruments in time of war is radio broadcasting and, if the war is to be won, it must absolutely be controlled by the Government.

6. It is the business of the publicity department of the Government to encourage false pacifism abroad, and one of the most effective instruments is, of course, the radio.

7. It is the function of the aircraft to spread, not only bombs, but also leaflets in the enemy territory.

8. The total war means a total blockade by every means at the disposal of the High Command, namely by submarine, warships, and by airplane.

9. The first thing that the airplane should be used for after the outbreak of war is for the attack on railroads and aerodromes.

10. With air mastery over a territory you can advance more troops hundreds of times faster than Napoleon ever dreamed of military movements. This is the Blitzkrieg of today.

11. To wage a successful war for a long period of time a nation must be self-sufficient and this can only be achieved by using artificial methods to replace materials which can be cut off by a blockade. This was one of General Ludendorff's suggestions which Germany followed so carefully that she developed many new artificial and synthetic industries.

12. Next it is indispensable to attack all the enemy's centers of production so that he cannot produce war materials or carry on peacetime business with which to obtain foreign exchange to purchase the nation's requirements abroad. Ludendorff emphasized the importance of total industrial mobilization and total industrial destruction by airplane bombardment.

---

[1] New York: Harper Brothers, 1941.

13. He also hinted at bacteriological warfare to be used against agricultural crops. By destroying the soil, you destroy the food which makes for the resistance of the enemy.

14. In speaking of military equipment one of the points he drove home consistently, especially in regard to airplanes, was the danger of obsolescence. For this reason Germany used very inexpensive airplanes which after several hundred hours of flying can be rebuilt. If the airplane was shot down, the loss in equipment was not great. A fighting plane does not require the same standards as a transport plane which is built to fly many thousands of miles. This idea was followed very carefully by the farsighted General von Seeckt when he was Chief of Staff several years ago.

15. The strangest suggestion that came from General Ludendorff, who commanded the Hindenburg Line of trenches for three long years, was: "in the future no trench warfare." He favored a war of maneuver employing armored and motorized divisions. In its early campaign the German Army is reported to have had 18 mechanized division units, each with about 200 tanks.

16. Last but not least, Ludendorff emphasized the cardinal importance of the element of surprise. This is the one point the Nazis certainly did not forget. Hitler kept the whole world guessing as to what his next move would be. Then when he moved, he struck with devastating rapidity a hard decisive blow.

The degeneration in international conduct since 1939 and the evils of total war have produced profound public consequences. There is no longer a battle front in the conventional sense; there is no longer a defined and limited zone of combat occupied by military forces, by men who are expected to run the risks of soldiers, leaving a rear territory inhabited by civilians not subject to the same hazards under the old concept of warfare. Mr. James Burnham, in *The Coming Defeat of Communism*, comes down to cases and asks: "Who is a 'recognized' combatant? A man in military uniform, following specific orders? a guerrilla or partisan in rags? a saboteur in a business suit? a fifth columnist running a factory or editing a newspaper? a short-wave broadcaster?

"Who is a 'military man,' who a 'civilian'? The general who has won battles and studied tactics? or the scholar who has mastered nuclear physics and biological chemistry? the expert in naval gunnery? or the expert in propaganda, who can unify the national will, and break down enemy morale? Is naval strategy a military field, and the construction of filters for uranium fluoride a civilian occupation? Is the businessman who reports on the chemical industry abroad a spy? Is the general in charge of psychological warfare a soldier, and the educator who teaches the errors of foreign ideologies a man of peace?"

Today the total population is involved; the needs of technological developments embrace so much organization for armament and for supply that the battle front has moved into every city, town, and village. There is no rear; there is no escape; and there is no shield of legal status. That is one of the most calamitous consequences of the degeneration in the sense of values which began with the Industrial Revolution and culminated in the crass materialism of Communism and the cynical secularism of the Nazi philosophy of the State. The dignity of human personality and the inalienable rights of individuals were made subservient to the fascination of mass production, mass movements, mass results, and massed power. The sky lines of Christendom bear testimony to the competition of spirit and matter. Huge, ugly chimney stacks, belching clouds of factory smoke and gaseous fumes, jostle the cross-tipped spires of Gothic cathedrals. What is of immediate concern, then, is definition and clarification of the issue raised by President Truman's reference to necessity and the welfare of the United States, followed by his authorization to proceed with production of the hydrogen bomb.

Direct assault launched against us by an enemy who is known to have the atomic bomb — and no power would now attack the United States without it — raises one type of question not too difficult to answer. We should have no alternative but to retaliate in kind. A second question is more compelling and it is with this that we are here concerned: Would the United States be justified in launching an immediate atomic attack against an enemy power before it could use that devastating weapon against our cities?

Under any hypothesis, the answer is extremely difficult to formulate, both for ethical and historical reasons. Our every tradition and instinct as a people, as well as conscience itself, recoils before such a dread alternative even in self-defense, although few moralists will insist that we must wait until the enemy delivers the first atomic blow. Under the new conditions of the atomic age such an aggression might very well be fatal, not only to a vast number of individuals, as is obvious, but to our entire system of national defense and to our existence as a nation.[2] Clearly, atomic bombs would be used under title of defense only, a claim that would be set up by every nation. Hence, the concept and term "defense" must be clarified, both by definition and through application to concrete circumstances.

The use of force for legitimate self-defense is conferred by the natural law. This moral justification to repel an unjust aggressor by means reasonably adapted and proportionate to the nature of the attack, is the right not only of individuals but of the State as well. In the case of the State, it goes further still; it becomes an obligation, in view of the duty incumbent on government to safeguard the lives, the liberty, and the temporal welfare of citizens viewed individually and collectively. In total war the attack is no longer limited to acknowledged military targets; it is leveled against whole peoples as peoples.

It has been asserted that a rocket bombardment of the United States could one day originate from an inland base such as the area stretching from Lake Baikal to Kamchatka in Siberia. Or from launching platforms erected in the Baltic regions so jealously guarded by Soviet Russia. There is great significance in the fact that an unarmed American military plane flying over the waters of the Baltic in April, 1950, was ruthlessly shot down by Soviet fire with total loss of plane and crew. That incident revealed how successfully Russian geopolitics have operated to make a *mare nostrum* out of the Baltic Sea.

A survey made by Mr. Curt L. Heymann, an Associated Press staff correspondent, and dated April 29, 1950, illustrates the meaning and progress of Soviet planning. Six hundred miles of coast line in the strategic Baltic area have been transformed into a Soviet zone of fortifications and armament centers for naval and air operations. Already in control of Pechenga on the northern tip of Finland, this area, from Kaliningrad (old Königsberg) to the frontiers of the British zone of occupation near Lübeck in Germany,

---

[2] The number of persons killed at Hiroshima by the first atomic bomb, either killed outright or wounded to a degree leading to death at a later date, has been put at 200,000.

has been converted into one of the most concentrated war plants on the continent of Europe.

Supplied by nature with numerous harbors and coastal advantages, the area is crowded with military installations, submarine plants, and shipbuilding facilities, such as the Vulkan yards and the Neptune Works, all operating at full blast. German vessels taken over by the Soviets: e.g., the *Hansa,* the *Oceana,* and the *Cordillera,* were being converted into troop transports. Stettin is the principal naval construction base for Soviet Russia in Central Europe; Swinemünde is the headquarters of the Baltic fleet. The port of Memel is equipped with "bunkers" for the most modern U-boats; Kolberg and Peenemünde are closely guarded testing grounds for rockets and V-bombs. Munition dumps abound. The entire area is manned by an army of laborers and engineers engaged in working the assembly plants and constructing military highways to the hinterland. Security precautions are severe and the shore patrol is said to be composed of the same type of Mongolians whom I encountered in 1945 in Brandenburg guarding the Autobahn from Helmstedt to Berlin. The significance of this mobilization of war industries in this particular area may be judged from the geographic location. It was here that Hitler located his testing ground for new weapons. From this same southern shore of the Baltic he launched some of his most dangerous air and sea attacks.

Now turn to the Orient on a map of the world, preferably a global projection; measure the air distance and bombing range from Soviet bases such as Anadyr in eastern Siberia, or from Petropavlovsk, or from the Komandorskie Islands, or over the Polar Cap, to the heart of North America. We are no longer invulnerable behind wide expanses of water but exposed on both flanks, and over the top, to air assault. A 5000-mile cruising range (not impossible) will bring not only Canada but entire continental United States under air bombardment. The strategic boundaries of Soviet power are no longer lines on a map but peripheral zones which are being pushed constantly outward from Moscow, thus providing both depth for defense of the center and forward bases for offensive installations. To be sure, the argument runs both ways and Soviet targets are equally near, as the crow flies. But American policy includes no program of aggression nor fixed resolve

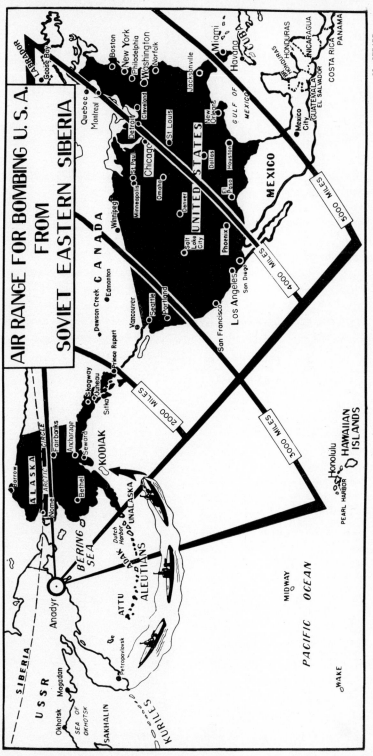

AIR RANGE FOR BOMBING U.S.A. FROM SOVIET EASTERN SIBERIA

M. GERARD

to achieve world domination. The active opposite components of the Soviet mind are the decisive factors in attempting to set up a balance of future probabilities.

Although the effective range of V-2 rockets was short and experimental when the Nazis bombarded London with them, it is no secret that much progress has been made in the past five years toward achieving intercontinental range for guided missiles capable of carrying an atomic warhead. Nazi technicians were improving and expanding rocket warfare so rapidly that the fate of England might have been wholly otherwise if the collapse of Hitler's empire had not come when it did. America would have been his next target and we must not run the danger of miscalculating the progress Soviet science has accomplished from the point where the Nazis ended. In his report of 1945 General Marshall points out: "Göring stated after his capture that it was a certainty the eastern American cities would have been under rocket bombardment had Germany remained undefeated for two more years. The first attack would have started much sooner." Albert Speer, Hitler's Minister of Armaments, made even more specific prophecies in his final statement at Nuremberg in 1946:

In five to ten years this war technique will present the possibility of firing rockets from continent to continent with uncanny precision. . . . As former Minister of the highly developed [Nazi] armament system it becomes my last duty to affirm that a new large scale war will end with the destruction of human culture and civilization. Nothing will prevent the unleashed technique of science from completing the destruction of humanity, on which it had [only] started in so dreadful a form in this recent war.

What Soviet Russia has accomplished with the schnörkel type of submarine, taken over from defeated Germany, is a fair index of the potentialities of the rocket program inherited at the same time. The first warning might be the appearance of a cloud of unidentified missiles suddenly appearing on the radar screens of the American protective network and approaching North America at a speed of something like 2000 miles per hour. V-2 rockets have already achieved incredible speed. At the Long Range Proving Ground, Cocoa, Florida, a captured V-2 German rocket was successfully tested on July 29, 1950. It was a combination missile composed of a parent rocket weighing 14 tons with a 700-pound rocket mounted on top of it. The larger V-2 attained a speed of 2727 miles an hour and reached an altitude of 9 miles. At that point, the "WAC corporal" detached itself automatically from its carrier and continued eastward over the Atlantic at a speed of 3600 miles per hour. Or the attack could come from a fleet of schnörkels suddenly surfacing along the Atlantic or Pacific seaboard and discharging special types of atomic bombs from properly contrived launching devices. It is suspected that at least one Soviet submarine has already made a reconnaissance survey off the west coast of the United States.

The problem, then, involves questions relating to the certainty and immediacy of an attack under given circumstances as well as to the nature of the defensive weapon. In the evolution of human relationships from primitive to modern and complex, the elements of certainty and immediacy have varied in step with the development of weapons of attack. Primitive man was justified in exercising his right to strike a preventive blow when he saw a bare fist descending on him at arm's length, or a stone lifted against him. In the course of time he saw an ax uplifted, a dagger drawn, then a sword thrust at him, then a spear leveled, then an arrow fitted to a bowstring. The danger though moving back in space was still immediate and certain in time. With the invention of gunpowder, the assailant moved farther and farther away; but no basic change was introduced in the elements of certainty and immediacy of attack. Then, long-range artillery, though discharging explosives from emplacements even out of sight and miles away, could menace life and limb with equal certainty and immediacy.

Now comes the age of air power, with military aviation carrying flaming death from bases located 3000–5000 miles away. Aircraft carriers far out at sea, flying bombs, guided missiles, jet bombs, and atomic explosives can now be a certain and immediate menace from ever growing distances in this era of global-minded warfare. Who shall maintain that the substantive and inherent right of self-defense is canceled out by an accidental circumstance or by the ingenuity of an aggressor in a chemical laboratory?

The Japanese air force which bombed Pearl Harbor was carried to a point designated for the take-off by a fleet of war vessels including carriers, which, we now know, left the northern Japanese port of Tankan Wan on November 26, 1941, for the attack delivered on December 7. The attacking planes took off from the decks of their carriers at a point approximately 230 miles north of Pearl Harbor. It would be a tortured interpretation of the right of self-defense to deny the corresponding right to have intercepted and destroyed that advancing menace at any point, near or far.

We know, moreover, from testimony presented in 1946 to the Congressional Committee on Pearl Harbor, that the Japanese Government, on December 2, 1941, had instructed its Washington embassy to destroy certain code machines and machine codes. The message had been intercepted by Army Intelligence and the decoded information handed to the proper authorities of government in Washington; similar secret messages ordering the burning of codes were intercepted by the Navy before the attack on Pearl Harbor, decoded and communicated to President Roosevelt. On the evening before the attack, i.e., December 6, 1941, the first thirteen paragraphs of the final Japanese reply, which was to be handed to Secretary Hull at 1:00 p.m. the following day, had already been intercepted, decoded, and communicated to President Roosevelt. It was testified that on reading them, he turned to Harry Hopkins who was with him in his study and said, "This means war." Early in the morning of December 7, at 4:37 a.m., a Japanese message was intercepted by the Navy in Washington laying special emphasis on "one o'clock" as a deadline; something was scheduled to happen at that precise hour, which was about dawn in Honolulu. The fourteenth and final paragraph of the Japanese note was in the hands of the State Department, decoded, and handed to President Roosevelt by 10 a.m. on December 7, the day of the attack, which was launched at 1:00 p.m. Washington time. The first news of the attack reached Washington from Pearl Harbor at 1:50 p.m. The Japanese envoys handed their note to Secretary Hull at 2:05 p.m., after the attack had begun.

The interception and decoding of secret messages was a feat of ingenuity not limited to American experts. Japanese code breakers in Tokyo were equally efficient. From testimony revealed during the trial of Tojo and his associates before the International Military Tribunal for the Far East, 1947–1948, we now know that President Roosevelt's last, personal appeal to Emperor Hirohito had been intercepted by the Japanese. The cable reached Tokyo at noon and its contents were known to Japanese officials during the course of the afternoon. It was not delivered to the American Ambassador until 9 p.m. that night. As soon as he had decoded the message Mr. Grew called on Foreign Minister Togo at 15 minutes after midnight but was refused an audience with the Emperor. When Mr. Grew took his leave of the Foreign Minister at 30 minutes after midnight, the two countries were already at war in accord with the timetable set in the Japanese naval operations orders.

The question naturally arises: if the right of self-defense is as unassailable as contended in the reasoning above, why were appropriate and positive measures not taken in advance? The answer does not lie in any weakness of evidence respecting an imminent attack but in the false judgments made somewhere in Washington respecting the place where the first blow was to fall. It was known that a Japanese fleet of combat vessels and troop-ships was steaming southward in the Pacific, presumably toward Indochina and the Kra Peninsula. Hence it was supposed that the first blow would be struck in that area. Meanwhile the true menace was creeping nearer and nearer to Pearl Harbor in the North Pacific. The ghastly sequel is too well known to require repetition here. But, should history repeat itself and produce a Soviet feint in some remote area of Asia or the Middle East, it will be the signal for those burned once in the fire of such deceit to keep their eyes fixed on the Northwest and Arctic sector of our American defense system. If the Government of the United States has sound reason to believe (that is, has moral certitude) that a similar attack is being mounted and ready to be launched against this country from any source, then it would appear that President Truman would be morally justified to take defensive measures proportionate to the danger. That could mean use of the atomic bomb, as no power would launch a surprise attack on the United States without an adequate supply of atomic bombs. Should large numbers of civilians be harmed by American necessity to use the bomb in self-defense, that regrettable effect, not intended as such, would be attributable to what moralists describe as the *indirect voluntary*. An attack against us would have to be sudden, unannounced, sufficiently devastating, and so widespread in coverage as to cripple our powers of reprisal; the reply to any partial crippling would be so overwhelmingly atomic that no aggressive government would risk the gamble without certainty of success. Losing the gamble under present conditions of warfare would mean practical annihilation.

This argument presupposes, as its crucial premise, accuracy of information, honest information, competent information, and an alert intelligence service. If time permitted, a warning or an ultimatum to an enemy found to be preparing such an attack should be given. But, with or without ultimatum, I personally see no immorality, though much tragedy and horror of consequences, in the government of the United States choosing the lesser of two evils. Neither reason nor theology nor morals require men or nations to commit suicide by requiring that we must await the first blow from a power with no moral inhibitions and when, as in the case now under consideration, the attack would surely include a bombardment of atomic bombs. Even Christ Himself did not disdain to seize a lash and drive the hypocrites out of the Temple. But what an appalling responsibility is now laid on Military Intelligence, on diplomatic vigilance, and on all related security agencies which gather and analyze information in this atomic age.

The measure of certitude, moreover, must be convincing, as high and firm as is humanly possible, in view of the gravity of the decision at stake. Some moralists who reluctantly accept the alternative of lesser evil would require in addition that the use of atomic weapons be limited to military targets insofar as military installations can be segregated from civilian surroundings. Still others would require a United Nations decision, not merely an American interpretation of urgency to act.

A final, perhaps more perplexing problem yet remains to be faced. Would the argumentation thus far developed apply to another country about to be attacked by Soviet Russia, i.e., one of the Atlantic Pact countries or Iraq or Iran or Greece or Turkey or India? With regard to the areas included in the Atlantic Pact, defense of which has already been considered as essential to the security of the United States, a political answer in the affirmative has already been given by President Truman. In his crucial pronouncement of April 6, 1949, he declared that use of the atomic bomb would be authorized if the welfare of the United States and the democracies of the world are at stake. The phrase "democracies of the world" will need clarification even from the point of view of political expediency, prescinding for the moment from the moral justification.

It is probable that the term "democracy" was not used by the President in a strictly analytical sense as signifying countries whose governmental structure corresponded to the American understanding of desirable political organization. England is a constitutional monarchy as are Belgium, Sweden, Denmark, and Norway. It would be unreal to conclude, even without the Atlantic Pact, that these vigorous types of the democratic spirit were not to be included in the President's broad delineation of nations meriting the support of the United States against Soviet aggression. It would be safe to assume that any non-Communist State whose sovereignty and freedom are endangered by Soviet aggression and whose membership in the United Nations entitles it to the assistance of other free and sovereign peoples would be included in the collective security which is the very essence and purpose of the United Nations' organization. That is in the bond.

Hence, having entered on a military operation in fulfillment of its pledge, the United States would next have to determine the nature and extent of the weapons it would use under given circumstances in developing the defense. The conditions enumerated earlier in this chapter would then operate, provided the natural right of legitimate self-defense against a certain and immediate danger is honestly established in favor of the aggrieved people whose cause in the premises we have made our own. This is a logical consequence of our having signed the charter of the United Nations. The developments in Korea make apparent what probably has not yet been fully realized: we are committed to an entirely new and heavy international responsibility — but a collective responsibility. If, as previously set forth, we should be morally justified in using the atomic bomb for our particular defense, and since we have accepted the principle of collectively guaranteeing the security of United Nations' members, because of the common danger, we must be consistent in our moral conclusions.

In my opinion, consequently, use of the atomic bomb against an aggressor named as aggressor by the United Nations, even though the invasion be not immediately directed against the United States, would not violate Christian morality. We may be spared any pangs of conscience by suddenly learning to our amazement on some tranquil Sunday morning that other nations have atomic bombs and will not scruple to use them. Defense of allies or friends unjustly treated by an aggressor was included by theologians and jurists among the legitimate titles for armed intervention long before Grotius codified the law of Nations.[3]

What if a nonmember of the United Nations should be attacked? What of Ireland, Spain, Austria, Germany, and Japan? If the answer in respect to Austria, Germany, and Japan is obvious because of our presence and responsibilities in those zones, it is not less affirmative for the others. Defense of human freedom and our obligations to the spiritual values of Christendom do not repose solely on legal or contractual grounds but on understanding of the issue and the challenge. The danger arises *per se* from the advance of World Communism; every new conquest by the Kremlin is an added menace to Christian civilization, and to the Hindu and Moslem world as well. That is the issue which must be met, at least if life on this planet is to be worth the living.

Ex-Governor Stassen, now president of the University of Pennsylvania, evidently reacted deeply to this conviction. In August, 1950, he proposed that an ultimatum be addressed to Soviet Russia with an actual declaration of war to follow should Moscow continue her aggressions by attacking any other country at any point in the world, whether by direct assault or by the indirect technique of organizing and supporting a Communist uprising in the designated land. This measure he would accept as hard alternative to the possibility of seeing American armed strength "dissipated and spread out in jungles and mountains and valleys in distant parts of the world." After passage of such a resolution by Congress, the General Assembly of the United Nations would be asked to approve the decision.

There is a certain logicality and sense of alternatives in this

---

[3] E.g., Francisco de Victoria, at the University of Salamanca, 1532.

attitude. It is the practicality that gives pause. Such a resolute position presupposes something that does not yet exist — the ability to enforce it. "Preponderant power" was the phrase used to describe the crux of the problem by Mr. Walter Lippmann who dissented with much asperity from ex-Governor Stassen. Under our present limitations and in view of the present inadequate re-arming of western Europe, how, he asks, could we successfully meet the "armed hordes of Eurasia" if they take to the field? Again, the only ready answer lies in the atomic bomb, which if used to halt such an invasion of western Europe would probably destroy as many of our friends as enemies. That is the tragic impasse now weighing on the Christian conscience and it would be folly to deny that the atheistic Politburo is profiting daily from the debate.

But to return to the catalogue of affirmative steps which the times demand. With the indicated measures for strengthening and exemplifying the meaning of a workable democracy in a spiritually chastened population well in progress, economic assistance to liberty threatened abroad will carry not only material support but the powerful argument of good example. A bad idea is best driven out by a good idea, unless the evil aggressor succeeds in paralyzing his prospective victim before the prophylaxis becomes effective. Hence, military assistance, to the extent assumed by the terms of the Atlantic Pact, and by the enlarged emergency created in the Far East, is a reasonable adjunct in the circumstances. President Truman's Report to the Congress, January 8, 1951, presented a point-by-point enumeration of the measures proposed both on the international and the domestic front.

1. Appropriations for our military build-up.
2. Extension and revision of the Selective Service Act.
3. Military and economic aid to help increase the strength of the free world.
4. Revision and extension of the authority to expand production and to stabilize prices, wages, and rents.
5. Betterment of our agricultural laws, to help obtain the kinds of farm products we need for the defense effort.
6. Improvement of our labor laws to help provide stable labor-management relations and to make sure that we have steady production in this emergency.
7. Housing and training of defense workers, and the full use of all our man-power resources.

8. Means for increasing the supply of doctors, nurses, and other trained medical personnel critically needed for the defense effort.

9. Aid to the states to meet the most urgent needs of our elementary and secondary schools.

10. A major increase in taxes to meet the cost of the defense effort.

The cost of these combined preventives of future wars will indeed be staggering but must be weighed in the balance with the alternatives. There is need of complete thinking at this point, not spurts of enthusiasm, of volatile sentiment, nor unfounded fears nor programs for the partial containment of Soviet aggression. The cost of a needed commodity or of an essential service is not truly stated by the price tag but by the foreseeable consequences if it is not bought. A fire extinguisher for a modest home or a sprinkler system for an industrial establishment may seem expensive in terms of the present income of the respective buyers; it can be inmeasurably more expensive, possibly fatal, not to have them on hand and in working condition when a fire breaks out.

There is a fire aflame in the world today, kindled and fanned by a band of international arsonists bent on spreading the conflagration as widely as possible. The Revolution is on the march from Berlin to Korea. Eight nations have had their freedom burned to ashes already. The final confrontation now has come and American blood has been shed in a major war. The two central figures, whose emergence Stalin predicted, are committed to combat in the Far East while their diplomats sit facing each other across conference tables which stretch from the Kremlin to the English Channel, from Brussels and Paris to New York and Washington. The unprecedented character and stark realism of the conflict became evident when the President of the United States could bluntly declare a year ago that he could no longer put faith or credence in any promise made by Soviet Russia.

The President's later analysis of the Soviet program, in his Report on the State of the Union, compared it with the imperialism of the Tzars. Previous Russian expansionism, he pointed out, "has been replaced by the even more ambitious, more crafty, and more menacing imperialism of the rulers of Soviet Russia . . . they are willing to use this power to destroy the free nations and win domination of the whole world. . . . The gun that points at them points at us, also." This forthright language conveyed no news to informed students of the Russian Revolution and probably not to the Congress. The news element derived from the official pronouncement of it by the President of the United States before such a legislative assembly, followed by an impressive catalogue of positive countermeasures. The known facts became acknowledged facts for incorporation in a State paper as public basis for stronger public policy.

In normal times such statements from the head of a government would have meant instant rupture of diplomatic relations and a probable full mobilization for war on both sides. But we are not engaged in conventional diplomacy under accepted standards of international decency such as prevailed at Vienna in 1815 after the Napoleonic Wars. We are embarked on a kind of cosmic poker game for the highest stakes in history. Some there are who believe one of the players has been prolonging a colossal bluff which began at Yalta and Tehran and which succeeded notably against the leading player on the opposite side, who was then in failing health. The government of the United States finally decided to call for a showdown on the Korean crisis and was supported by the United Nations. Had both done so earlier, the odds in favor of true peace in Europe and Asia would have been far more favorable and Soviet Russia would not have scored the gains that began with the desertion of Poland by her former allies. On the issue, when the cards eventually fall, may well depend the quality and quantity of human freedom for generations to come.

The record is clear and the designs of Soviet Russia were never unclear. Her gamble in Korea was logical perfidy. Edmund Burke in 1772 warned Europe that the partition of Poland by Prussia, Austria, and Russia would not be the end of the feasting. It was, he pointed out, only a breakfast for the great armed powers; but where would they dine? He knew that neither history nor appetite for power ever stops short.

The true question before the American people and before their representatives in Congress is not so much the cost in dollars, though heavy, but the alternative possibilities. If the grim record of the past five years of Soviet-American relations has achieved anything, it has clarified the cold war down to a basic consideration. The debate is not whether we can afford to do the necessary things for the defense of Christian civilization — but can we afford not to do them?

APPENDIX I

Last Will and Testament of Peter the Great

In a book published in the eighteenth century as the posthumous memoirs of the Chevalier d'Eon de Beaumont, there appeared a very remarkable document purporting to be the will of Peter the Great. The notorious D'Eon is known to have gone to Russia in the disguise of a woman, as a secret envoy from France. It is said that his intimacy with the lascivious Empress Elizabeth gave him extraordinary opportunities for making important discoveries, and that he transmitted his document to Louis XV, in 1757.

Doubts have been cast upon the authenticity both of the memoirs and of the so-called will; historical scholarship has declared the latter a forgery ("The Testament of Peter the Great," in *The American Slavic and East European Review*, VII, pp. 111–124, April, 1948). Independently, however, of its authenticity, the will possesses great intrinsic interest, as embodying principles of action which have been notoriously followed out by Russia during the last hundred years, with such modifications as time and circumstances, and the variations of the European equilibrium, have rendered necessary.

✿   ✿   ✿   ✿

The document begins thus:

"In the name of the holy and indivisible Trinity, We, Peter, Emperor and Autocrat of all the Russians, etc., etc., to all our successors on the throne and in the government of the Russian nation.

"Forasmuch as the Great God, who is the author and giver of

our life and crown, has constantly illumined us with his light and upheld us during his support," etc.

Here Peter sets out in detail that, according to his view, which he takes to be also that of Providence, he regards the Russian nation as destined hereafter to exercise supreme dominion over Europe. He bases his opinion on the fact that the European nations have for the most part fallen into a condition of decrepitude, not far removed from collapse, whence he considers that they may easily be subjugated by a new and youthful race, as soon as the latter shall have attained its full vigor.

The Russian monarch looks upon the coming influx of the northerners into the East and West as a periodical movement forming part of the scheme of Providence which, in like manner, by the invasion of the barbarians, effected the regeneration of the Roman world. He compares these emigrations of the polar nations with the inundations of the Nile, which at certain seasons fertilize the arid soil of Egypt.

He adds that Russia, which he found a brook and should leave a river, must, under his successors, grow to a mighty sea, destined to fertilize worn-out Europe; and that its waves would advance over all obstacles, if his successors were only capable of guiding the stream. On this account he leaves behind him for their use the following rules, which he recommends to their attention and constant study, even as Moses consigned his tables of the law to the Jewish people (from Kelly's compilation of Karamsin, Tooke, and Ségur [London, 1854]):

1. The Russian nation must be constantly on a war footing to keep the soldiers warlike and in good condition. No rest must be allowed, except for the purpose of relieving the state finances, recruiting the army, or biding the favourable moment of attack. By this means peace is made subservient to war, and war to peace, in the interest of the aggrandisement and increasing prosperity of Russia.

2. Every possible means must be used to invite from the most cultivated European states commanders in war, and philosophers in peace: to enable the Russian nation to participate in the advantages of other countries, without losing any of its own.

3. No opportunity must be lost of taking part in the affairs and disputes of Europe, especially in those of Germany, which, from its vicinity, is of the most direct interest to us.

4. Poland must be divided, by keeping up constant jealousies and confusion there. The authorities must be gained over with money, and the assemblies corrupted so as to influence the election of the kings. We must get up a party of our own there, send Russian troops into the country, and let them sojourn there so long that they may ultimately find some pretext for remaining there for ever. Should the neighbouring states make difficulties, we must appease them for the moment, by allowing them a share of the territory, until we can safely resume what we have thus given away.

5. We must take away as much territory as possible from Sweden, and contrive that they shall attack us first, so as to give us a pretext for their subjugation. With this object in view, we must keep Sweden in opposition to Denmark, and Denmark to Sweden, and sedulously foster their mutual jealousies.

6. The consorts of the Russian princes must always be chosen from among the German princesses, in order to multiply our family alliances with the Germans, and to unite our interests with theirs; and thus, by consolidating our influence in Germany, to cause it to attach itself spontaneously to our policy.

7. We must be careful to keep up our commercial alliance with England, for she is the power which has most need of our products for her navy, and at the same time may be of the greatest service to us in the development of our own. We must export wood and other articles in exchange for her gold, and establish permanent connexions between her merchants and seamen and our own.

8. We must keep steadily extending our frontiers northward along the Baltic, and southward along the shores of the Black Sea.

9. We must progress as much as possible in the direction of Constantinople and India. He who can once get possession of these points is the real ruler of the world. With this view we must provoke constant quarrels — at one time with Turkey, and at another with Persia. We must establish wharves and docks in the Euxine, and by degrees make ourselves masters of that sea, as well as of the Baltic, which is a doubly important element in the success of our plan. We must hasten the downfall of Persia; push on to the Persian Gulf; if possible, re-establish the ancient commercial intercourse with the Levant through Syria; and force our way into the Indies, which are the storehouses of the world; once there, we can dispense with English gold.

10. Moreover, we must take pains to establish and maintain an intimate union with Austria, apparently countenancing her schemes for future aggrandisement in Germany, and all the while secretly rousing the jealousy of the minor states against her. In this way we must bring it to pass that one or the other party shall seek aid from Russia; and thus we shall exercise a sort of protectorate over the country, which will pave the way for future supremacy.

11. We must make the house of Austria interested in the expulsion of the Turks from Europe, and we must neutralize its jealousy at the capture of

Constantinople, even by allowing it a share of the spoil, which we can afterwards resume at our leisure.

12. We must collect around our house, as round a centre, all the detached sections of Greeks which are scattered abroad in Hungary, Turkey, and South Poland; we must make them look to us for support; and thus, by establishing beforehand a sort of ecclesiastical supremacy, we shall pave the way for universal sovereignty.

13. When Sweden is ours, Persia vanquished, Poland subjugated, Turkey conquered — when our armies are united, and the Euxine and the Baltic in the possession of our ships, then we must make separate and secret overtures, first to the court of Versailles, and then to that of Vienna, to share with them the dominion of the world. If either of them accepts our propositions, which is certain to happen if their ambition and self-interest is properly worked upon, we must make use of one to annihilate the other; this done, we have only to destroy the remaining one by finding a pretext for a quarrel, the issue of which cannot be doubtful, as Russia will then be already in the absolute possession of the east and of the best part of Europe.

14. Should the improbable case happen of both rejecting the propositions of Russia, then our policy will be to set one against the other, and make them tear each other to pieces. Russia must then watch for and seize the favourable moment, and pour her already assembled hosts into Germany, while two immense fleets, laden with Asiatic hordes, and convoyed by the armed squadrons of the Euxine and the Baltic, set sail simultaneously from the Sea of Asof and the harbour of Archangel.

Sweeping along the Mediterranean and the Atlantic they will overrun France on the one side while Germany is overpowered on the other. When these countries are fully conquered the rest of Europe must fall easily, and without a struggle, under our yoke. Thus Europe can and must be subjugated.

APPENDIX II

The Prophecies Respecting Russia by De Tocqueville (1835) and Donoso Cortés (1850)

The following passages contain the prophetic warnings of two distinguished Europeans writing on the destiny of Russia as it appeared to them over a century ago. Donoso Cortés was a brilliant Spanish author and diplomat (1809–1853). De Tocqueville's *Democracy in America* first appeared in 1835.

. . . There are, at the present time, two great nations in the world which seem to tend toward the same end, although they started from different points: I allude to the Russians and the Americans. Both of them have grown up unnoticed; and while the attention of mankind was directed elsewhere, they have suddenly assumed a most prominent place among the nations; and the world learned their existence and their greatness at almost the same time.

All other nations seem to have nearly reached their natural limits, and only to be charged with the maintenance of their power; but these are still in the act of growth; all the others are stopped, or continue to advance with extreme difficulty; these are proceeding with ease and with celerity along a path to which the human eye can assign no term. The American struggles against the natural obstacles which oppose him; the adversaries of the Russian are men; the former combats the wilderness and savage life; the latter, civilization with all its weapons and its arts: the conquests of the one are therefore gained by the plowshare; those of the other by the sword. The Anglo-American relies upon personal interest to accomplish his ends, and gives free scope to the unguided exertions and common sense of the citizens; the Russian centers all the authority of society in a single arm: the principal instrument of the former is freedom; of the latter servitude. Their starting point is different, and their courses are not the same; yet each of them seems to be marked out by the will of Heaven to sway the destinies of half the globe (De Tocqueville, *Democracy in America*, Part I, Chap. XIX).

*　*　*　*

When there are no longer standing armies in Europe, as a result of their having been liquidated by the revolution; when there is no longer any patriotism in Europe, as a result of its having been snuffed out by socialistic revolutions; when the great confederation of Slavonic peoples has become an accomplished fact in Eastern Europe; when in the West there remain but two great armies, the army of the despoiled and the army of the despoilers, then, Gentlemen, Russia's hour will strike on the clock of the ages; then Russia will be able to traverse our Fatherland unmolested, armed to the teeth; then, Gentlemen, the world will be witness to the greatest punishment within the memory of history (Donoso Cortés, *Speech in Spanish Parliament,* January 30, 1850).

APPENDIX III

Basic Doctrines, Strategy, and Tactics of World Communism

The classic sources of Communism are chiefly found in the writings of Marx, Engels, Lenin, Trotsky, and Stalin. Taken in their totality, these teachings permit us to understand why Communism exercises such a vitalizing influence on its adherents. Marxists the world over have inherited an identical creed with four components of power. It is a kind of secular mysticism. It is a philosophy of history with a special methodology for interpreting it. It is a deposit of faith expressed by a succession of political, social, and economic dogmas which are declared to be infallible because scientific. It supplies a Machiavellian code of conduct for ruthless conspirators who have become crusaders by mystical elevation and held to their course by dogmatic certitude of success. Whether one considers Communist teachings as colossal lies, subtle half-truths, or calculated entrapments of immature minds, he cannot ignore the objective record of an entire generation thrown into turmoil by their dissemination.

The fundamental concepts were further elaborated in the theses and resolutions of the Third International during its heyday, in the manifesto of its successor, the Cominform, and in the interpretative writings of representative leaders. An integrated anthology of such key statements would require a thick volume such as *A Handbook of Marxism* by Emile Burns (1935). He required 1087 pages to do it. Taken in conjunction with the citations introduced into the body of the present book, the following selected passages, arranged chronologically, present a condensed epitome of the Communist scriptures and reveal the purposes which still motivate the Politburo in 1951. They demonstrate the continuity of ideas and the unchanged character of the Russian Revolution in its role as the spearhead of World Communism.

* * * *

The Marx-Engels Period

1. The history of all hitherto existing Society is the history of class struggles. . . . Society as a whole is more and more splitting up into two great hostile camps — bourgeoisie and proletariat. . . . Of all the classes that stand face to face with the bourgeoisie today, the proletariat alone is really a revolutionary class. . . . The Communists disdain to conceal their views and aims. They openly declare that their ends can be attained only by the violent overthrow of all existing social conditions. . . . The proletarians have nothing to lose but their chains. . . . Working men of all countries, unite!

The Communist Manifesto, 1848.

2. The final causes of all social changes and political revolutions are to be sought, not in men's brains, not in man's better insight into eternal truth and justice, but in changes in the modes of production and exchange. They are to be sought, not in the philosophy, but in the economics of each particular epoch. The growing perception that existing social institutions are unreasonable and unjust, that reason has become unreason, and right wrong, is only proof that in the modes of production and exchange changes have silently taken place, with which the social order, adapted to earlier economic conditions, is no longer in keeping.

Engels — *Socialism: Utopian and Scientific.*

3. . . . Now, insurrection is an art quite as much as war or any other, and subject to certain rules of proceeding, which, when neglected, will produce the ruin of the party neglecting them. Those rules, logical deductions from the nature of the parties and the circumstances one has to deal with in such a case, are so plain and simple that the short experience of 1848 had made the Germans pretty well acquainted with them. Firstly, never play with insurrection unless you are fully prepared to face the consequences of your play. Insurrection is a calculus with very indefinite magnitudes the value of which may change every day; the forces opposed to you have all the advantages of organization, discipline, and habitual authority; unless you bring strong odds against them you are defeated and ruined. Secondly, the insurrectionary career once entered upon, act with the greatest determination, and on the offensive. The defensive is the death of every armed rising; it is

lost before it measures itself with its enemies. Surprise your antagonists while their forces are scattering, prepare new successes, however small, but daily; keep up the moral ascendancy which the first successful rising has given to you; rally those vacillating elements to your side which always follow the strongest impulse; and which always look out for the safer side; force your enemies to a retreat before they can collect their strength against you; in the words of Danton, the greatest master of revolutionary policy yet known, *de l'audace, de l'audace, encore de l'audace!*

> Written by Engels and printed under name of Marx, 1851–1852, *New York Daily Tribune,* in a series of articles on revolution and counterrevolution in Germany during the period 1848–1849.

4. The great basic question of all, and especially of recent, philosophy, is the question of the relationship between thought and existence, between spirit and nature. . . . Which is prior to the other, spirit or nature? Philosophers are divided into two great camps, according to the way in which they have answered this question. Those who declare that spirit existed before nature, and who, in the last analysis, therefore, assume in one way or another that the world was created . . . have formed the idealist camp. The others, who regard nature as primary, belong to the various schools of materialism.

> Engels — *Ludwig Feuerbach.*

5. Freedom is the recognition of necessity. Necessity is blind in so far as it is not understood.

> Engels — *Anti-Dühring.*

6. In the eyes of dialectic philosophy, nothing is established for all time, nothing is absolute or sacred. On everything and in everything it sees the stamp of inevitable decline; nothing can resist it save the unceasing process of formation and destruction, the unending ascent from the lower to the higher — a process of which that philosophy itself is only a simple reflection within the thinking brain.

> Engels — *On Dialectical Materialism —*
> passim — in his works.

7. In such great developments, twenty years are but as one day — and there may come days which are the concentrated essence of twenty years.

> Marx — *Exchange of Letters with Engels,* Vol. III, p. 127.

8. Two errors robbed the brilliant victory of its fruits. . . . The proletariat stopped half-way; instead of proceeding with the "expropriation of the expropriators," it was carried away with dreams of establishing supreme justice in the country. . . . The second error was unnecessary magnanimity of the

proletariat: instead of annihilating its enemies, it endeavored to exercise moral influence on them.

Marx — *The Civil War in France*
(The Paris Commune of 1871).

9. During . . . the past four weeks I have read all sorts of things. Among others Darwin's work on Natural Selection. And though it is written in the crude English style, this is the book which contains the basis in natural science for our view.

Marx — *Letter to Engels.*

10. Religion is the opium of the people. . . . The criticism of religion is the beginning of all criticism.

Marx — *Critique of the Hegelian Philosophy of Right.*

11. . . . The last vestige of a creator external to the world is obliterated.

Engels — *Anti-Dühring.*

12. Man, at last the master of his own form of social organization, becomes at the same time the lord over nature, his own master — free.

Engels — *Socialism: Utopian and Scientific.*

*   *   *   *

The Lenin-Stalin Period

13. The roots of modern religion are deeply imbedded in the social oppression of the masses . . . it is a kind of spiritual intoxicant.

Lenin — *On Religion.*

14. During this past year a very great part of the work of the Polit-Bureau consisted in deciding every question having to do with politics which arose in the course of the work, combining the activities of all Soviet and Party organizations and of all organizations of the working class and conducting the entire work of the Soviet Republic. The Polit-Bureau decided all questions of international and domestic policy. . . .

Lenin — At the Ninth Party Congress
on March 29, 1920, in the report of the Central Committee.

15. Without a revolutionary theory, there cannot be a revolutionary movement. Only a party guided by an advanced theory can act as a vanguard in the fight.

Stalin — *Leninism.* Lecture at Sverdlov University, April, 1924.

16. Revolutionary theory is a synthesis of the experience of the working class movement throughout all lands — the generalized experience. Of course, theory out of touch with revolutionary practice gropes in the dark unless revolutionary theory throws a light on the path. But theory becomes the greatest force in the working class movement when it is inseparably linked with revolutionary practice; for it, and it alone, can give the movement confidence, guidance, and understanding of the inner links between events; it alone can enable those engaged in the practical struggle to understand the whence and the whither of the working-class movement.

Stalin — *Leninism*. Lecture at Sverdlov
University, April, 1924.

17. Tactic is the determination of the line to be taken by the proletariat during a comparatively short period of the ebb or flow of the movement, of advance or retreat of the revolution; the maintenance of this line by the substitution of new forms of struggle and organization for those that have become out of date, or by the discovery of new watchwords, or by the combination of new methods with old, etc. Whereas strategy is concerned with such wide purposes as the winning of the war against tsarism or the bourgeoisie, tactic has a narrower aim. Tactic is concerned, not with the war as a whole, but with the fighting of this or that campaign, with the gaining of this or that victory which may be essential during a particular period of the general revolutionary advance or withdrawal. Tactics are thus parts of strategy, and subordinate thereto.

Stalin — *Leninism*.

18. As long as Capitalism and Socialism exist side by side we cannot live in peace. One or the other will finally triumph. One will hold the funeral oration for either the Soviet Republic or World Capitalism. It is only postponing war.

Lenin — *Collected Works*, Vienna-Berlin, Vol. XXV, p. 643.

19. To wage war for the overthrow of the international bourgeoisie, a war which is a hundred times more difficult, more prolonged, more complicated, than the most bloodthirsty of wars between States, while renouncing beforehand the use of maneuvering, of playing off (though for a time only) the interests of one foe against the other, of entering upon agreements and effecting compromises (even though these may be of an unstable and temporary character) — would not such renunciation be the height of folly? We might as well, when climbing a dangerous and hitherto unexplored mountain, refuse in advance to make the ascent in zigzags, or to turn back for a while, to give up the chosen direction in order to test another which may prove to be easier to negotiate.

Lenin — *Works*, Russian Edition, Vol. XVIII, p. 158.

20. A vanguard alone will not lead to victory. To hurl the vanguard into the fray before the masses are ready to support it, or, at least, are willing to remain neutral, would not only be the height of folly but a crime. Agitation and propaganda do not suffice to bring the masses to a suitable frame of mind. They need also to be schooled by political experience. This is the law which lies at the root of all far-reaching revolutions, a law which has been confirmed in a striking manner both in Russia and in Germany. The Russian masses, uneducated, often illiterate, and the German masses, whose education and culture are at such an incomparably higher level, had each in turn to learn by bitter experience all the powerlessness, the listlessness, the helplessness, the servility of the governments carried on by the leaders of the Second International — henchmen of the bourgeoisie. The masses had to learn by experience that either of two dictatorships was inevitable: the dictatorship of the ultra-reactionaries (such as Korniloff in Russia and Kapp and Co. in Germany), or the dictatorships of the proletariat as a definite step on the road to Communism.

Lenin — *Works*, Russian Edition, Vol. XVII, p. 173.

21. To be a revolutionist, to be a socialist or communist sympathiser, is not enough. It behooves us to find, at any given moment, that particular link in the chain to which we can cling in order to keep the whole chain together, and subsequently to pass on to the next link. . . . For the nonce, the particular link is the stimulation of commerce on the home market, and its effective control and guidance by the State. Commerce is a "link" in the chain of historical events, in the transitional forms of our socialist construction; and we must cling to this link for dear life.

Lenin — *Works*, Russian Edition, Vol. XVIII, Part I, p. 412.

22. Never play with insurrection; but, having begun one, make up your mind to go through with it to the end. At the right place, and when the time is ripe, assemble forces greatly outnumbering those of the enemy — for otherwise the latter, better prepared and better organized, will annihilate the insurgents. Once the rising has begun, it is essential to act with the utmost resoluteness, and, without fail and unconditionally, to assume the offensive. "A defensive attitude is fatal to an armed rising." We must try to take the enemy by surprise, to seize the moment when his forces are dispersed. We must endeavor to gain some success, however small, day by day (hour by hour, even, if we are operating in a town), so that at all costs we may maintain a superior "morale."

Lenin — *Works*, Russian Edition, Vol. XIV, Part II, p. 270.

23. We may consider that the time is ripe for the decisive struggle: when all the class forces arrayed against us are in a state of confusion, are sufficiently embroiled one with another, have been sufficiently weakened in combats for which their strength is inadequate; when all the vacillating, unsteady, un-

stable intermediate elements (the petty bourgeoisie, the petty-bourgeois democracy, in contradistinction to the bourgeoisie) have exposed themselves enough before the people, have made a sufficient parade of their utter bankruptcy; when there has arisen and spread widely among the proletariat a strong feeling in favor of decisive and unhesitatingly bold revolutionary action against the bourgeoisie. Then the time is ripe for revolution. Then, if we have kept good account of the before-mentioned conditions, and have chosen our moment well, our victory is assured.

Lenin — *Works*, Russian Edition, Vol. XVII, pp. 180–181.

24. But is there such a thing as Communist ethics? Is there such a thing as Communist morality? Of course there is. Often it is made to appear that we have no ethics of our own; and very often the bourgeoisie accuse us Communists of repudiating all ethics. This is a method of shuffling concepts, of throwing dust in the eyes of the workers and peasants.

In what sense do we repudiate ethics and morality?

In the sense that they were preached by the bourgeoisie, who declared that ethics were God's commandments. We, of course, say that we do not believe in God, and that we know perfectly well that the clergy, the landlords and the bourgeoisie spoke in the name of God in order to pursue their own exploiters' interests. Or, instead of deducing these ethics from the commandments of morality, from the commandments of God, they deduced them from idealistic or semi-idealistic phrases, which were always very similar to God's commandments.

We repudiate all morality that is taken outside of human, class concepts. We say that this is deception, a fraud, which clogs the brains of the workers and peasants in the interests of the landlords and capitalists.

We say that our morality is entirely subordinated to the interests of the class struggle of the proletariat. Our morality is deduced from the class struggle of the proletariat.

The old society was based on the oppression of all the workers and peasants by the landlords and capitalists. We had to destroy this, we had to overthrow this; but for this we had to create unity. God will not create such unity.

This unity could be created only by the factories and works, only by the proletariat, trained, and roused from its age-long slumber; only when that class was formed did the mass movement begin which led to what we see now — the victory of the proletariat revolution in one of the weakest countries in the world, a country which for three years has repelled the attacks of the bourgeoisie of the whole world. And we see that the proletarian revolution is growing all over the world. We now say, on the basis of experience, that the proletariat alone could create the compact force that could take the lead of the disunited and scattered peasantry, that could withstand all the attacks of the exploiters. This class alone can help the toiling masses to unite, to rally and completely build up, Communist society.

That is why we say that for us there is no such thing as morality taken outside of human society; such a morality is a fraud. For us, morality is subordinated to the interests of the class struggle of the proletariat.

> Lenin — Speech Delivered at the Third All-Russian Congress of the Russian Young Communist League, October 2, 1920.

25. Every Marxist, if he is not a renegade, must put the interests of socialism above the right of nations to self-determination. Our Socialist Republic has done what it could for the self-determination of Finland, the Ukraine, and other countries. Nevertheless, if the situation demands a choice between the existence of the Socialist Republic, which is being endangered, and the right of self-determination of several nations, it is clear that the conservation of the Socialist Republic is predominant.

> Lenin — Issue No. 34, *Pravda,* 1918.

26. The dictatorship of the proletariat is the fiercest and most merciless war.

> Lenin — *Left Wing Communism.*

27. The dictatorship [of the Proletariat] means nothing more nor less than power which directly rests on violence and is not limited by any law or any absolute rules. Dictatorship means unlimited power resting on violence and not on law.

> Lenin — *Collected Works,* Vol. XXV, pp. 436, 441.

28. The working class without a revolutionary party is an army without a general staff.

> Stalin — *Leninism* (New York, 1932–1933), Part I, pp. 163–165.

29. We should not forget for a single instant the intrigues of international reaction, which is hatching plans for a new war.

> Stalin — 1946 May Day Order to the Red Army.

30. What is the meaning of the impossibility of the complete and final victory of socialism in a single country without the victory of the revolution in other countries? It means the impossibility of having full guarantees against intervention, and hence against the restoration of the bourgeois order, without the victory of the revolution in at least a number of countries. To deny this indisputable fact is to abandon internationalism, to abandon Leninism.

> Stalin — *Problems of Leninism.*

31. The scientific difference between Socialism and Communism is clear. What is generally called Socialism was termed by Marx the "first or lower phase of communist society." In so far as the means of production become

public property; the word "Communism" is also applicable here, providing we do not forget that it is not full Communism.

Lenin — The State and Revolution.

32. Years and years of firm rule of the proletariat are necessary, because only the proletariat is capable of defeating the bourgeoisie.

Lenin — The Deception of the People.

33. The transition from Capitalism to Communism represents an entire historical epoch.

Lenin — The Proletarian Revolution and the Renegade Kautsky.

34. We are not doctrinaires. Our philosophy is not a dogma, but a guide to action.

Lenin — Collected Works, Vol. XXI (1), p. 133.

* * * *

Trotsky

35. Events can neither be regarded as a series of adventures, nor strung on the thread of some preconceived moral. They must obey their own laws.

Trotsky — History of the Russian Revolution, Preface.

36. The different stages of a revolutionary process, certified by a change of parties in which the more extreme always supersede the less extreme. . . . Without a guiding organization, the energy of the masses would dissipate like steam not enclosed in a piston-box. But, nevertheless, what moves things is not the piston or the box but the steam.

Trotsky — History of the Russian Revolution, Preface.

37. Only from a theoretical height is it possible to observe it [struggle for power] fully and correctly understand it.

Trotsky — History of Russian Revolution, Vol. I, Chap. XI.

38. A revolutionary conception without a revolutionary will is like a watch with a broken spring.

Trotsky — History of Russian Revolution, Vol. I, Chap. XV.

39. The mystic doctrine of spontaneousness explains nothing.

Trotsky — History of Russian Revolution, Vol. I, Chap. VIII.

40. And I can assure you that the communist workers who actually form the core of this army, consider themselves to be not only the protecting troops

of the Russian Socialist Republic, but also the Red Army of the Third International. . . . When the time comes and our brothers of the western countries call to us for aid, we shall answer: We are here, we have in the meantime learned how to use these weapons, and we are ready to fight and to die for the cause of the World Revolution!

> Trotsky — Statement at the First Congress of the
> Communist International in March, 1919.

41. The revolution in the Soviet Union is a part of the world Revolution, its commencement and the basis for its development.

> Stalin vs. Trotsky — *Once More concerning the Social-Democratic Aberration in our Party,* State Publishing House of the Soviet Union, December, 1927, p. 35.

❋   ❋   ❋   ❋

Third International

42. One of the most important tasks of the cultural revolution affecting the wide masses is the task of systematically and unswervingly combatting religion.

> *Program of the Third International at Sixth World Congress,* Moscow, 1928.

43. The Communists fight with courage and devotion on all sectors of the international class front, in the firm conviction that the victory of the proletariat is inevitable and cannot be averted. The Communists disdain to conceal their views and aims. They openly declare that their aims can be attained only by the forcible overthrow of the existing social conditions. Let the ruling class tremble at a communist revolution. The proletarians have nothing to lose but their chains. They have a world to win.

> *Program of the Communist International,* 1928.

44. The dictatorship of the proletariat cannot come about as a result of the peaceful development of bourgeois society and bourgeois democracy.

The conquest of power by the proletariat does not mean peacefully capturing the ready-made bourgeois state machinery by means of a parliamentary majority. The bourgeoisie resorts to every means of violence and terror to safeguard and strengthen its predatory property and its political domination. . . . Hence, the violence of the bourgeoisie can be suppressed only by the stern violence of the proletariat. The conquest of power by the proletariat is the violent overthrow of bourgeois power.

> *Program of the Communist International,* 1928.

45. To Comrade Stalin, the Leader, Teacher and Friend of the Proletariat and the oppressed of all the world!

In the name of the million-strong army of the fighters for the proletarian World Revolution, in the name of the workers of all countries, we turn to you, Comrade Stalin, our Leader, and the faithful disciple of the work of Marx, Engels, and Lenin, to you who with Lenin have welded together the party of the new type, the party of the Bolsheviks, the party which brought about the victory of the great proletarian October Revolution and the victory of Socialism in the Soviet Union. We turn to you, beloved Leader of the international Proletariat and of all the oppressed, with fiery greetings. More than ten years have passed since we lost Lenin, this giant of the revolutionary idea and action, the unforgettable leader of the World Revolution. To you, Comrade Stalin, fell the gigantic task of replacing him at the helm in the struggle for the liberation of all toiling humanity.

Under your leadership, Socialism prevailed in the Soviet Union, and the unshakable foundation of the proletarian World Revolution was laid. You swore at Lenin's grave to strengthen the ties which bind the active workers in all the world together, the ties which are represented by the Comintern, and the communists in all countries are realising this oath in their heroic struggle under your guidance.

Now, when the capitalistic world is entering upon a new stage of revolutions and wars, the Proletariat possesses the surest guarantee of its final victory which it did not have during the first cycle of wars and revolutions, namely the mighty Union of Socialist Soviet Republics, the land of victorious Socialism, and the Comintern, the uniform world party of Communism. Under your leadership the U.S.S.R. has become an impregnable bulwark of the Socialist Revolution, the bulwark of the struggle against Fascism, Reaction and War. Let the gentlemen of the Bourgeoisie try today to ask the peoples of the world whether they want War or Peace, Fascism or Socialism. The peoples of the world do not want War and they do not want Fascism. They turn more and more to the Soviet Union and look with hope and love to you, Comrade Stalin, the Leader of the active workers of all countries.

The victory of Socialism in the Soviet Union opens up the new stage in the proletarian World Revolution.

The Seventh World-Congress of the Communist International assures you, Comrade Stalin, in the name of the sixty-five communist parties, that the communists everywhere will keep faith with the great and unconquerable banner of Marx, Engels, Lenin, and Stalin forever. Under this banner Communism shall triumph in all the world.

> Ercoli (i.e., Togliatti—Italy) — The Seventh World Congress of the Communist International, Moscow, 1935.

❋   ❋   ❋   ❋

The Cominform

46. Because of the above, the imperialistic camp and its directing force, the United States of America, show a growing aggressive activity. This activity evolved at the same time in all spheres — in the sphere of military and strategic activities, economic expansion and ideological warfare. The Truman-Marshall plan is only a farce, a European branch of the general world plan of political expansion being realized by the United States of America in all parts of the world. The plan of the economic and political subjugation of Europe through American imperialism is complemented by plans for the economic and political subjugation of China, Indonesia, and South America. The aggressors of yesterday — the capitalist tycoons of Germany and Japan — are being prepared by the United States of America for a new role — as tools of the imperialistic policy in Europe and Asia of the United States of America.

Manifesto of the Cominform, October 5, 1947.

47. We should not forget that the imperialist agents, through their clatter regarding the danger of war, try to intimidate vacillators and weaklings and thus gain through blackmail concessions for the aggressor.

In the same way as the appeasement policy of Munich led to Hitler's aggression, today concessions to the United States of America and the imperialist camp may cause its instigators to grow even more shameless and aggressive.

Manifesto of the Cominform, October 5, 1947.

✳   ✳   ✳   ✳

Miscellaneous

48. Our Army . . . is the Avantgarde of the World Proletariat. Our Army is an international Army. By victories in other countries also, the Proletarian Revolution will create new detachments of the Red troops. The Red Army is the Avantgarde of the armed forces of the World Revolution.

Voroshilov — Declaration at Session of the Moscow Soviet on the Tenth Anniversary of the Red Army, *Pravda,* No. 50, 1928.

49. As we observed the tanks driving by us, and the airplanes flying past us in the air, we observed from the Red Square the military power not only of the working class of the Soviet Union, but rather the strength and the power of the Revolutionary Proletariat on a world-wide scale.

The Soviet Government, Comrades, is the government of the Proletariat, and the Soviet Government protects the interests of the workers, the producers, the oppressed throughout the world. The interests of the Soviet Government — are the interests of the World Proletariat. . . .

When you (our Russian brothers and sisters) strengthen the fighting force of the Red Army, you not only strengthen the power of the Soviet Union, but also the power of the World Proletariat.

The Soviet Union and its Red Army are the guardians of peace among nations. The Soviet Union is the citadel of the Proletarian World Revolution.

> Dimitrov — Speech made in the Hall of Columns
> of the Town Hall, May 1, 1935.

50. . . . in the propaganda of Marxism-Leninism the chief decisive weapon must be the press . . . and oral propaganda should occupy the place of a secondary aid.

> Party Decision on the Press — in *History of the*
> *All-Union Communist Party,* 1938, Moscow.

51. War psychosis instigated by the efforts of the militarist and expansionist circles of certain countries, United States of America occupying the foremost place among them, is continually spreading and assuming all the more menacing character.

A furious campaign in the press, mainly in American press, and in the press of the countries following obediently the U.S.A., like Turkey, is being spread already for a considerable lapse of time for the purpose of coaxing the public opinion in favor of a new war. All means of psychological influence — newspapers, magazines, radio, cinema — have been used.

War-hungry psychosis is stimulated in every way among the American public, excited and fanned by militarist and expansionist circles of the U.S.A.

> Vyshinski's Speech at the United Nations General
> Assembly, on September 18, 1947.

52. The Revolution does not simply *happen,* it must be *made.*

> E. Browder — *What Is Communism?* New York, 1936.

53. The Soviet Union signed a pact with Germany, fully assured that peace between the peoples of the U.S.S.R. and Germany is in the interests of all peoples, in the interests of universal peace. Every sincere supporter of peace will realize the truth of this. This pact corresponds to the fundamental interests of the working people of the Soviet Union and cannot weaken our vigilance in defense of these interests. This pact is backed by firm confidence in our real forces, in their complete preparedness to meet any aggression against the U.S.S.R.

This pact, like the unsuccessful Anglo-French-Soviet negotiations, proves that no important questions of international relations, and questions of Eastern Europe even less, can be settled without the active participation of the Soviet Union, that any attempts to shut out the Soviet Union and decide such questions behind its back are doomed to failure.

The Soviet-German Non-Aggression Pact spells a new turn in the development of Europe, a turn towards improvement of relations between the two largest states of Europe. This pact not only eliminates the menace of war with Germany, narrows down the zone of possible hostilities in Europe, and serves thereby the cause of universal peace: It must open to us new possibilities of increasing our strength, of further consolidation of our position, of further growth of the influence of the Soviet Union on international developments.

There is no need to dwell here on the separate clauses of the pact. The Council of People's Commissars has reason to hope that the pact will meet with your approval as a document of cardinal importance to the U.S.S.R.

The Council of People's Commissars submits the Soviet-German Non-Aggression Pact to the Supreme Soviet and proposes that it be ratified.

> Molotov — Speech before the Council of the Union and the Council of Nationalities of the Supreme Soviet of the U.S.S.R., August, 1939.

54. In the pamphlet Regarding the Questions of Leninism, Comrade Stalin very clearly showed wherein the significance of the Proletarian Dictatorship really lies. He showed us three fundamental sides of the Proletarian Dictatorship: (1) The full use of Proletarian Power for the suppression of the exploiting classes, for the protection of the country, for strengthening the relations with the proletarians of other countries, for bringing about and insuring the victory of the Revolution in all countries. . . .

> Molotov — During the Fifteenth Session of the Seventeenth Party Congress of the Communist Party (Bolshevik), Soviet Union, January-February, 1934.

55. There can be no respite in the ideological war. Any position which we abandon today will not remain empty — tomorrow the enemy will occupy it. And at the present moment our ideological enemies are extremely aggressive. They are attempting to gain ground, and wherever we, representatives of Soviet art, permit it, they will not only attempt it, but will actually gain ground.

We should and shall fight on the ideological front. That follows naturally from what we have been taught by the party of Lenin and Stalin. That follows naturally from our traditions, from our character, trained by the periods of the five-year plans, tempered during the days of the war.

Our enemies find that we are stubborn and unpleasant. We have no intention of changing, however unpleasant they find us. We take this as a compliment, coming from our enemies.

We declare at the tops of our voices, to the whole world, from the tribune of our art, that we are fighting and shall continue to fight for communism; that we consider communism the only worthy future for mankind; that our communist ideals were, are, and always shall be unchangeable; and that no one can ever cause us to falter.

And to those who languish for "pure" art, we say:

There are different views on beauty in art and beauty in life. One view holds that beauty in life is found outside the limits of struggle, labor, and suffering; accordingly, beauty in art is likewise found outside their limits. But there is another view which holds that it is exactly within the limits of struggle, labor, and suffering that the greatest beauty of life lies, and accordingly that the beauty of art is also found within these limits. That is our view of life and art. This is a view which takes sides. We approve of it. More than that we are proud of it.

Constantine Simonov — *Litraturnaya Gazeta*,
November 23, 1946.

56. In literature and on the stage we must show the Soviet person — the builder of the future — in such a light that the audience and the whole world will see the moral and spiritual superiority of people who have been reared in a socialist society.

Our diplomats speak from the world tribune with such brilliance and so convincingly not only because they are great statesmen and orators, but also and mainly because, in spite of the lies and libel spread about them, they alone speak the truth about humanity, a truth supported by our entire people. It is the moral and ideological superiority of our people which makes our representatives superior to all others in the world tribune.

Constantine Simonov — *Litraturnaya Gazeta*,
November 23, 1946.

57. The dictatorship of the proletariat cannot arise as the result of the peaceful development of bourgeois society and of bourgeois democracy; it can arise only as the result of the smashing of the bourgeois state machine, the bourgeois army, the bourgeois bureaucratic machine, the bourgeois police.

Lesson III, in *Outline of Marxist-Leninist Fundamentals for
Class Use or Self-Study*, distributed by Communist Party
of United States. Exhibit 51, p. 123, U. S. Brief before
Supreme Court, October term, 1950, on appeal of eleven
Communists against their conviction in New York.

58. *Summation of Communist Strategy and Tactics in Supreme Court of The United States.*

The goal of the Communist Party is to seize powers of government by and for a minority rather than to acquire power through the vote of a free electorate. . . . Violent and undemocratic means are the calculated and indispensable methods to attain the Communist Party's goal. It would be incredible naïveté to expect the American branch of this movement to forego the only methods by which a Communist Party has anywhere come into power. In not one of the countries it now dominates was the Communist Party chosen by a free or contestable election; in not one can it be evicted by any election. The international police state has crept over Eastern Europe by deception, coercion, *coup d'état,* terrorism and assassination. Not only has it overpowered its critics and opponents, it has usually liquidated them. The American Communist Party has copied the organizational structure and its leaders have been schooled in the same technique and from the same tutors. . . .

The Communist Party alone among American parties past or present is dominated and controlled by a foreign government. It is a satrap party which, to the threat of civil disorder, adds the threat of betrayal into alien hands.

> Mr. Justice Jackson in *American Communications Association v. Douds,* 339 U. S. at 427.

APPENDIX IV

Selected Dates in the Chronology
of the Russian Revolution Since 1905

1905: First attempt to establish Soviets in St. Petersburg. Defeated by Tzarist government. The Revolution goes underground.

1917: Fall of Romanov dynasty. Return of Lenin. Bolsheviks seize power on November 7. Revolution triumphant.

1918: Treaty of Brest Litovsk. Revolution retreats before German advance. Lenin saves the Revolution by compromise.

1919–
1920: Civil wars, counterrevolution. Lenin founds Third International as external agent of Revolution.

1921: New economic policy in face of impending famine. Modified and controlled Capitalism permitted. Revolution again retreats.

1922–
1923: The great famine. Revolution invites co-operation with non-Communist States. The Revolution survives civil wars and famine.

1924: Death of Lenin. The Revolution falters. Internal feuds over leadership.

1924–
1927: The Trotsky-Stalin duel. Elimination of Trotsky and victory for Stalin. The Revolution resumes its progress.

1928–
1932: First Five-Year Plan to strengthen the Revolution internally. Non-aggression pacts signed with neighboring States. Diplomatic measures used to achieve acceptance of the Revolution.

1933: Recognition by U.S.A. Roosevelt-Litvinov Agreement.

1934: The Revolution enters the League of Nations.

1935: A major zigzag is ordered by the managers of the Revolution in view of the rising menace of Hitler. Communists throughout the world ordered to co-operate with bourgeois governments. The Trojan Horse technique. The common front advocated.

1939: August 23, the Nazi-Soviet Pact. Stalin becomes partner of Hitler. As Germany invaded Poland, the Russian Revolution began its advance into western Europe and attacked Finland. League of Nations expels Soviet delegation.

1940: Lithuania, Latvia, and Estonia annexed to U.S.S.R.

1941: Hitler invades Soviet Russia. The Russian Revolution retreats. Soviet lands occupied by a competing Revolution.

1942–
1943: Low water mark of the Russian Revolution. Last stand at Petrograd, Moscow, and Stalingrad.

1944: Recoil and recovery of the Revolution. Pursuit of the retreating Nazis.

1945: Triumph over the Nazi Revolution by joint forces of Allied powers. Capture of Berlin by Soviet forces. End of World War II.

1946–
1948: The Russian Revolution reverts to classic Communist program. Maneuvers for world domination. Founding of Cominform. Blockade of Berlin countered by the airlift. Consolidation of satellite system.

1949–
1950: Zenith in progress of the Revolution. Triumph in China, compromise in Europe in view of Marshall Plan, the North Atlantic Alliance, and defiance by Tito. The Revolution advances into South Korea.

1951: Rearmament of United States. Stiffening of will to resist in western Europe. General Eisenhower returns to Europe as Commander in Chief of European forces. Heavy losses in Party membership in Italy, France, Germany, etc. Reduction in Party membership ranges from 31 per cent in Italy to 84 per cent in Luxembourg. United Nations forces in Korea stem Chinese advance and drive them back toward North Korea. The Revolution agrees to another conference of Foreign Ministers. The Politburo shifts its attention to the oil resources of Iran.

Index

ABC of Communism, official text, 65

Absorption of border states, Soviet process of, 81 ff

Acheson, Secretary, and Alger Hiss conviction, 167

Adoratsky, on dialectical method, 110

"Aesopian language," Soviet use of, 199, 203, 218

Aggression, not in American plans, 248 f; UN commitments versus, 255 f; use of A-bomb versus, 255

Agreements with Soviet Russia, caution needed in, 20 ff; the 1933 agreement, 25; Russia's violation record, 26

Alaska, importance to U. S., 155 f; Soviet designs on, 241

Albania, Russia's seizure of, 94, 139

Alternatives to Communism, 258 f

America, chances for war with Russia, 149; Communist Party in, 97 f, 103 f; De Tocqueville's prophecy, 265; discovery of, economic motivation, 74; discovery of, importance, 30. *See also* United States

American Communists, collaborators, 95 ff; directives from Stalin, 130 f; education in Russia, 120; motives for aiding Communism, 101 ff; sympathizers, 97 ff; trial of eleven, 105, 137

American genius, technical, 27

American indifference, toward Communism, 137 f, 166 f

American mind, analysis of, 174 ff

American Relief Administration, and famine in Russia (1921–1923), 5 ff, 72

American Revolution, crossroad of history, 32; results of, 37

Anglican Church, and dialectical materialism, 134

Appeasement, F. D. R. and, 226; futility of, 212

Asia, Soviet plans for expansion in, 140

Atomic bomb, effects of, 243 f; improvements in, 249; Russia and, 168; use justified, 246 ff

Atomic control, Russia's attitude on, 164 f, 243

Austria, Peter the Great and, 263; Russian influence in, 147, 164, 170

Baltic, the, Peter the Great and, 263, 264; scene of Russian rearmament, 247 f

Beard, Prof., on F. D. R. and Soviet-American relations, 221

Bednyi, early Soviet poet, and concept of man, 92

Beneš, Mr., relations with Moscow, 83, 240

Bentley, Elizabeth, confession of, 95, 148

Berle, Adolph, on F. D. R. at Yalta, 221

Borah, Senator, onetime Soviet advocate, 96

Bourgeois society, as enemy of the Revolution, 88

Brest Litovsk, Treaty of (1918), 48 f, 139, 189

Browder, Earl, cited, 279; overtures to Catholics, 124 f; at Seventh World Congress (1935), 26; on training of Communist leaders, 121

Brownson, Orestes A., on recognition of truth and error, 206

Budenz, Louis, confession of, 95, 148

Budkiewicz, Msgr. Constantine, liquidated, 13 ff, 17, 191

Bulgaria, Communist control in, 94, 114, 139, 140, 147, 169, 185

285